BLACK LAWYERS, WHITE COURTS

BLACK LAWYERS, WHITE COURTS

The Soul of South African Law

KENNETH S. BROUN

With a Message from
NELSON MANDELA

Foreword by
JULIUS L. CHAMBERS

Ohio University Press
ATHENS

CONTENTS

A MESSAGE FROM
NELSON MANDELA

THE LAWYERS whose stories appear in this book are men and women I know well, either in person or by reputation, and I admire them all greatly. All have overcome the burdens of apartheid to become lawyers and to help the downtrodden of South Africa through their knowledge of law. They suffered through the evils of an educational system calculated to limit their achievement. Despite that system, they attained a degree of knowledge and sophistication that their oppressors would have thought to be impossible. Two, Dikgang Moseneke and Fikile Bam, were my fellow prisoners on Robben Island.

Fix Bam and I read law together in the early days of our imprisonments. Godfrey Pitje was a clerk in my law firm in the 1950s and I watched him start on a career of dedication to service to the people of this country. Dullah Omar has been my lawyer and my Minister of Justice. I have known most of the others through their dedicated work in the struggle against the oppression of apartheid and their outstanding efforts after the adoption of the new constitution.

The stories of these lawyers are especially important because they illustrate the strength and courage of people to rise up in a society bent on keeping them down. Their struggles, as described in this book, are a vivid example of the struggles of all South African black people.

But for apartheid, how many more black men and women would have risen to careers in the law or other professions? We will never know the answer to that question, but we can at least take pride in the accomplishments of those who were able to overcome the system calculated to defeat them. The benefits of their success go not only to them and to their clients, but to the entire nation of South Africa.

Sadly, Godfrey Pitje has passed away. But the other individuals in this book are still actively part of the South African legal profession. Indeed, in many ways, they form the backbone of our new society. They have experienced oppression firsthand and also know the joys of freedom. They know the role that law can play to accomplish wrong, as under apartheid, and they also know what good it can accomplish in a free society. These men and women are the heroes of yesterday and the hope of tomorrow. I salute them and their histories set forth in this book.

NELSON MANDELA
President
Republic of South Africa

FOREWORD

I VISITED South Africa in 1983 as part of a team designed to work with black lawyers of South Africa. Our objective was to develop an organization of black South African lawyers similar to the NAACP Legal Defense and Educational Fund.

The late Judge Leon Higginbotham led the team, which also included Judge Thelton Henderson and Ms. Sara Cherry. My wife, Ms. Vivian Chambers, accompanied me and was an important member of the team.

The trip was sponsored by the Carnegie Foundation with the hope that through law, with a trained cadre of black attorneys, racial apartheid could be eliminated peacefully.

I had had extensive experience as a civil rights attorney with the Legal Defense Fund. Judge Higginbotham had significant trial experience and was a leading United States jurist and legal scholar. Judge Henderson also had extensive civil rights experience and served as a Federal District Court Judge in the Northern District of California. Sara Cherry was a great writer and researcher who assisted Judge Higginbotham with a number of his research projects.

Our team visited with black lawyers in all of the major cities of South Africa. Many of these lawyers are discussed in Kenneth Broun's book, *Black Lawyers, White Courts: The Soul of South African Law*. We heard their experiences as described by Professor Broun. We stayed in their homes and visited with them over fourteen days. We exchanged experiences, describing similar experiences of black lawyers in the United States. We talked about cases like *Griggs v. Duke Power* and others that we thought might be employed in South Africa even under a different South African Constitution which sanctioned racial apartheid.

It was painfully clear, however, that there were major differences

PREFACE

W[HEN] I think of the black lawyers of South Africa, I sometimes visualize them as lawyers doing things that lawyers do everywhere—going to court, winning and losing cases, struggling to get clients and to make a living. The lawyers of this book certainly have done and continue to do all those things. But these are South African black lawyers and my image of them is altered by the unique situation in that nation. So I think about Godfrey Pitje in the Johannesburg suburb of Boksburg refusing to sit at a table in the courtroom specially reserved for blacks. I see Ismail Mahomed moving from room to room in his advocates' chambers because the Group Areas Act prevented him from having his own office. I envision Dullah Omar calling a wife or parent of a Robben Island prisoner as a witness in a trial on the island, not because her testimony had any value to the case at hand, but rather to give his client the opportunity to see a loved one.

Because it is South Africa, I also have mental images of these same lawyers in circumstances not directly related to the practice of law. I visualize Dikgang Moseneke on Robben Island, sixteen years old or so, breaking up rocks and conjugating Latin verbs with his teacher, Stanley Mogoba. I see Yvonne Mokgoro thrown into a township police van after having her baby ripped from her arms because she came to the defense of a man being arrested for no cause. I again see Godfrey Pitje, this time not as a lawyer, but rather as a father forced to sit in a car rather than be at the graveside for the funeral of his ten-year-old son.

This is a book about these individuals and other lawyers. It tries to tell their stories, through their own words, both as lawyers and as people struggling to deal with a society that openly and systematically discriminated against them because of their race. Their histories demonstrate their impor-

tance to the protection of whatever meager rights the apartheid government
offered to individuals. The same stories also show the significance of the
experience of these men and women in the old legal system to the success of
the new South Africa. Their words also give some insight into these individuals as people. How could they become professionals under an educational
system diabolically structured to keep them as hewers of wood and drawers
of water? What enabled their spirit to persevere under circumstances where
most of us would have resigned ourselves to our governmentally designed
destiny?

   I first went to South Africa in 1986 to conduct trial advocacy programs
for the Black Lawyers Association–Legal Education Centre. My companion
on that trip and on many others over the next thirteen years was James E.
Ferguson II. "Fergie," a fellow North Carolinian, is one of America's great
trial lawyers. Under the auspices of the National Institute for Trial Advocacy
(NITA) and with substantial funding provided through the United States
–South Africa Leader Exchange Program (USSALEP), Fergie and I and a
dozen or more American trial lawyers have taught trial advocacy to hundreds of South African black lawyers. We received superb teaching assistance in South Africa, both from many of the black lawyers whose stories
are told in this book and from sympathetic white South African lawyers and
judges.

   The idea for this book came from many evenings and late nights spent
with the participants in these programs—both students and teachers. They
talked about their practices and their struggles in a matter-of-fact way,
always assuming that they would eventually overcome the terrible hand that
fate and apartheid South Africa had dealt them. I thought then and I think
now that someone other than a few American lawyers ought to hear their
stories. I went to South Africa for the first five months of 1996 armed with
a tape recorder and, I hoped, some good will that would give me access to
the histories of these remarkable people. I was successful in interviewing
twenty-seven lawyers. At least a part of each of their stories appear here.
Obviously, these are not the only black lawyers in South Africa whose stories are worth telling. I hope only that they represent a cross-section of the
roughly 1,500 black lawyers in South Africa (out of a total of approximately
10,000 lawyers) and that their accounts are representative of others.

   I have used the term *black* in this book in the broader sense—to include all nonwhite people. Some of the lawyers interviewed were classified as "Indian," a few others as "Coloured."* Most are black Africans. Although all nonwhite groups suffered in South Africa, the apartheid government treated black Africans as the lowest on the totem pole.

I do not mean by this narrative to neglect the considerable contribution of many white lawyers and judges who actively opposed the regime. Like that of their black colleagues, their work was meaningful and courageous. Lawyers frequently mentioned by the people interviewed for this book— Arthur Chaskalson, now president of the Constitutional Court; George Bizos, one of the nation's leading human rights advocates; Bram Fischer, who gave his life for the cause; and many others—deserve prominent mention in any chronicle of the South African struggle. Their efforts are worthy of another book. But this is a book about the special problems and role of black lawyers. South Africa was, and to a large extent still is, a nation obsessed with race. As Cornel West says, race matters, and in South Africa race matters very much, even in distinguishing between groups of equally good and courageous individuals.

*The terms "Coloured" and "Indian" are the creation of the apartheid government. Both racial categories comprised individuals of several ethnic groups. I have chosen not to enclose the terms in quotation marks to avoid drawing undue attention to them.

ACKNOWLEDGMENTS

THE REAL authors of this book are the twenty-seven lawyers who permitted me to interview them. I am grateful to them for their time and the sharing of their stories. Whatever weaknesses this book may have are in my editing and organization, not in their narrations. The courage with which these lawyers have conducted their lives and the enormous talent that they bring to the legal profession are the essence of the book.

My travels to South Africa to conduct trial advocacy programs, through which I got to know the black lawyers of South Africa, were made possible by the financial support of the Black Lawyers Association—Legal Education Centre, the National Institute for Trial Advocacy (NITA), and the United States–South Africa Leader Exchange Program. The programs themselves have also received support from the United States Agency for International Development, the Ford Foundation, and the American Bar Association Section of Litigation.

Funding for my extended stay in South Africa in order to conduct the interviews for this book was provided by a Kenan Research Leave granted by the University of North Carolina. The University of North Carolina School of Law, especially my dean, Judith W. Wegner, provided significant additional support in funds, research assistance, facilities, and encouragement. While in South Africa, I was graciously provided office space and other amenities by the Faculty of Law at the University of the Witwatersrand, by the Faculty of Law at the University of Cape Town, and by the Black Lawyers Association—Legal Education Centre. Some of the preparation of the manuscript was done with the assistance of the University of San Diego School of Law.

I was simply one of many American lawyers who volunteered their time and experience to help impart some advocacy skills to South African black

xx   ACKNOWLEDGMENTS

lawyers. All of the American lawyers gave enormous blocks of their time and worked without monetary compensation. The work done by these individuals contributed significantly to the quality of work done by South African black lawyers. Most especially, my deepest gratitude goes to my closest partner in that venture, the great lawyer James E. Ferguson II and to his law firm, Ferguson, Stein, Wallas, Adkins Gresham & Sumter, P.A. of Charlotte, North Carolina. Fergie showed me not only what an excellent lawyer can accomplish in his own country, but how that skill, knowledge, and experience might successfully be exported to professionals working in another system. Two other members of Fergie's firm, Geraldine Sumter and Henderson Hill, also have been leaders in the success of our programs and thus may take credit, but not blame, for the substance of the book. Another member of the firm, Adam Stein, was involved in the first program and gave consistent support to our efforts. Other American participants in those programs, who deserve not only my gratitude but that of lawyers everywhere for their professionalism and dedication to an important venture, include Charles Becton, Jim Fuller, Ken Frazier, Isabelle Gunning, Rudy Pierce, Mike Tigar, Greg Weeks, and Mariah Wooten. A special thanks goes to Rudy Pierce, who not only contributed enormously to the program in South Africa, but supported Fergie's and my efforts to continue NITA's support for it.

Particular thanks go to the staff of the Black Lawyers Association–Legal Education Centre, most particularly to my great friend Faith Mandiwana as well as to her husband, Thom, who kept me thinking about music instead of fretting over law. I am also indebeted to an outstanding former Centre director whose busy schedule kept her from being one of the subjects of the book, Mojanku Gumbi.

Thanks go to Helen Frühauf at the University of the Witwatersrand for her diligent and expert typing of the transcripts of the tapes of all of the interviews contained in this book and to my student research assistant at Wits, Candice Pillay.

Helpful advice, including excellent readings of this book and comments, were given by Catherine Admay, Penelope Andrews, Susannah Arwood, Walter Bennett, Patricia Bryan, Bob Byrd, Martin Chanock, Frank Kirschbaum, Jonathan Klaaren, Deanne Siemer, Howard Willens, and Rosemary Waldorf. Much advice and support was also given by Sheridan Johns, John Conley, Rich Rosen, and Lou Bilionis.

I particularly want to thank my editors, Gillian Berchowitz, Nancy Basmajian, and the staff at Ohio University Press for their many contributions. Gillian, in particular, showed immediate interest in the book and offered invaluable encouragement, patience, and advice throughout the process.

With deep sadness, I also acknowledge the advice and moral support I received on this project from the late Professor Etienne Mureinik of the University of the Witwatersrand Faculty of Law. Etienne's encouragement and assistance in Johannesburg during the period when most of the research for the book was being done were enormously valuable. More significantly, his contribution to the South African legal community and to the rule of law will be sorely missed.

Most importantly, I would like to thank my family for their support in this project. First and foremost, I thank my wife, Margie, for everything during the long course of this project, including perhaps the most helpful readings of early drafts of the manuscripts. If there are things in the book that are not interesting or readable, it is clearly not her fault. I am particularly indebted to my son, Dan, and daughter-in-law, Joal, for helpful readings of parts of the manuscript. I am also grateful to my son Jonathan and daughter-in-law Becky for their encouragement and moral support and to grandson Harrison for just being there.

ABBREVIATIONS

ANC   African National Congress
APLA   Azanian People's Liberation Army, military wing of the PAC
ASSECA   Association for the Educational and Cultural Development of
            the African People
AWB   Afrikaner Weerstandsbeweging (far-right-wing organization)
BCP   Black Community Programme
BLA–LEC   Black Lawyers Association–Legal Education Centre
BPC   Black People's Convention
CBD   central business district
CALS   Centre for Applied Legal Studies at the University of the
            Witwatersrand
CPSU   Cape Peninsula Students Union
IEC   Independent Electoral Commission
IFP   Inkatha Freedom Party
JORAC   Joint Rent Association
LRC   Legal Resources Centre
MK   Umkhonto weSizwe (Spear of the nation), military wing of
            the ANC
MVA   Motor Vehicle Act
NADEL   National Association of Democratic Lawyers
NAIL   New Africa Investments, Ltd. (black-owned investment
            company)
NEUM   Non-European Unity Movement
NUSAS   National Union of South African Students
PAC   Pan Africanist Congress
SABC   South African Broadcasting Corporation

SACOS	South African Council of Sport
SASO	South African Students Organisation
SRC	Student Representative Council
TATA	Transvaal African Teachers' Association
TLSA	Teachers' League of South Africa
UCM	University Christian Movement
UCT	University of Cape Town
UDF	United Democratic Front
UNISA	University of South Africa
USSALEP	United States–South Africa Leader Exchange Program
UWC	University of the Western Cape

BLACK LAWYERS,
WHITE COURTS

1

⚖

GODFREY MOKGOMANE PITJE

Teacher, Scholar, Attorney, Father

GODFREY PITJE was certainly not the first black lawyer in South Africa. In 1912 a black lawyer named Pixley Seme organized the group that became the African National Congress (ANC). Such luminaries as Mahatma Gandhi, Nelson Mandela, and Oliver Tambo (head of the African National Congress in exile) also preceded Pitje. But Godfrey's story precedes as well as spans the time of all the other lawyers whose stories are contained in this book. In many ways, his life raises the issues that the other stories expand upon. Therefore, I give his complete history as my first chapter.

Godfrey Pitje was a person of such great warmth and unfailing dignity that the outrages he suffered at the hands of the South African authorities were singularly appalling. Godfrey, or G. M., as he was often called, cared deeply about the struggle of his people and especially about the role of black lawyers in South African society. He was proud of his heritage, proud of the education he had managed to obtain, and proud to be a member of the legal profession. He was also a deeply religious person; his Christian faith sustained him through times of horrendous difficulty. Although he had much reason for bitterness, Godfrey was not a bitter man. He would refer to

1

"white bastards," but it was clear that you were only a white bastard if you set out to harm black people.

Godfrey Pitje was the first lawyer that I met when I came to South Africa in 1986. At that time he was the director of the Black Lawyers Association–Legal Education Centre. We had many conversations, or, more accurately, sessions in which I listened to Godfrey tell about life and the practice of law in South Africa. He visited me in the United States and stayed at my home, where the discourse continued. His first communication with Oliver Tambo in more than twenty-five years occurred by telephone from my house.

When I first met Godfrey, he had a deep rasp in his voice. The rasp was the product of a knife wound to his throat, delivered by the disgruntled husband of a client he had represented in a divorce case. Although apartheid South Africa was reputed to have superb medical care, at least for whites, Godfrey felt that he could not get the treatment there that he needed. He received medical advice from physicians in Chapel Hill, North Carolina, and eventually recovered fully.

I conducted formal interviews of Godfrey Pitje on two occasions, once in 1992 and again in 1996, at two different private law offices he occupied in Johannesburg. On both occasions, one on a Saturday morning, his small office area was jam-packed with litigants or potential litigants, old friends with no apparent reason for being there, and staff. Neither office was a luxurious lawyer's suite; both felt like inner-city law clinics. Both were located in old buildings in Johannesburg's quickly deteriorating central business district. The furniture was modest; no expensive art work adorned the walls. But his offices were places where poor people could comfortably go to seek assistance from a respected elder who would intercede for them with the powers that be.

Early Years

Godfrey Pitje was born in Pokwani, in what was then the Northern Province of South Africa, in 1917. His tribal language, which was spoken exclusively at home, was Sepedi. His mother was completely illiterate, his father barely able to write his name. They were devoted members of the Ba-Pedi Lutheran church, an African offshoot of the German church.

There were eight children, three boys and five girls. One of the other boys became a schoolteacher, the other a businessman in Pretoria. None of the girls went beyond standard 4, the equivalent of sixth grade in an American school.

∞ I went to the local primary school. It was a mission school of the Berlin Lutheran Church. Their priests came to South Africa under the aegis of the Berlin Missionary Society. Beginners, as they called us, would have no classrooms. You had lessons under a tree. If it was a bit chilly, you would go into some old dilapidated ruin with no roof and a blackboard patched on the wall. Our teacher was an old black evangelist, who I guess would have passed standard 4. I don't think he had a teacher's certificate. He was the local evangelist of the Lutheran church. He taught us during the week and held church on Sundays. He also prepared candidates for confirmation. He was highly respected and was called Meester.

Meester would write on the board for beginners and then write on the board for the sub-As [the next youngest pupils]. My recollection is that I quickly caught up with this beginners' class and advanced to the sub-A class. I would write the same things as the sub-As and would sheepishly present my slate when that class was called upon to do so. He would take me aside because he thought I was a little too young. He did not like my trying, as it were, to "jump the class." I was only six years old. I was kept back for a year because they thought I was too young for promotion.

The system was geared towards confirmation. At seventeen, you were eligible for confirmation class. We looked forward to the Sunday when Meester would announce "my seventeens." If you reached standard 4 before you reached seventeen you repeated standard 4 until you reached the age of seventeen. After that you would go out and seek work. However, my brother—the one in Pretoria—broke the rules after passing standard 4 and went to the local Methodist school, which offered standards 5 and 6. Consequently, when I passed standard 4, I followed him to the Methodist school.

My brother was in standard 6 [eighth grade] when I was in standard 5 and we did more or less the same type of work. We were taught by the same teacher, Shadrack Matlala, a very good teacher. He was the father of Reverend Stanley Mogoba, the present Bishop of the Methodist Church of South Africa.[1] He taught us every subject. I went to the Methodist school in 1931 and 1932 to do standards 5 and 6.

Because of the excellence of my teacher, when we first presented ourselves for standard 6 [national] examinations, I had no doubt that we would pass. Indeed, I was surprised that only two of us passed the standard 6 examination in 1932. The other was Isaac Mogoane, who was a year or two older than me. He came from a well-to-do family. But once confirmed, he joined the stream of migrant workers to town. In later years, I found him in Germiston, where he was a senior clerk at the Germiston Hospital.

Pitje repeated standard 6 in 1933, because he was not yet old enough to be confirmed. He also took temporary employment as a private teacher for the children of the police in a nearby village, Nebo.

In 1934 I was confirmed, and therefore I could now go to town to work. My brother in Pretoria was keen that I should join him in Pretoria. He was in domestic service at that time. He sent me ten shillings to pay for the bus from Pokwani to Middelburg, then our nearest town. As I came down the steps from the bus at the Middelburg railway station, I heard a voice say, "This child looks like a Pitje child." When I looked, I saw an old lady with her eyes fixed on me. I literally fell into her hands. I soon discovered that she was the sister of my paternal grandmother, Rufus Kgothadi. I had often heard of her. She suggested I could stay at her house while I looked for work.

After going to her house, I walked ten miles from Middelburg to the Botshabelo training institution, a teacher training institution run by German mistresses. I was told that there might be work at the school. When I went there, I tried to see an old man known to my aunt. He was the official driver for the superintendent of the college. I finally got to see him and then saw the superintendent of the institution. The superintendent suggested if I could get accommodations in the village, he would persuade the staff to take me on the following day—not as a worker but as a student. My aunt and her husband easily agreed that I should stay at their house.

The Germans were very strict. The girls were on the extreme eastern

end of the grounds and the boys on the western side, with the college itself more or less in between. We were not allowed to sit with girls, not
even in the classroom. The medium of instruction was English. The majority of the students were Sepedi-speaking, but we had students from all
over. The school was open to anyone who belonged to the Lutheran
church. I remember two from Mafikeng, one from Kimberley, and three
or four from the Eastern Transvaal, but the main source seemed to be
northern Transvaal. They would be SePedi-speaking, except that there
were dialectal differences in language.

After three years at Botshabelo, Pitje became a qualified teacher. He
took a teaching post in Pretoria at a small school established by the Dutch
Reformed Church. He was the only teacher at the school, which had thirteen students and went to standard 2 (fourth grade). While teaching, Pitje
continued his studies privately and, in 1939, got what was known as a junior certificate. The qualification entitled him to six pounds rather than the
five pounds earned by other teachers and enhanced his chances of being
made a principal. He used the extra money to buy a bicycle for £1 10s.

Obtaining the junior certificate enabled Pitje to enter his matriculation
studies. Matriculation, or matric, as it is commonly called, refers to the last
one or two years of secondary education in South Africa, which prepared
graduates to take a national examination that would enable them to enter a
university.

‹⁊ At the end of 1941, I wrote and passed the matriculation examination
and immediately applied to Fort Hare to do a degree. I was at Fort Hare
from 1942 through 1944. Fort Hare University was a very interesting
place when I was there. [At the time, Fort Hare was the only university in
South Africa for blacks. A small number of blacks attended some of the
white universities.] Firstly, I come from a rural background, and Botshabelo Training Institution was also in a rural setting. For instance, we didn't
have toilets. We went into the bush. We did not have any facilities for
washing. We went to the nearest stream to do our washing. And so, Fort
Hare was quite an experience for me. I found a more sophisticated group
of students—most sophisticated stuff, I thought.

I spent the year of 1942 quietly. But in 1943 there was a strike led by

Oliver Tambo. Tambo had completed his degree in 1941 but came back
in 1942 to do a teacher's diploma. He was the head student of my hostel,
which was St. Peter's, or Peter Hall as they called it. I was too junior to
understand the real reason behind the strike. It started with friction between the house committee and the white bishop, Ferguson Derby.

After meeting with the bishop, the house committee came back to
the students and it was decided that we would begin a policy of noncoop-
eration with him. We were instructed that we should reply to the first
thing said in the service and then keep quiet. We did that and the poor
bishop didn't know just how to handle the situation. My recollection is
that he quickly mumbled something in the service and closed it. When he
couldn't resolve the differences between himself and the house committee
and the students, who were now virtually not cooperating with him, he
appealed to the principal of the college. We in turn were given an ultimatum that we either renounce this strike or we quit. Tambo quit. I am one
of those who relented. Whether I was wise or unwise, I am not prepared
to say, but I relented and wrote my examinations at the end of '43.

Teacher and Scholar

∞ At the end of '44, I passed my B.A., and in '45 I was employed as a
secondary school teacher at what used to be called Orlando High School
in Soweto. Simultaneously, I enrolled as a part-time student at Wits [the
University of the Witwatersrand, in Johannesburg], the intention being to
do an honors degree in social anthropology. I was aware of no restrictions
on me at Wits as a black person. As part-time students, we were not really
regarded as part of the student body.

In 1946, on the advice of a professor at Wits, Hilda Kuper, Pitje returned to Fort Hare to continue his studies. His work also took him to the
Eastern Transvaal, to an area called Sekhukhuniland, where he did research
in social anthropology. He completed a paper entitled "Traditional and
Modern Systems of Education among the Pedi and Cognate Tribes" and
was awarded a master's degree in 1948. During that period, he also served as
a junior lecturer in anthropology and as assistant curator of the F. S. Malan
Museum of Ethnology.

∞ Nineteen forty-eight was a significant year because not only was I on the staff at Fort Hare, but my political awareness had now taken a definite shape. The change arose from my experience at Orlando High, where I found the students were politically alive. There was clear evidence that after school they were exposed to the Tambos, the Mandelas, Sisulus [Walter Sisulu, an ANC leader and close associate of Nelson Mandela and Oliver Tambo] and others. One felt a little uneasy to have students who seemed to be more advanced than their teachers in extracurricular activities. So in 1948 I was prepared mentally to do as much work outside the lecture room as inside. And that saw us establish a branch of the ANC Youth League at Fort Hare. We were supported by some of the professors. The other students included Chief Mangosuthu Gatsha Buthelezi,[2] who was a student in social anthropology with me, Dr. Nthato Motlana,[3] and Robert Sobukwe.[4]

Pitje's work with the Youth League brought him into conflict with the authorities. By 1949 he was feeling uneasy and resigned his post at Fort Hare. He took up a teaching position near Johannesburg, at a school called the Wilberforce Institute. From there he became headmaster of the Jane Furse School. While at these schools, he began to take an active part in the Transvaal African Teachers' Association (TATA), and was elected to its executive.

∞ Towards the end of 1953, two friends of mine were teaching at separate schools in the Walmansthal district of Pretoria. They invited me to be their guest speaker at parents' day, an event to which they also invited one of the members of the Eiselen Commission on Education, Dr. P. A. W. Cooke. The commission supported the Bantu education bill then before Parliament. It was clear that they anticipated that I would speak favorably about Bantu education from "the African view." I accepted the invitation and I spoke after Dr. Cooke. I gave the real African view. The meeting was on a Saturday. I slept in Pretoria and went back to Jane Furse on Sunday. When I opened the school on Monday, there was a panel of white inspectors pouncing on my school. They clearly had been offended by what I had to say at Walmansthal. They had gotten the impression that I was

more of a political teacher and condemned, as far as they could, the quality of the work I was doing at Jane Furse.

Pitje's references to Bantu education are to the South African government's policy that there should be a totally separate educational track for
blacks—a track aimed at insuring that they not rise above the level of manual laborers or domestic servants. The policy was embodied in the Bantu
Education Act of 1953. Under the act, most of the mission schools that had
contributed so beneficially to the education of Pitje and contemporaries
such as Nelson Mandela and Oliver Tambo were closed. In many ways, although their education never came close to matching that available for
whites, blacks who were educated before the mid-1950s had significantly
better opportunities than those of the next generation. When Pitje says he
gave the "real African view," he means that he expressed strong opposition
to the proposed new educational scheme. The impact of Bantu education is
more fully discussed in chapter 4.

Mandela & Tambo

✍ So I commenced the year 1954 feeling very uneasy about whether I
could continue teaching. At the end of 1954, there was a conference of
the TATA at which a constitutional problem arose. The conference decided that the problem should be referred to lawyers and its choice of
lawyers was Mandela & Tambo. I was asked to consult them with regard
to the problem. And this is what brought me to law.

I went to Mandela & Tambo, who had an office in Johannesburg on
Fox Street near the Magistrates Court. They were the only black law firm
in Johannesburg, indeed in all the Transvaal at that time. I chose to speak
to Oliver Tambo about this problem of the teachers.

In his typical style, instead of applying his mind to the problem I had
brought, his first words were, "When are you going to join us?"

I said, "Why?"

"Your teaching is going to be viewed as antigovernment because of
your political views. We have space for you here as an articled clerk."

I agonized on his suggestion. He told me that he came into the office on Sundays. So Sunday morning I strolled into his office and inquired more about law. He told me that, among other things, I had to have matric Latin. I had never had a word of Latin. When I expressed fear, Oliver said, "Well, it's a dead language—you could swat it."

I accepted Oliver Tambo's advice. I went back to Jane Furse and gave notice that I would terminate my services as a teacher on the 31st of March, 1955. I started articles [the apprenticeship required of all aspiring attorneys] on the 1st of April, 1955, at Mandela & Tambo. At the same time, I enrolled as an external student at the University of South Africa to do correspondence courses in law and Latin. The law course was three years. I finished the third year in '57. My articles continued into 1958. I was admitted finally on the 24th of March, 1959.

I did many things as an articled clerk with Mandela & Tambo. I did a lot of interviews with clients in all kinds of cases. They were essentially criminal lawyers, but they also had some very interesting civil cases. They would apply for interdicts [in American parlance, injunctions] on behalf of their clients. One that I remember specifically was a case involving a chief being deported by government order. We successfully challenged the deportation order, although I think the law was immediately amended to deter anybody who intended to use the same law. In any event, it was a varied practice, a mixed bag.

There were two clerks. The other was a chap named Meinrad Msimang, who is the present ambassador to London.

Mandela and Tambo were already under a banning order that limited their activity. [*Banning* refers to a governmental order that restricted a person's activity, for example, limiting one's ability to attend meetings or leave a particular community without permission from the police. The extent of the limitation varied, depending on the person and the extent to which the government feared his or her political activity. As he discusses later, Pitje himself was eventually subject to such an order.] I don't remember the exact restrictions, but certainly it interfered with their work. One of the conditions I had to accept was that I cease to be politically active so that at least there would be one member of the firm who would not be restricted. They would be politically active and I could do the running of the office and deal with the clients.

We would have general discussions about the political situation. The firm was a hive of activity. Many politicians called at the office, either for discussions or formal meetings, or just to pop in to see Mandela and Tambo. From that point of view, one felt very close to the political scene.

Nelson Mandela and Oliver Tambo were very effective lawyers. I would say, taking the whole of South Africa from the Cape to the Limpopo River [part of the northern border of South Africa], that they were the first to break through the racial barrier and be recognized as good lawyers. Indeed, although there had been other black lawyers in the past, they were the only lawyers in the Transvaal. There may have been one or two in the Transkei or in the Cape, but no others in the country. They weren't restricted as black lawyers in terms of appearing in courts, but they had their share of difficulties with the courts, with the magistrates, with prosecutors, and with the police.

They did a lot of spade work, so that those of us who followed in their footsteps found the fields had been at least tilled. They would take a stand against a magistrate who didn't accept a black lawyer in his court. We lost a number of cases because of the prejudice on the bench. We took them on appeal and had a lot of success at higher court, which enhanced all of our dignity. It made many magistrates take note that they were dealing with the same sort of lawyers that they thought they had in the white community.

I would say that they were generally treated well by other lawyers, but at that stage there would still be lawyers who were racially biased who would not look kindly towards them. That was also my experience when I started in practice. There were no black advocates at that time, so we would instruct white ones. [Like the United Kingdom, South Africa has a divided bar. In South Africa, lawyers who would be barristers in England are called advocates and lawyers who would be solicitors are called attorneys. Although the situation has changed somewhat since 1995, advocates traditionally were the only lawyers who appeared in the higher courts. Advocates ordinarily do not have client contact, but instead are "instructed" by the office lawyers, the attorneys. Attorneys can and frequently do appear in the magistrate courts, the lower courts dealing with less significant matters.[5]] They sort of concentrated on certain advocates, people like

George Bizos, Jules Browde, or Joe Slovo—if it was a senior matter, Bram Fischer [white, antiapartheid advocates].

After two years as an articled clerk, I could begin to appear in court. I handled a mixed bag of cases, both criminal and civil. I remember walking to court with Nelson, going to the clerk of the court's office. Nelson was walking in front of me. He went past the door labeled Natives and entered the door labeled White. I sort of took a fright at the thought of us going into a "white" area but followed him into the office, whereupon a young white clerk asked him what he was doing there. This particular clerk was one of those people whose complexion was not officially white. Mr. Mandela reacted by saying, "What are you doing in here?" which in effect said to him, "You are not white. Why are you in that office?" But almost simultaneously as Mr. Mandela gave this reply, a senior magistrate walked in and said, "Yes, Mr. Mandela? What can we do for you?" And that was the end of that incident. But it's something that taught me that you can stand up to these white bastards.

Godfrey Pitje was the only lawyer associated with Mandela & Tambo to remain in active practice after the political turmoil of the early 1960s. His principals, Mandela and Tambo, went on to achieve a place in history as fathers of the new South Africa. Meinrad Msimang went into exile. The firm's decision that Pitje would try to avoid politics freed Mandela and Tambo for more political and perhaps more important work.[6] It also permitted Pitje, despite enormous impediments, to continue to practice law in Johannesburg, to help hundreds, perhaps thousands of individuals, and to serve as a role model for others who followed.

Segregation in the Courtroom

∞ Mandela and Tambo had a way of springing work on me. In other words, instead of giving me a file ahead of time, they would give me a matter in the morning, which I felt in duty bound to take without question because they were my bosses. So one morning I arrived and I was given a file by Oliver, who discussed the case with me. It was a case of a Coloured man in Boksburg who was trading without a license. He had been arrested and I was to appear for him. Unknown to me, Oliver had previously appeared for this man. Oliver had been asked to take a segregated table and chair in the Boksburg Magistrate's Court and had declined. When the magistrate insisted, he withdrew from the matter. Before withdrawing, Oliver had asked for permission to talk to the accused and tell him that he was withdrawing and that he would then ask for a postponement so that he could get himself another lawyer.

Now, this was the postponement date and I was to be the lawyer. I got to Boksburg and the prosecutor, who didn't even have the courtesy to look at me, told me that my case was not being handled by him. Rather it was being handled by the senior public prosecutor, which surprised me. This was really a minor case, in my judgment. I moved from him towards the door to go and find the senior public prosecutor. At the door, I was accosted by a court interpreter who drew my attention to the small table and chair at the door.

In not so many words, he was trying to say to me, "Please don't kick up any fuss. Go over to that table and let's finish with this case." I hardly had time to answer him, when the senior public prosecutor walked in, oppressively, to take his position in the courtroom. At the same time, the magistrate walked in and I moved from where I was to the defense desk— to the regular defense desk, a long table across the room.

I positioned myself right in the middle of the table. The magistrate then said, "Get away from there."

And I said, "Why?"

That caused an altercation which eventually landed me with a contempt of court conviction. He convicted me of contempt right there on the scene. He said five pounds or ten days, and I went down to the cells rather than pay the fine. I spent only half a day in the cells. By midday, I was told that somebody had paid the fine for me and that I could go. When I came out, I saw the first edition of the Johannesburg *Star,* which said that a native was found guilty of contempt of court for refusing to take a segregated chair and table.

We appealed the contempt conviction. We lost in the Supreme Court in Pretoria and lost then in the appellate division in Bloemfontein. My counsel was George Bizos. There was no law requiring separate counsel table; it was a court practice and the issue was whether that practice could continue. When George Bizos appeared in the appellate division, the chief justice said to him, "Mr. Bizos, if I tell one of my woman advocates here to leave the defense table and take a separate table and chair, can she refuse?" By asking that type of question, he really removed us from where we thought we were arguing, namely the principle of segregation in court. It put it as a question of authority. Can you disobey the order of a magistrate if he says, for whatever reason, "Get away from there; go and sit there?"

I did not take any interest in whether the practice continued in Boksburg after my case. I do know that I experienced the same thing in other courts and, rather than make another scene in those courts, I did sit at the segregated table. The practice really ended with the liberalization of the courts after attacks by some lawyers against the practice.

Pitje's description of the events is corroborated by the official report of the case as decided by the Appellate Division of the Supreme Court of South Africa, *Regina v. Pitje,* South African Law Reports 709 [1960 (4)].

In the course of the opinion, Chief Justice Steyn states:

✑ A magistrate, like other judicial functionaries, is in control of his courtroom and of the proceedings therein. Matters incidental to such proceedings, if they are not regulated by law, are largely within his discretion. The only ground on which the exercise of that discretion and the legal competence of the order might in this instance be called in question, would be unreasonableness arising from alleged inequality in the treatment of practitioners equally entitled to practice in the magistrate's court. . . . But from the record it is clear that a practitioner would in every way be as well seated at the one table as at the other, and that he could not possibly have been hampered in the slightest in the conduct of his case by having to use a particular table. Although I accept that no action was taken under the 1953 Act [which would have permitted the court to officially segregate the facilities], the fact that such action could have been taken is not entirely irrelevant. It

shows that the distinction drawn by the provision of separate tables in
this magistrate's court, is of a nature sanctioned by the Legislature, and
makes it more difficult to attack the validity of the magistrate's order
on the ground of unreasonableness. The order was, I think, a competent order.

The court concluded that the contempt citation was appropriate because Pitje, despite repeated warning, willfully disregarded the order of the
court. The decision set a precedent that, at least in theory, permitted an ab-
horrent practice to continue for decades. But, in fact, not many courts had
segregated tables for nonwhite lawyers, despite the condoning of the practice in *Regina v. Pitje*. Perhaps even the government found the court's argument that a practitioner forced to sit at a separate table "could not have been
hampered in the slightest" too ludicrous to withstand even the limited public scrutiny of apartheid South Africa.

Practice on His Own

∽ I was licensed in 1959 as an attorney. On the first of April, I started in
my own office in Johannesburg. My first office was at the corner of President and Fraser, in an old dilapidated building. Among the tenants was
Senator George Ballinger. We struck up a friendship and so I worked in
his office. He was not an attorney. He was a trade unionist from England
who came to help the labor movement in South Africa. I practiced out of
that office and had a general practice. At that stage, Mandela and Tambo
were virtually out of practice and full time in politics. I continued to have
contact with them, and I did some of their cases which they couldn't do at
the time. I inherited a few files from their office.

There were many problems associated with my practice. The first
problem was influx control. [*Influx control* refers to laws that regulated
where blacks could legally live and work within South Africa. In addition,
each black person was required to carry a pass that indicated the areas in
which his or her presence was permitted.] I had been given permission to
article with Mandela on the understanding that when I completed my articles, I would go back whence I came. In defiance, after I qualified I didn't
go back to my homeland, but rather I set up practice illegally in Johannes-

burg. It was illegal because of influx control. That was how Senator George Ballinger became important to me. I could occupy his office and hide the fact that I was practicing law.

When you came into Johannesburg from outside, the influx control regulations compelled you to go to the Labour Office, I think they used to call it. There, the first requirement was that you must be examined by a doctor, who must certify that you were free of disease. Otherwise, the assumption was that you were bringing disease into the area. So you stripped down, stood in a line, and the doctor walked around with a stick, looking at your private parts. Sometimes he picked it up. You didn't know what he was looking for. Anyway, at the end of the exercise, he put a stamp in your pass to say that you were given a nice bill of health. It happened to me in Pretoria when I first came to town, and it happened to me here in Albert Street when I came in 1955. I don't think there were exemptions.

The pass laws meant that I had to carry my pass on me at all times. When I was still a clerk, I stayed in Sophiatown,[7] and I developed a habit of coming into work early so I could put in an hour or so before other people came into the office. I would get off a train at Diagonal Street and walk along West Street. One morning, at the corner of West and Market, I was intercepted by what was then called the Ghost Squad, police in mufti—private clothes. One of them, a black chap, sort of touched my arm, to which I objected. I said, *tch* [a clicking noise]. He took offense at that and immediately handcuffed me. When I looked, I found there was a line of black men handcuffed. I was the last one in line. I didn't know why I was being handcuffed. Another black policeman said to the one who had handcuffed me, "What are you going to charge him for?" He replied, "Failing to produce." By that stage, I had taken out my reference, or pass book. It was in my hand.

But he said, "Well, as of the time I handcuffed you, you didn't have it. You have now produced it, so the charge will be failing to produce."

At about quarter past nine, Oliver Tambo got to the office and apparently received a report that I was somewhere in the street. He came along and spoke to the police. They turned out to be Xhosa chaps and he spoke to them in Xhosa to let me go. They obviously knew him and had respect for him so, without much ado, I was released from the handcuffs, protesting that I wanted to go to court and defend myself because I didn't think I had done anything. At that stage, a double-decker bus carrying whites from the suburbs stopped at the robot [traffic light].

They looked through the window and said, "Ha, a bunch of robbers, housebreakers. Look at them."

The assumption was that we were all criminals. It hurt to hear those words from white people in the bus. Anyway, I was released and I went back to the office, still protesting. Tambo's attitude was that even if they didn't release me, I was not going to go to court. Rather, they would drive all over until the van was full. Then they would go to the police station, not to court. He said, "You may not even appear in court today; they will lock you up." On that basis, it was better to have me released.

I had trouble with my pass when I went into practice by myself. Somebody had to sign my pass. When I was a clerk, this would have been Nelson Mandela. When he was not available, I was subject to arrest under Section 29 for being a loafer. I could have explained to them that I now had no boss, except that would expose the fact that, contrary to what I had said when I began my articles, I was still in Johannesburg after completing my articles.

There were also curfew regulations. You had be out of town by 10 P.M. [Under the laws then in effect, blacks could work in Johannesburg, but had to be outside the city after 10 P.M. unless they had specific permission to be there.] I used to do cases outside Johannesburg and I would invariably come back after 10 P.M. and be harassed by the police. A doctor friend of mine showed me an exemption by the native commissioner exempting him from curfew regulations. I then approached my local commissioner for an exemption.

His attitude was, "Why do you need an exemption? You don't need to be out at night. In case of an emergency, it is a simple thing; you go and get permission from the police"—which, of course, was rubbish because the police would then arrest me for being in town without a permit. But that was the commissioner's attitude.

Then there was discrimination in the courthouse itself. Many buildings had one entrance for whites and another for blacks. You might walk to court with a white attorney. When you got to the building, he went through one entrance, normally the front entrance, and as a black attorney, you would have to go around back. Inside the building there would be a consulting room that would be for whites. No provision was made for a black attorney. You stood in the corridor and took your statements and consulted with your client.

You went into court and talked to the prosecutor. At least you tried to talk to him. He was negative; he didn't want to know what you were doing there. In many cases, by the time you followed him into his court, he had not spoken to you. He didn't know what you had come to do. Once he became aware of your case, he took the file and put it at the bottom. He did all the cases and when he came to yours, he would ask for a postponement because it was late. From the economic point of view, it ate your heart out. A simple case which you could dispose of in an hour or so now had to take you another day. Even on that day you had no guarantee that your case would be heard.

Magistrates were hostile by and large. They didn't believe you were qualified. Some of them actually demanded to see your admission certificate. When you produced the certificate, they still didn't believe you could be a good lawyer. You faced the prosecutor on the one side and the magistrate on the bench, clubbing against you and making sure whenever possible that your client was convicted.

The white attorneys were no better. A white attorney would walk into court, not sit next to me, but take a seat at the other extreme end. In some cases, he came and sat next to the prosecutor and both of them conducted the case to make sure that you didn't succeed. The white attorneys in a sense were even worse than magistrates and prosecutors.

Because of this rough treatment and the fact that magistrates went out of their way to convict clients, clients tended to shun the black attorney in favor of a white attorney. In fact, there is a SePedi expression, *di chueu ga di tsoane*, which means that a white man will never fight with another white man. In essence, you're safer defended by a white man than by a black man.

One other problem in court was the court interpreter. [Interpreters, invariably blacks, were provided primarily for witnesses and litigants who would not be fluent in the official court languages, English and Afrikaans.] He could win a case for you and he could lose a case for you. If he wanted to help you, he interpreted and twisted the evidence of the witness to your favor. Because, by and large, the prosecutors and magistrates didn't understand the language, you would get away with it. On the other hand, if he decided he was against you, he would interpret in such a way that your client would be convicted. That's quite apart from the fact that some of them had linguistic difficulties. You take a case of rape. As a matter of politeness, an African woman will not say that "this man had sexual intercourse with me." She will say literally, "he slept with me" and stick to that wording. If the court interpreter keeps on using the words "he slept with me," at the end of the case there is no case because all the requirements for rape are not there.

I remember my first case in the magistrate's court. I found an interpreter who took a liking to me. In fact, he said, "We win this one." It was a case of theft by a boyfriend of money which was on top of the wardrobe in the room of his girlfriend. The interpreter's way of making sure that my client would be acquitted—and therefore I would look like a good lawyer—was to interpret properly as long as the woman was saying something that didn't incriminate my client. As soon as she mentioned something that was incriminating, he got into an argument with her.

The magistrate would say, "What's the problem?"

He would say, "I am talking about the window and she is talking about the door."

The magistrate would come down hard on the interpreter and say [to the witness], "You don't have to answer the question."

But the witness would get flustered and before I knew what was happening, I had stopped my cross-examination. The prosecutor had no other witness and my client was acquitted.

I cannot point to a specific year, but the situation got better. It was a gradual process and also depended on the individual and the type of practice he engaged in. I mean even as late as the nineties, when I had no difficulty, I would see a young attorney experiencing the same difficulty that we had experienced earlier on because of the attitude of the white magistrates.

Indignities of the sort suffered by Godfrey Pitje were not unusual for black lawyers who proceeded or followed him. Mohandas Karamchand Gandhi, known later as Mahatma Gandhi, came to South Africa from India in 1893, dressed in the barrister's uniform of frock coat and patent leather shoes. He had come to represent one Indian business firm in a court battle against another. He stayed for almost twenty-two years, practicing a little

law and a lot of politics. His first encounter with South African racism came
in the infamous incident of his removal from the first-class section of a
South African train. Gandhi also successfully fought a magistrate's order for
him to remove his turban in a Pretoria courtroom. Foreshadowing the
struggles of other black lawyers, he also overcame the opposition of the
Natal Law Society to become admitted as an advocate.[8]

Political Trouble

As I have said, I was articled at Mandela & Tambo on the strict condition that I wouldn't participate in politics. But it was difficult. For example, I would be invited to tea in the suburbs [areas of Johannesburg outside the central business district populated exclusively by whites] and I
innocently would go to have this tea. I thought I was going to meet the
owner of the house and his wife and family. I remember that a minister of
education from India came to the country. I was invited on the basis that
I was a former teacher; they needed an educator to talk to this chap. I
went to that house and there was this Indian minister of education. Before I knew what was going on, we were having a full-blown political discussion, never mind that it was centered around education.

Tambo noticed this and he called me aside and said, "Look, the best
way of attracting a ban [a banning order] is what is happening. If you're
going to keep off politics, let's decline this invitation."

But by then it was too late. The people who had invited me to the
house were white communists. I didn't know that. I mean as a child of
God from the rural areas, I took every white man on his face. It became
regular. It was tea; it was lunch; it was a dinner, some innocent coming of
people together.

Then the ANC was banned. The PAC Pan Africanist Congress] was
banned. [The year was 1961.] I became both an ANC and PAC lawyer. I
was compelled to brief advocates on behalf of both. The ANC became affiliated with a body called Defence and Aid, which was responsible for
collecting funds for political cases. I think the main funding was through
England. There was a local committee here running that fund. I think at
one stage I represented the ANC in the meetings dealing with funding.
Unknown to me, the government planted one or two informers who informed them of the activities of Defence and Aid.

Then some money came into the country and was given to various individuals to use politically. Evidence emerged of money not being properly used. People would get money and buy a car or furniture or whatever.

At that stage, Walter Sisulu approached me and said, "We will give you money which you will disburse. We can trust you. We will give you a lump sum and you disburse it in terms of our instructions. The money will come from the Right Reverend Arthur Blaxall of the Anglican Church."

In due course, I went to see Reverend Blaxall. He would give me a lump sum and I would disburse the money to the PAC and ANC people in terms of my instructions.

Blaxall was in charge of the School of the Blind, in Roodepoort, and I became a very frequent visitor there. In fact, he used to call a couple of what he considered African leaders on the Reef [the Witwatersrand (the white water's reef): the Johannesburg area] to this place to have political discussions. His school was on a *koppie* [a hill] sort of towards the valley. The Special Branch [the security police] would camp on top of the koppie, see us as we came in, take the number plates of our cars, and would be able to say on Sunday, 10 May, you were at such and such a house and driving this type of car.

The first hint that trouble was coming was when I got home one evening and I was told some Special Branch police had been there. They left their telephone number and address and they said, if possible, report to Benoni [the white town near where Pitje lived] tomorrow morning. As I remember the interview, I got there the following morning and I was asked if I knew Bishop Ambrose Reeves.

I said, "Yes."

"Who is he?"

"He's my Bishop."

"Well, tell us more about your relationship with him."

"It's one between a bishop and a congregant."

"Oliver Tambo?"

"That was my principal."

"Do you know where he is?"

"No, I don't know."

"Do you correspond with him?"

"No."

"Well, what do you hear of him?"

"Nothing."

"Nelson Mandela?"

"That was my principal."

"Are you in touch with him?"

"No."

"Do you know where he is?"

"No."

"Come on then, are they corresponding with you?"

"No."

(Mandela and Tambo were now underground. At least at that time, I was not aware that Tambo had skipped. Mandela I knew was still around because I used to meet him in disguise.)

"You know Reverend Blaxall?"

"Yes."

"What is your relationship with him?"

"A congregant and priest. We belong to the same church."

"Have you been to his place in Roodepoort?"

"Yes."

"What are you discussing there?"

"Oh, religious affairs."

"On a certain Saturday, you were there with so-and-so and so-and-so. What was going on?"

"Oh, friendly discussion about the church."

"Okay."

They let me go.

After a day or two, there were headlines: Blaxall Arrested. The police immediately descended on my office. I was interrogated from 10 A.M. to 8.00 P.M. When I said I had court work, they said, "Give us the cases that you have for today. We will communicate with the courts."

Just when I was sure that I was spending the night in jail, they said to me, "Let's go to the magistrate's court." That's when I discovered that the courts were in fact on twenty-four-hours duty in political cases. I found a beehive of activity in the magistrate's court. I was interviewed by one of the prosecutors, a Mr. Theron, who disclosed to me that he was the senior public prosecutor in Boksburg when I was found guilty of contempt of court. He actually said to me that he drew the attention of the magistrate to the fact that I was defiant. Anyway, now the prosecutor was very nice to me and said, "Well, I am surprised. They are wrong in bringing you here today. But your name has been tossed around very frequently. Have you not been banned?"

I said, "No."

He said, "As far as I know the ban has been signed." I found out shortly thereafter that he was right. But I was released that day.

Then Blaxall was prosecuted and I was called as a state witness. Blaxall was defended by Rex Walls, Q.C. I took advice from my own advocate. I think I consulted either Sydney Kentridge or Jack Unterhalter. [Walls, Kentridge, and Unterhalter were white, antiapartheid advocates.] They said, "Just make sure that you don't incriminate anybody, including yourself."

I asked what that meant. They said, "You acted in good faith: you didn't know (a) where the money came from; (b) what it was being used for; (c) you acted on instructions from your clients, the main client being Sisulu."

So I gave that evidence. Blaxall was found guilty and given a jail sentence but spent only one day in jail. He was released and he immediately went back home to England.

Before Reverend Blaxall was convicted, I would get cases from the PAC and the ANC. A number of the leaders of both groups were personal friends, so it was natural for them to look towards me. When Blaxall was arrested, the funds were frozen. At that stage, I owed a number of advocates, but I was helpless. [Attorneys are responsible for paying advocates who they have briefed on a particular case.] I couldn't get money from Blaxall, and the advocates, one by one, said, "What has that to do with me? I was briefed. I've done the work. How you're going to get funds is not my business."

I remember Unterhalter, having said that, came back to me to say, "I have made inquiries from Defence and Aid in England and they said that Defence and Aid in South Africa have to pay. But the Defence and Aid locally said we pay only for cases that come through us. If they go directly to you, that's your bill."

I really shudder to think of what would have happened if the Law Society had nosed around my office in those days. I don't know how many times I was blacklisted. If an attorney doesn't pay an advocate, the attor-

ney is blacklisted until the advocate is paid. That means that you can't
brief an advocate. And that means that if a case is to go to the Supreme
Court, you can't handle it because attorneys have no right of appearance
there. When you paid, they then lifted the blacklisting.

Banning

∞ On 1 October 1963 I was called to police headquarters, the Special
Branch in Main Street. I was served with a banning order. Five years. I
had to be at home from 8 P.M. to 6 A.M. during week days; on weekends
from 3 P.M. on Saturday to 6 A.M. on Sunday; report at the police in
Benoni once a week; not enter any premises where printing is done; not
enter a Coloured township; not enter an Indian township; not go anywhere near a school or be seen teaching any child; no social gatherings. It
was then interpreted as two is company, three is a crowd. As long as we
were two it was all right; when a third person walked in I was breaking my
ban, which was pretty stiff.

That was 1963. In 1965 my son died; he was ten years old. I needed
a permit to go and see him at the hospital. After his death, I was told by
the authorities that I had to sit in my bedroom and let those who, by
African tradition, would come to commiserate with me, come one by one.
Comes the funeral, they said I needed a special permit to go and bury my
child. They said that in the car must be you and members of your immediate family. They drew a route from my house to the cemetery. I had to
take that route and not say one word either at home or in church. I was to
come back by the same route. It was unpleasant, but I got through it.

Then would come Law Society conferences. I was then virtually the
only black lawyer in Johannesburg. I would apply for permission to attend the conference, and the chief magistrate of Johannesburg would give
me a permit saying that I was permitted to travel to Pretoria for a law conference. "Report your departure at Marshall Square [police headquarters];
take the straight route to Pretoria, report your arrival to Pretoria Central;
go to the conference by the shortest route; don't say a word in the conference. After the conference, report your departure to Pretoria Central; go
to Johannesburg; report your arrival at Marshall Square and then go directly home."

The original ban restricted me to Benoni, which was the town where

I lived, and Johannesburg, which was where I had my office. Then they discovered that in order for me to go from Benoni to Johannesburg, I must go through Boksburg and through Germiston, so they amended the order to permit me to go through those two towns.

The ban on social gatherings hit me very hard. I liked going to church, and the order prevented me from going to church. It was considered a social gathering. It was terrible. I got into trouble once over that part of the ban. My brother's daughter was being married, and the first thing was that *lobola* had to be paid [the traditional payment paid by the African groom to the family of his bride]. I took my wife and family to Pretoria. My intention was to drop them at the gate, come back, and fetch them later but not to go into the house. As I entered Mamelodi [the township where his brother lived], I saw a Volkswagen. I just ignored it. I didn't realize it was a police van. I got to the house and I was invited in to eat. I was just about to eat when the message came through to say that the police wanted me outside. I immediately realized what the position was, and I went into an outer room. They invited the police to come to me, and they reluctantly did but immediately took me to the police station. They charged me with breaking my ban. I went to court, where I was defended by Ivor Schwarzman [another white, antiapartheid advocate]. I was acquitted because we were able to prove that I didn't mix with the other people. If I had been convicted of breaking the ban, I would have gotten either a cautionary discharge or a suspended sentence. I don't think they would have really sent me to jail.

The banning order lasted eleven years, eleven months. It went first from 1 October 1963 to 1 October 1968; it was renewed for another five years, 1 October 1968 to 1 October 1973; renewed for another five years on 1 October 1973, but withdrawn during the course of the year in 1974. I don't quite know why it was withdrawn. The first five years I was advised that there was no hope of challenging the order. The second five-year ban, there was still that same feeling. But the third ban, we felt there was an argument.

What had I done in the ten years to deserve the ban? The order said, "Whereas I, so-and-so, minister of justice, am convinced that you are taking part in the furtherance of communism . . ." What had I done in ten years to do that? I approached Advocate Unterhalter, who went into the matter and he tried to speak to the minister. He made representations that I was living a clean political life, confined myself to law, and I was not aware of anything that could be regarded as subversive. He came back and said the minister says you don't have a chance. I approached the Law Society through its president, S. W. van der Merwe; he also came back and said they said you don't have a chance. I tried Helen Suzman, who was then a member of Parliament, and she came back with the same reply. I also tried Dr. Phatudi, who was chief minister of Lebowa [a homeland]. I don't think he succeeded either, although after the order was withdrawn in 1974, he claimed that it was because of his representations.

My banning had another sidelight. My son, Legwai, did his junior certificate at a school in Pietersburg. I felt that I wanted him to change schools, to bring him to St. Barnabas in Western Native township. I applied there, and he was accepted. Then the principal came with a rider: this is a Coloured area; he will need a permit to come here. We tried for a permit through Jack Unterhalter and he came back with a negative response. The reply was, "Oh, there are so many black secondary schools; he doesn't need to go there."

So that hit me hard. Eventually I had to take him to Natal to do matric. Later, I tried my best to get him to Fort Hare, because I didn't like the University of the North in Turfloop. But they refused on the ground that it was not possible, and eventually the only university I could send him to was Turfloop.

Those were just sidelights related to my banning: my son's death, my son's education.

During the time I was banned, I could no longer do political cases for the ANC or the PAC. My criminal cases would be largely in the magistrate's court and in the native commissioner's court: things like trespass, being in a restricted area for more than forty-eight hours, failing to produce a pass, Section 29 [influx control] cases. I did a little bit of civil work: seduction claims, defamation. The going was tough.

Then I got into the divorce court, and what helped me there was my involvement with a white lawyer called Henry Helman. He was a bully in the courts. He was a household name in the townships, and it was difficult to have a case in either the commissioner's court or the divorce court without having him as plaintiff's attorney or defendant's attorney. There were many attorneys who were afraid of facing him, but I had no choice. I found myself being on the other side in many cases, and word went round that there was one lawyer who could stand against Helman, and gradually my work accumulated until I basically was a divorce lawyer and had very little to do in the other courts. Eventually, I was on very good terms with the bench and could get away with many things that others couldn't get away with. I continued to do that kind of work, and that became my specialty from the time of my banning order all the way through until today.

The Black Lawyers Association

∾ As a result of all the difficulties I have discussed relating to the practice of law, and as our numbers picked up, I called the black lawyers together to make common representations to the authorities to be allowed to have offices in town and to be freed from influx control, pass laws, the lot. These lawyers used to meet in my office. Sometimes there would be three or four or five. The number gradually increased so that by 1978, when Dikgang [Moseneke] was admitted, there were more than ten of us. I remember this because Dikgang had hit a snag with his admission [see chap. 6]. We met and agonized over the situation. We briefed Jules Browde to represent us. From that point onwards, we met on a regular basis. Later, it was agreed that we would formalize the body, draw up a constitution, and have a properly constituted body. Throughout that period, I was chairman and leader of this group. I remember one year we agreed that we were going to storm the Law Society conference to attack them for discrimination, etc. It fell on my lot to lead the assault.

There was a young man at Wits, Ramaruma Moname, who was attached to [Professor] John Dugard in the Centre for Applied Legal Studies [at the University of the Witwatersrand; CALS]. Through that body, he went to America and came back with the idea that we could get black lawyers from America into the country to come and assist us. Through him, we got Judge Higginbotham [A. Leon Higginbotham Jr., then a judge of the United States Court of Appeals for the Third Circuit], Judge Henderson [Thelton E. Henderson, a judge of the United States District Court for the Northern District of California], and Julius Chambers [then director of the NAACP Legal Defense Fund] to come as our guests.

Before they left, they suggested to us that we needed to improve our organization. We ought to have an office. We ought to have some pamphlets to tell people who we were and what we were doing.

They came a second time in 1984, and this time we engaged them in a discussion of what we could do in this country to improve the lot of black lawyers. What were the problems facing us? At that time, there was only one university taking black candidates, the University of the North. It had a very poor law library. Most of the lecturers there were Afrikaans-speaking, and they struggled to teach in English. Consequently, the quality of that degree was not what it should be. Even if someone qualified there, he needed articles. There were no black firms to article you; the white firms would not accept you. If the young person completed his articles and he tried to set up practice, he had no funds, no library, no books. He could hardly get offices.

We decided that those of us who were qualified to take on articled clerks should take as many articled clerks as the law permitted. But we had no money to pay them. Therefore, we created a fund through which we could help pay these articled clerks. We also had young persons struggling to express themselves in court, struggling to conduct a case. They needed to improve their skills. What was the answer? The answer was to have an education center where these young people could be brought together, be lectured by experienced lawyers, have seminars, demonstrations.

Based on the discussion with the American judges and lawyers, the Black Lawyers Association applied for and received funds from various foundations based in the United States and elsewhere, including the Ford and Carnegie Foundations. A Legal Education Centre was established. When some younger lawyers, including Dikgang Moseneke, turned down the opportunity, Godfrey Pitje became the first director of the center. Beginning in 1984, he served as the full-time director of the center for more than three years.

The Present

∞ I left the Legal Education Centre in 1987 and came back into private practice. In 1994, out of the blue, Nelson Mandela literally ordered me to go to Pietersburg to help formulate the government of the Northern Province, and I have since remained there. I joined a team of about ten lawyers. We were told that our first task was to draw up a constitution for the province. Then I was asked to be one of the two administrators of the province. That has been phased out. When my coadministrator went back to his job in Pretoria, I was asked to remain in the government of the province and was later appointed chairman of the Tender Board [a review board dealing with government contracts]. I then became head of the legal team in the premier's office.

Godfrey Pitje declined to talk about what was perhaps the greatest tragedy of his life, the murder of his son, Legwai. Legwai Pitje was one of the only black advocates in Johannesburg in the 1980s and early 1990s. He was viewed by many of the young lawyers with whom he worked as a leader and a role model for all black advocates.[9] Legwai was murdered by an off-duty police officer in 1993. His friends and legal colleagues associate his death with his involvement in the Goldstone Commission's investigation of the role of the South African police in the ANC-Inkatha Freedom Party violence of the early 1990s. No linkage between that activity and his death has ever been established.

Godfrey Pitje died on 23 April 1997, after a short illness. People speaking at his memorial service and funeral included President Nelson Mandela, Chief Justice Ismail Mahomed, Minister of Justice Dullah Omar, and James E. Ferguson II, who represented all of the American lawyers (including myself) who had been involved in the trial advocacy programs conducted through the Black Lawyers Association–Legal Education Centre.

Godfrey Pitje was a remnant of the small generation of black lawyers that included Oliver Tambo and Nelson Mandela. In some significant respects, there were distinct generational differences between him and many of those who followed him in the profession, particularly recently. As in the case of the other more senior lawyers whose stories appear in other chapters, Godfrey was relatively fortunate to have gone to school before the days of Bantu education. But his rural religious upbringing set him apart even from others close to his age. He was educated in mission schools and delighted in both the education and the religious training he had received there. His education was modest when compared to what the average white was exposed to in his day, but he always seemed to have teachers he cared about and who cared about him. He was wary of white people, yet cognizant of the efforts that many made on his behalf. Also, as reflected in the incident where he was handcuffed by the police on the streets of Johannesburg, he was concerned about what whites thought of him.

His struggles, first as a lawyer actively involved in representation of clients in political cases, including his onerous banning order, and later as a divorce lawyer, exemplify the problems of his contemporaries and presage the careers of other black lawyers.

Arguably, Godfrey Pitje's greatest and most lasting accomplishment was his role in the formation of the Black Lawyers Association. His words appear again later in this book when he discusses the relationship between the Black Lawyers Association and liberal white lawyer groups (chap. 9).

2

⚖

SOME BEGINNINGS

I N S O M E senses, the family histories of black lawyers bear little in common with those of most other blacks in South Africa. Their families were usually better off economically; their parents' educational level was frequently higher. More than half the lawyers interviewed for this book had at least one parent who was a teacher. Often both parents were teachers. In other cases, parents were doctors or nurses. Virtually all the lawyers speak of the high premium placed on learning by their parents, even in those families where the parents had little education. It was and still is common for South African black parents to split up for many reasons, including the husband's need to find work in mines or factories far from his wife and children. Yet, the lawyers of this book generally came from intact families.

In other ways, the families and early education of these individuals were no different than those of other blacks. Almost all were poor when compared to the average South African white. They had few physical comforts. Most of their schools were overcrowded, inadequately staffed, and lacking in proper physical facilities. Perhaps of greatest significance for people whose careers would depend in large measure on their ability to use the English language, few grew up with English as their first language. As in the case of Godfrey Pitje, most black Africans grew up speaking one of the African languages. The first language for those classified as Coloured was likely to be Afrikaans. Even the acceptability of Afrikaans in the courts would not diminish the need for English in commercial transactions. Some black lawyers with good language aptitude learned to speak both English and Afrikaans fluently, along with half a dozen or more African languages. Others still struggle with English.

Fikile Bam

After ten years as a prisoner at the infamous Robben Island penitentiary, Fikile Bam became a well-regarded attorney and advocate. He serves today as president of the Land Claims Court, a court set up to deal with the claims of individuals who lost their property due to governmental action. Although born twenty years later than Godfrey Pitje, Bam was still fortunate enough to have the benefit of missionary schools whose educational policies were not dictated by the government under the Bantu Education Act. His experience was different from that of Pitje, but also reflects the impact of church-run schools on young black people.

I was born in the Transkei in a little town called Tsolo, very close to Umtata on the way towards Natal. It's quite a historical little place because the English colonials settled in Qumbu and Tsolo during the annexation of the Pondomise [part of the Xhosa nation]. They had camps there and that's how those two little places got important enough to become towns. I was born in 1937, on July 18th. That's according to my mother. My grandfather had 16 July 1938 written in his bible, so there was quite a discrepancy. My mother was the daughter of a missionary of the Moravian church, a German church. She came from a very deeply religious and missionary family. She went to a missionary school and first became a teacher and ultimately became a nurse.

My father also was a teacher. His education, for that time, was quite good. He had a degree in education from Fort Hare. He went to teach immediately after getting his degree. He came from what you would call a political family. His own father was a long-time member of the Pondo Bunga–the Transkei Territorial Council. After teaching for a while, my father became chief advisor and secretary to the paramount chief of the Pondo Bunga. Then off he went to the war.

My father was a staff sergeant. He did a lot of typing and at some stage he did a bit of work with first aid. He did go to the front but he was not in the artillery or anything like that; he was on the administrative side. There were black units within the South African army. They were mostly not armed when they were in this country. They only got armed if they were fighting outside the country, in Italy and in North Africa. There have recently been commemorations of them. For a long time, when we grew up, we were never even told that they existed. We heard about them from our fathers, not from the schools. These African soldiers played a tremendous role during the war. They made a lot of sacrifices, won medals. So my father came back from the war with all these stories. Not all of them were 100 percent truthful, but very entertaining all the same! He came back from the war and worked as a civil servant. He died in 1952.

In 1939 my father had to leave home to go to the army. My mother had to look after herself so she, in turn, left Tsolo to go and look for a teaching post. She didn't find one. She first went to work in Pondoland, where she got a post working as a housekeeper for Rev. Norton, a priest of the Anglican church. Subsequently, she worked in the house of a medical doctor, Dr. Drew, who was a superintendent of the mission hospital in Pondoland, at a place called Holy Cross, near Flagstaff. As a result of this work, she became interested in nursing. So I really grew up in this mission hospital at Holy Cross. That's where I first went to school. The important thing about it is that Oliver Tambo taught at this school at the time. I found him there as a teacher. It was an Anglican mission school; I doubt if it was subsidized at all by the state.

I was in that mission school until I passed my standard 2, which means that I spent four years there. After that my mother and I moved to Johannesburg. This was at the end of the war, 1946. We moved in order to be with our father, who was coming back from the war. We decided that it was probably better for us to settle in Johannesburg because he had better chances of getting a job there.

I continued with my education at an Anglican mission school, St. Cyprian's, in Sophiatown. St. Cyprian's was run by an Anglican religious order called the Community of the Resurrection. It was well known because Trevor Huddlestone, when he first came to South Africa, came to be a superintendent priest in this order. [Huddlestone was a well-known activist and associate of Nelson Mandela.] From St. Cyprian's, you almost automatically qualified and went to St. Peter's, which was the high school or secondary school which took people from other poor communities. A number of well-known people were there at the time including Hugh Masekela, the jazz trumpet player, and Jonas Gwanga, the trombonist. Oliver Tambo had taught at this primary school.

I went to high school in 1951 and was there until the school closed in 1956. The school closed because of the Group Areas Act. [The Group Areas Act divided South Africa into areas to be occupied by different racial groups. Under the act, there were separate areas set aside for whites, blacks, Indians, and Coloureds. With some limited exceptions, nonwhite groups were precluded from living in most white cities. Each group would live and of course have its segregated schools in its own designated township.] St. Peter's was in an area in the south of Johannesburg that subsequently became a white area under the Nationalist government. It had to move or become a white school. Those things happened to us. We had to close down St. Peter's. But the buildings are still there, the classrooms are still there, and the church is still there. It changed its name to St. Martin's and became a white school for the time that apartheid legislation was effective. Now it has again become an open multiracial school, predominantly white. It is still called St. Martin's.

At the time it was closed down as St. Peter's, the school had been in existence as a black school for well over fifty years. It was black in the wider sense that it had taken so-called Coloureds and people who were Asiatic, but it was predominantly black African. It was predominantly for the Anglican children and other denominations whose parents couldn't afford to send them to private schools. You went there mostly on a bursary, or scholarship, if you had done well at your primary level. Then the priest would make sure that you had some free education at St. Peter's. You would probably just pay for your clothing but not for your tuition. It was not a very big school, but it had a good reputation and lots of people still remember it.

We got as good an education as was available at the time for black children. It wasn't the same as the private schools to which white children went. Incidentally, St. Peter's did have a sister school, St. John's, which was white and which to this day is still one of the top white private schools. You couldn't compare life at St. John's to St. Peter's, but I think the substance of the learning was very good.

I finished matric in 1956 at St. Peter's. It closed just as I was leaving. I worked for a while. Then I got two scholarships, one of which was a medical scholarship. Sometimes I kick myself for not having taken it because it was a very lucrative scholarship. I could have gone that way, earned a lot of money and not landed in jail! I didn't like hospitals because both my mother and two of my sisters had been nurses, and just visiting them at hospitals was very unpleasant. One of my sisters was a theater nurse, and several times when I went there to see her I would see these people coming out bleeding all over, or their arms and things broken. I said, this profession wasn't for me. So I then took up a much smaller scholarship, which I had got through my headmaster, Michael Stern, to study anything, anywhere. I took this scholarship and I went to the University of Cape Town and I started to study in 1957.

I didn't register full-time in 1957 because I first tried to work in Johannesburg. My work didn't turn out well. At the beginning of 1957, I was having an unpleasant time with my employers because of discriminatory practices within the workplace. It was a bookshop and I unpacked books, shelved, categorized, and priced them. In a bookshop, you have to know which books you have and how much they cost and sometimes also a little about what is in them. But there was racial discrimination. They actually were quite fond of me. They liked me, but then they got another girl, a white girl who also had just passed her matric, to come in and work. As she came in a full two months after I had come in to do the job, she learned all that she had to learn about the job from me. Then lo and behold, she was already earning more than I was. She really did not have the same qualifications; she was even a year younger. She came in a bit later than I did to work and left a bit earlier. I was teaching her the work. She told me that her very first salary was substantially more than what I was getting, so that was one gripe I had against the employers. The second thing was, I was also raising other issues like half an hour lunch time allowed to black workers and the sort of conditions people were working under. Although it was a bookshop, we had to go and eat at the back. It was dirty and damp, and I said something about that, which wasn't very well taken.

I think the final straw came with what was called the Alexandra bus boycott in 1957. [Alexandra is a black township adjoining Johannesburg.] The buses that ferried people from Johannesburg to Alexandra and back raised the fares. I was staying in Alexandra. In protest, we decided to walk back and forth, which meant that we were often late at work and got there very tired and slept. The employers didn't think that our bus boycott was a good decision for us to have taken in the first place and said, "Look, you either come to work on time or you get fired." Well, I couldn't come in on time and I wouldn't stop boycotting the buses, and ultimately we had to part company. It was just as well because it was then that I decided to look around for bursaries [scholarships to university]. I just resigned and they were happy for me to go.

Phineas Mojapelo

Phineas Mojapelo is now a prominent attorney in Nelspruit, a small city in the far northeast province of Mpumalanga, not far from the vast wildlife preserve Kruger National Park. He was born and lived his early years in roughly the same rural section of the country as Godfrey Pitje. Although it was almost thirty-five years later, their early experiences had much in common.

Mojapelo was born in 1951 in Pietersburg, in the Northern Province. His father died when he was an infant and he was brought up by his mother and grandparents. The family spoke SePedi (also called Northern Sotho).

He grew up in a rural area. His first school consisted of two rooms in an abandoned farmhouse. His mother was one of the three teachers. The school moved to more formal surroundings when he was in standard 1 (third grade), but there were still the same three teachers. All of the teaching was in SePedi.

In 1963 Mojapelo began standard 3 (fifth grade) at a Roman Catholic school.

 I wasn't Roman Catholic, but I went there because of problems at the village level. The community in which the school we were attending was located would not admit us to that school anymore. The Roman Catholic school became the only option. My people, the Mojapelo people, had for a long time been involved in a fight to try to regain their tribal land and their chieftainship, which had been taken over. The Mojapelo people had a small piece of land in an area which didn't have a school. When they did not want to fall under Chief Molepo, the Molepo people refused them permission to send their children to their school.

The distance between my home and the school which I first attended I would estimate would be something in the order of five kilometers. We had to go past a river and some bushes and travel quite a long distance to get to the school. Of course, when the farm school moved that meant we had to travel even further. We still walked, there was no other way. And when I had to change schools at the end of 1962 that meant that I had to travel even further—probably ten kilometers. We had to go past one river, up a mountain, down the mountain, up the next mountain, and down that mountain. I walked to school barefoot until I passed my standard 6 in 1966.

In 1964 it looked as if there were hopes for the Mojapelo people to get back their tribal land. In order for the tribe to reassert its relationship with the land which was the original land that they had owned, they established a school there even before they moved there, which meant that I had to travel much longer distances to school. I attended that school through standard 6 [eighth grade].

I was also a herd boy. I had to look after my grandfather's cattle, and even if my grandfather did not have cattle, in that environment every young boy had to look after the community's cattle. In the perception of my grandparents and all the villagers where I grew up, looking after cattle was just as important as going to school, if not more important. The tribal people had to look after their cattle lest they cross onto a white man's farm, where the cattle would be impounded. Cattle were the basis of their wealth and whatever they had. We were therefore divided into pairs, and on the one day you would go and look after cattle and you wouldn't go to school. On the second day, you would go to school. Until I did standard 6, I would actually attend school for two days in one week and three days in one week on a continual basis. Funnily enough, I would always find that at the end of the year I was able to catch up. But the system left quite a lot of people behind, of course.

Mojapelo passed his national standard 6 examination with a first class, an exceptional achievement, given the humble circumstances of his early education.

∽ Nineteen sixty-six, the year in which I passed my standard 6, was also an interesting year in many respects. I still remember very vividly the radio had just come into South Africa and it was an in thing, and each school had to have its own radio. There was a radio period, where the school would break and go and listen to the radio. I remember in 1966 the news coming that the then prime minister of South Africa, Dr. Verwoerd, had been stabbed to death in Parliament. With all the land issues and the other problems which our people experienced at that time, the question of a head of state being stabbed to death in Parliament struck me as quite an irony. I will tell you that in South Africa a knife is used for cutting; it's a domestic instrument. Only the *tsotsis,* the rough guys, the people who don't behave, actually kill each other with knives. So here was a head of state actually being killed like a tsotsi. I remember my principal actually getting us to discuss this issue. The general view in that small classroom was, beware! That is exactly how they treat people; that's exactly how they are going to die. They live a dishonorable life and they will die a dishonorable death.

When I went to standard 7, the school I was to go to was, by far, much further than my other schools. I would have had to walk for close to a day before I got to school. So my mother put together all the money she could to put me in a boarding school. It was an interesting boarding school—it had no running water and no electricity. The name of the school was Tshabela, and it was in the Molepo area, approximately thirty to forty kilometers east of Pietersburg. For the first time in my life I had an opportunity to go to school every day, and, of course, we were taught for the first time in a language other than Northern Sotho. We were taught in Afrikaans and English: half the subjects in Afrikaans, half in English. Northern Sotho would be done only in Northern Sotho lessons. During the first years, you were taught some subjects in Afrikaans and some in English. During the last two years, the subjects that you had been taught in English had to be taught in Afrikaans and those that you had been taught in Afrikaans had to be taught in English. The result was that you actually learned mostly just concepts in different languages, and in terms of progressive learning of the substance itself, one didn't learn much.

Black schools did not have mathematics teachers except perhaps in the black townships, which had better schools than the rural areas. I remember at our school we had a mathematics teacher who came from Nigeria. How he found himself in that part of the world I still can't figure out. He was an excellent mathematics teacher, but he had other likings in life, including enjoying alcoholic drinks. He wouldn't be in class most of the time. When he came, it was excellent to be taught by this middle-aged man, as he then was. When we were doing our second year with him, he died. I don't know what the cause of death was, but I remember him losing weight, coming less and less to school, and eventually he died. I suspect it could have something to do with the type of life he was leading. But then the whole school was without a mathematics teacher, and at least for the four years that I was there, mathematics wasn't taught at our school. This kind of thing would account in the main for there being no black scientists, no black mathematicians, very few doctors, particularly from rural areas. There were no white teachers at all. I didn't have white teachers until I got to university.

There was an improvement while I was at that school in the sense that the school committee managed to buy a generator, and we could then switch on lights for reading. Before then, you had to have your own candle and light it, and if you didn't have enough money to buy candles, you had to make sure that you finished all your studying before it became dark. Of course we had to pay a petrol fee because the generator was operated on petrol. The generator was to be on in the evening for two hours. After two hours, they had to switch it off; otherwise we wouldn't be able to afford the petrol for the following day.

Ismail Mahomed

Ismail Mahomed, one of nation's most respected advocates and now chief justice of South Africa, was born in Pretoria in 1931.

∽ Both my parents were born in India, but the first generation that came here was my grandfather. I am the third generation in this country. My family has been in this country for over 100 years.

My father was a shopkeeper, but he is now retired. He is a man of great sensitivity, personalitywise, and my mother was very strong, but they didn't have education. My father could manage basic accounts and so forth for his business, but he had very little formal education. He did do some primary school in an Indian dialect in India, where he was born. My mother was the same. She could read the Qur'an in Arabic, but she didn't understand what she read. She communicated to her distant relatives in India in an Indian language in which she had gotten some primary education. Other than that, my parents were substantially illiterate.

We lived right in the middle of Pretoria, the administrative capital of South Africa. We lived in the central business district, in a street in which black South Africans of Indian origin traded and lived. It was one of two such areas in Pretoria. The other one was called the Asiatic Bazaar, and this one was called the Prinsloo Street area. The community in which I lived consisted mostly of shopkeepers whose ancestors were of Indian origin. We lived either in little residential units behind shops or in flats above the shop. It was impossible to expand our living quarters because there was a law which precluded the expansion of such properties without governmental permission, which was rarely obtained. The result was that large families grew up in very cramped quarters. Because we were in the center of the city, there were hotels and restaurants which we passed but were never permitted to go into. I never knew what the inside of a hotel looked like for most of my life.

There was a university close by which gave courses after hours to white students. Although I grew up virtually under the shadow of that university, I never had access to it. There was also a school nearby which white children peopled and which I never saw inside. We went to a school

approximately two or three kilometers away in the other area for South
Africans of Indian origin in Pretoria, the Asiatic Bazaar. The school had
only people of Indian origin. By law, we were not permitted to go to a
white school or a black school and so I was brought up in a school which
consisted 100 percent of South Africans of Indian origin, save for an occa-
sional Chinese student. The medium of instruction was English. I stayed
at that school for approximately twelve years, until I matriculated in
1950. In those days, there were not many students of Indian origin who
matriculated in Pretoria. My class at Pretoria Indian Boys High School
consisted of ten students. Today there are several hundred probably.

Lewis Skweyiya

Most blacks pulled themselves up by their own bootstraps in order to
achieve some sort of education. Occasionally, however, there was help from
sympathetic whites, especially teachers. Lewis Skweyiya is a nationally
respected advocate in Durban. In addition to his law practice, he has headed
several important official government inquiries. He was born in 1939 to
Xhosa-speaking parents.

∞ In those days the usual thing was to go to a boarding school, which
were missionary schools really. I went to a school known as Healdtown.
Healdtown was one of the ivy leagues of the black community. I was able
to go there because although my mother was not educated, she believed
that people have to go to school. You must struggle through it. Also, I
happened to have been doing well at school. When I passed my primary
education, I went to my principal and he asked me where I was going to
go to school next.

I said, "I am not going anywhere because I cannot afford to."

He then said, "No, you cannot just not proceed further. I will help
you."

So the principal of my school helped me through the rest of my
schooling. Of course my mother paid the bulk of my fees. I then went to
boarding school, which was *the* thing then.

The school I went to was the school to which Mandela went.[1] Healdtown was the center of education in the Eastern Cape. It was a Methodist

institution. Healdtown and another high school, Lovedale, were next to Fort Hare University. I did quite well at high school and again I had money problems. In fact, when I passed my standard 8, I had not applied to go back to school. The boarding master called me and said, "I believe you have not reapplied to come back next year."

I said, "Yes, my parents cannot afford it. I have no money. I will have to go and work a few years and then come back."

Then the boarding master said, "No, do apply. Here are the forms. Someone will pay for you, but she said you must not tell who she is."

So I filled in the forms. I went back the following year. I tried to find out who it was and ultimately I did find out. It was my maths [mathematics] teacher, a white lady who was a spinster who taught me maths at school. She, together with my science teacher, apparently decided to pay my fees to make sure that I would go back. She openly helped again when I was writing my final exams in matric.

3

$$\doteqdot$$

GROWING UP UNDER APARTHEID

Tʜᴇ ʀᴀᴄɪᴀʟ laws of apartheid South Africa were voluminous and complex. At one point, someone estimated that 60 percent of the nation's laws involved race in one way or another. Racial classifications determined where you could live and work, where you could go to school, and what kind of job you could hold. The differences were not only between blacks and whites. Each of the four major racial groups—whites, black Africans, Indians, and Coloureds—had its specific set of rights and, especially in the case of black Africans, limitations. The web of the legal implementation of apartheid often caught some of the lawyers-to-be and their families. These experiences could only have had a significant influence on the life and career choice of the young people involved.

Mahomed Navsa

Mahomed Navsa was an advocate and is now a judge of the High Court in Johannesburg.

∽ I was born 4 May 1957 in Edenvale, a town close to Jan Smuts airport [the major airport serving Johannesburg and Pretoria]. It was a white group area at that time. My father was a general dealer and later was a cinema manager. In relation to our friends and the people with whom we associated at school and socially, my father probably tried more than most to expose us to books. Every spare cent he had went on books. We had a bit of a library at home. My father's shop was at the edge of a massive African location that was relocated to Tembisa.

I am of mixed parentage. My father's father was Indian and his mother was Malay; my mother is Malay. There was a time when my father had to appear before the Race Classification Board because of his parentage. His father was his only parent who was officially registered. In terms of the old laws, he ought to have taken his father's race, Indian. But the board registered him as Cape Malay and he was therefore classified as Coloured. He remembers (he is seventy-nine now) with great resentment and bitterness the experiences of the Race Classification Board and also how he was picked up repeatedly by police and questioned about his ancestry.

Because of my father's reclassification, we moved from Edenvale to a Coloured group area, Reiger Park, when I was about fourteen years old. We felt resentment, not only from white people. I never felt I fitted in. Indian people used to expect me to converse with them in an Indian language. Coloured people used to see me as an outsider. It was a very trying time socially. I was also required to leave an Indian school, which was the only English medium school close to where I lived. There wasn't space in any Coloured school near us. The only school I could go to was in Kimberley [in the Northern Cape, approximately three hundred miles from Johannesburg], and that's where I finished my school.

I graduated from William Prescott School in Kimberley. It was an English and Afrikaans school. The real benefit for me in going to Kimberley was that there wasn't a separate Indian and Coloured school. It was one school. I lived with my uncle, A. R. Abass, who was the president of the South African Rugby Union. That was really the nonracial federation which was opposed to the status quo in the establishment. So in a sense, I had an increased politicization because of the situation in the home in which I boarded for two years while I was at high school.

Selby Alan Masibonge Baqwa

Selby Baqwa was born in 1951 to Xhosa-speaking parents. He practiced as an attorney and then an advocate in Durban before being named Public

Protector of South Africa, essentially an ombudsman for citizen claims against the government.

    ∽ I wasn't politically active in the years before I went to university. My father was not a person who was politically active. Teachers were not allowed to be politically active at that time. But if you lived in South Africa at that time, politics literally determined every minute of your life. However comfortable you may have been in terms of what your parents provided for you, immediately after you left the gates of your home, you couldn't help but meet the harshness of the system that existed around you.

    For instance, when we moved to the small town of Umzimkulu in the Transkei, where my father taught last, he tried to buy a house for us and entered into a contract with an Indian person. The house was nice and was situated in the comfortable side of town, which obviously was the white side of town.

    No sooner had he concluded the deal for that house, about which all of us were ecstatic, than he was reminded by the village management board that he couldn't live in the house because it was in a white section. The Group Areas Act was the law. We ended up in the poorer side of town, where there was no running water, the tap was 100 yards outside, and the sewerage was pit system. Facilities were rather scanty and life was not easy, but that's where the blacks lived and we had to suffer it.

    Even to the simple mind of a child you think, "My father had entered into a contract, and he had the means to buy that house, and somebody told him, No you cannot live there because you are black." I mean it started sending the message that something was wrong, something was not right out there. Through the formative stages at high school and so on, one started getting more of a sense that there was a lot that had to be put right in the country, and politics started creeping into my mind.

Dolly Mokgatle

    Not all black lawyers came from families with above-average education or incomes. Not an insignificant number had parents who struggled to put food on the table. Dolly Mokgatle was born in 1956 in Alexandra township, the poor and incredibly chaotic township bordering the wealthy Johannes-

burg suburb of Sandton. She is now senior general manager, the equivalent
of a senior vice president, at Eskom, South Africa's massive electrical utility.

∞ My father was a hawker. He started out as a tailor in Alexandra, and
he went out selling soft goods to bring up his children. He had eight children. My mother was a domestic worker until she got married and then
became a housewife. My father died in 1963, when I was seven years old.
Two years before that he had moved us to Springs, which is east of Johannesburg. He was born in Springs, and my father's family came from an
old township, which is now nonexistent, called Pineville, in Springs. Most
of his brothers and sisters had settled in Springs, and so he was the odd
one out living out in Alexandra. I think he was persuaded by his family to
move closer to home.

My mother brought us up single-handed. She never went back to
being a domestic. She was fortunate enough to find a job in a shop, a
department store in Springs. Her salary was not much higher than what
the domestics got. She had eight children to bring up. When she started
she used to earn R6.50 [rands] a week. I remember it was quite extraordinary because she went to work and we waited. We knew that the bus
would drop her at six o'clock. My home was the third house from the corner and the bus terminus was very close to the house and we would wait
outside or around the house—just waiting for that six o'clock bus to come
through. The minute she walked into the house, we would grab her bag
and look for what?—for bread. She was very health conscious. She bought
half a loaf of whole wheat bread every day and cut a slice to have with tea
in the morning, two slices with whatever at lunch, and another slice for
tea in the afternoon, and the rest she brought home. That was the best
treat you can imagine for us! It was quite a struggle. I don't know where
she got the strength, but she managed to raise eight children.

Timothy Bruinders

In many ways, the apartheid laws were most confusing and difficult to
comprehend for the group classified by the government as Coloured. There
were actually many different ethnic groups contained within the classification. Indeed, the entire grouping was a product of apartheid creativity.

Some were people of mixed race—for example, black African and white, black and Malay, or Malay and Indian, as in the case of Mahomed Navsa. Other Coloureds were people of full Malay descent. Although there are many Coloured people living throughout the country, by far the greatest number are concentrated in the Cape Town area. Timothy Bruinders, now an advocate in Johannesburg, reflects some of the confusion that others in his government-created racial group must have felt.

> ∞ I was born in District Six, Cape Town, in 1958. I lived there for the first couple of months of my life. Then my parents moved out on to the Cape Flats, first to Athlone [a Coloured township in the Cape Flats] and then to Grassy Park. But during the time we lived in Athlone and Grassy Park, my grandmother still lived in District Six, so I spent a lot of time there.
>
> The house that my grandmother lived in was an old double-story house which they rented from a local businessman, an Indian business-man actually. It was an old house where my mother was born. Her mother had lived in it when she was very young. It was shared between three or so families, so it was my mother and her cousin and another cousin, a lot of people living in the same house. Everybody lived there in District Six. It was an open area, a nonracially defined area. My mother lived in that house at a time when her neighbors were Africans, Jews, Coloureds, Muslims. It was a complete melting pot of cultures. She recalls vividly that the neighbors opposite were among the most educated people that she knew and they were African.
>
> My earliest memories of District Six, as a child, were spending the end of the year there, particularly during New Year's and Christmas, that sort of time. There were always carnivals. They call them minstrels now; then they were called Coons. As a kid I had these vivid memories of peo-ple who dressed up very weirdly in colorful psychedelic dress. There were people who were minstrels and people who we called the devils who dressed up like winged dinosaurs.
>
> The removals started in the late sixties after the Group Areas Act was promulgated. Ostensibly they were supposed to start in the late sixties, but I can't actually recall seeing people moving out. But in the early seven-ties, I can remember we used to call the removals the Group. The move-

ment from District Six was a combination of two things. The District was
declared a white area, so that anybody who wasn't white had to move out
from District Six. Secondly, there were sections of District Six that were
declared slums to get rid of people who didn't want to move. There was a
resistance to moving. Friends who were at high school with me in 1971,
just on the outskirts of District Six, came from the district. I recall that
they were moved out because not only was it a group area, but their
houses had been declared slums. They had to get out because the houses
had to be torn down. One day they were in their houses and the next they
were not. Kids at school would come and say, We have been moved out.

As in the case of Sophiatown, Johannesburg, the removals of nonwhite
people from District Six in Cape Town and the destruction of most of the
buildings in the area was a particularly gruesome example of the excesses of
the apartheid era. The events surrounding the end of District Six have been
the subject of considerable writing, both scholarly and popular.[1]

∽ My father was a bus conductor; my mother was a shop assistant. I
come from a mixed background. I think that my father was classified differently from the way we were classified. We were classified as Other
Coloured. My mother was classified as Cape Coloured and my father . . .
I can't remember. It was just strange; it was the Nationalist government.
They needed to pigeonhole people. My mother's father's family are of
Scottish descent. My mother's father was a very fair man whose parents or
grandparents were vaudeville Scottish actors who came out here. He had a
hooked nose. My mother's mother was of Moorish descent, so she was
very dark and also had a hooked nose. She was a bit of a mixture. She said
that one side of her family were Javanese. But she had sort of North
African features. It's quite bizarre actually that she was very dark and had
this hooked nose and had the same nose as her husband, who had come
originally from Scotland. My father's grandfather was Dutch. My sisters
have followed the family tree. I never really paid much attention to it,
partly out of reaction against the whole pigeonholing exercise of the
Nationalist government. To me, everybody was the same. In retrospect, it
was probably wrong of me. It would be interesting to know.

My father left school when he was thirteen or fourteen. My mother

left school at about the same age—standard 6. Both of them had older
brothers or sisters who died. They were the oldest and they literally had to
leave school to go and work to support younger siblings. All of my father's
brothers went to college. Two of them went to university and became
teachers. One of them is actually a presenter on television. My mother's
family, not one of them is well educated. They are all in factory work.

We spoke both English and Afrikaans at home. My father is
Afrikaans-speaking and always was. My mother spoke English, but it was
patois. We were completely bilingual. Our father would speak to us in
Afrikaans as kids, and we would answer in English because we thought
Afrikaans was the language of the oppressor. But we were just very young
and silly. Afrikaans actually is, as I discovered much later, not only a beautiful language but is a language that a lot of oppressed people have used to
express themselves very eloquently and poignantly. My father's brothers
read lots of Afrikaans poetry and literature. They would come from the
Eastern Cape and recite Afrikaans literature, a bit left of center (Breyten-
bach, Louw, that sort of thing) but the sort of stuff that a lot of conservative Afrikaners would also have read. They would read it and recite it.
They would also come down and watch rugby. They would support the
opposing team, the British Lions or the French, but would never support
the South Africans. Whether it was rugby or cricket, they would come to
watch a big match and the night before have lots of whiskey and talk
Afrikaans literature. The next day they would go there and support the
opposing team, whoever it was! It was a very strange way of growing up,
really.

I went to primary school in Athlone, up to standard 5. This was a
school that was reserved for Coloureds. If you talk racial features, there
was a particular point in my life where those things became completely
meaningless. I made a point of disabusing myself of even acknowledging
that people have different racial features. It was part of the process of
growing up under apartheid. But in my primary school, the people were
all classified as either Cape Malay, Cape Coloured, Other Coloured,
Rehoboth, Griqua. All those classifications. But people ranged from
people who looked completely white, to people who look like I do [dark-
skinned, but with few African features], to people who had features of
people who are African. They were all classified under the broader

umbrella of Coloured, and in that there were different classifications. Therefore, although there were no people at my school who were classified as white and no people there who were classified as African, the kids I went to school with were as light and lighter than most whites and a hell of a lot darker than I am. And I am pretty dark. So it was a lot more unhomogeneous than people think it was. We didn't have any white or African teachers. Our teachers were all classified as Coloured.

The school was in a poor community in Bridgetown in the Cape Flats. It was in a subeconomic housing estate. Although I went to school barefoot, I was a lot better off than half my classmates. There were kids who came to school with holes in their trousers. They never wore shoes, even through winter; they were too poor. It was a working class neighborhood, yet there were people who were qualified tradesmen in that area: printers, lithographers in the old printing trade before computers came, machinists, and so on. It was a bilingual area, Afrikaans and English, although not too much English was spoken—a lot of the mixture of the two really. Not too many kids from that school ended up at university. There was one kid at the school that I recall who was a neighbor. We knew from the day he could speak that he was phenomenally bright, and he is the only kid from my school that I recall having gone to university. In fact, he went to university in the United States on a scholarship. He became a chemist. He is from a Catholic family; there were thirteen kids.

4
♊

BANTU EDUCATION

THE Bantu Education Act of 1953 was a major step in the development of Grand Apartheid or "separate development." On its face, the act seemed routine enough. Funding and administration of education were transferred from missions and provincial authorities to the national government. In order to cement ethnic awareness, African vernacular languages were to be used as the medium of instruction for primary school students. The number of school places for blacks actually increased from 800,000 in 1953 to 1,800,00 in 1963.[1]

In actuality, Bantu education was a blueprint for maintaining blacks as an underclass. Then minister of native affairs (later prime minister) Henrik F. Verwoerd, speaking in support of the act in Parliament, stated that there was no place for Africans in white South Africa "above the level of certain forms of labor."[2] Curricula were to be redesigned with a view to eliminating "wrong expectations."[3] Separate curricula for black children were in fact developed for forty years—lesson plans geared toward the education of semiliterate manual laborers and domestic servants, not attorneys or advocates.

The primary targets of the Bantu Education Act were the mission church schools run by various Christian denominations. In 1948 there were over five thousand mission schools in the country.[4] Prior to Bantu education, a number of lawyers had received their education in church-run schools, including Godfrey Pitje, Fikile Bam, and Lewis Skweyiya. Many denominations, including the Anglicans, Roman Catholics, Presbyterians, and Methodists, had had excellent schools. The schools received some government subsidies and could develop their own curricula. They often provided a reasonably good educational experience despite inadequate facilities. After the Bantu Education Act, all private schools were required to be licensed and subsidies were usually unavailable.[5] A few, especially those sponsored by the Roman Catholic Church, continued to exist but struggled both for funds and for the ability to design their own curricula. Some of the lawyers interviewed had the advantage of going to those schools.

Yvonne Mokgoro

Yvonne Mokgoro was born in 1950 of Tswana-speaking parents. She is now a judge of the Constitutional Court of South Africa. She was one who attended a Roman Catholic school that survived under the dictates of Bantu education.

∽ I went to school at St. Boniface School from kindergarten up to standard 10. It was a Roman Catholic mission school in Kimberley. It was managed in the earlier part of the school by German nuns and in the high school by American Catholic missionaries. The school was quite renowned in the Northern Cape for its academic excellence. It was Catholic and it was missionary. During that time, the missionaries in their own way were very defiant of apartheid. Although we were part of the Bantu education system in that we wrote Bantu education exams, they tried, in defiance of course, to teach us wider or broader curricula than what Bantu education required them to do. Even the school's attitude was much more open-minded than what Bantu education imposed on schools. For that reason, students at the school always performed better than those at other local Bantu education schools.

It was an African school; definitely it was an African school. But then in my time we didn't have mixed schools. That was unheard of. We never even interacted with white schools. The nearest I could ever get to a white school were those that I passed every day when I went to my mother's workplace in the afternoon after school to assist her with minding the baby while she finished her work. I passed through those white suburbs, and I would see these immaculate schools and see these kids, participating in sports that we could only dream of, dressed in bright uniforms. With us, it didn't matter whether you wore a uniform. If you couldn't afford a uniform, you went without it. That was also one of the good things about going to that missionary school. School authorities were very compassionate, very sympathetic to the reality that we were poor and school uniforms were an unaffordable luxury.

I remember so well a thing that was very different from all the other schools in our township. They offered us a slice of bread every day! If you never had anything to eat before you went to school, you were at least assured of a slice of bread, which most of the time was our only "meal" for the day. That meant so much to some of us. In winter, each child was offered a cup of soup with a slice of bread. That too was something that all of us looked forward to when we went to school. In our neighborhood people would think we were privileged because we went to a school where we could get a slice of bread for the day.

Because it was a missionary school, the fees were very minimal. We only had to pay something like 25 cents a month. I think it was probably just a symbolic fee. Sometimes we would owe that 25 cents for a whole year because we couldn't afford to pay it. The nice thing about the school too was that we paid the 25 cents per family, not per head. If a family had more than one child at the school, they still paid 25 cents. Everybody wanted to get into St. Boniface, but it was a Catholic school and you had to be Catholic. Some people actually converted to Catholicism, not because they understood what it meant, but because they wanted a chance to get into the school! So with us nine children, you would find that we were four or five at the school at the same time, and we would only pay a total of 25 cents for school fees. But then, of course, you had the books to buy, and that was another question altogether.

I was fortunate in the sense that when I started standard 7, I got a scholarship from the Kimberley Rotary Club. They sponsored me from standard 7 to standard 10. I graduated from high school through the sponsorship that I got from the Kimberley Rotary Club. In return I had to perform well. I had to submit my annual school grades to them to have the scholarship renewed.

My mother was a washerwoman and was working for a white family. The man of the family, Mr. Adams—I remember him very well—owned a local men's outfitters. He was a member of the Kimberley Rotary Club. For some reason, my name came up as the subject of conversation between my mother and him, "her boss." If I may say so myself, I was a bright kid at the time and my mother mentioned this to him. She also mentioned how worried she was that I might not be able to do high school because she and my father could not afford the books. Then he suggested that she submit my school grades to him so that he could nominate me for a scholarship from the Kimberley Rotary Club. He did that and I got the scholarship. I had to resubmit my school grades every year in order to renew the scholarship for the following year. I managed to do that and that's how I managed to graduate from high school.

Because I had aid of the scholarship, I was the first one in my family to go up to standard 10 [twelfth grade, called matric]. My elder sister could only go up to standard 8, but then you could train as a nurse or a teacher with a standard 8. I was the first one in my family to get a university education—perhaps through my own efforts, too, because I studied part-time while I was working.

Dolly Mokgatle

In chapter 3, Dolly Mokgatle described the heroic efforts of her widowed mother to provide food for her family. Mokgatle attended state schools directly affected by the Bantu Education Act.

∞ I went to school in the local community schools and finished matric there in 1974. Like almost all blacks my age, I went through Bantu education. It's only our children who now have opportunities, through our efforts, to go to private schools. But we all went through Bantu education, and none of us had any choice unless you had parents who could afford either to take you overseas or to schools in Lesotho or Swaziland. People like Kgomotso Moroka [see next excerpt], for example, were not products of Bantu education. Her father was a doctor so she was taken to one of the best schools in Swaziland.

I think it gave me a good foundation. I eventually went to a black university. I am sure I would have made it even if I had gone to a white university because we were so used to hard work. I would have made it just the same, although the gap would have been much bigger.

Looking back, I think I could have done better. I am sure we would all have done better had we had education in areas or in schools that had much bigger and better facilities, but we didn't. There were very poor facilities in most African schools. I don't want to generalize too much, but you couldn't compare the facilities in township black schools to the facilities in white schools. First of all, our numbers, I learn now, were close to three times the size of normal numbers in white classes. We had sixty in a class. I am talking about lower primary, which is from grade 1 to standard 2. In the private school where my daughter goes, there have never been more than twenty-six kids in a class.

So the numbers were bad and the teachers were obviously teaching under very strenuous circumstances having to teach so many children. I am not going to blame them for any flaws in our education. They were really doing their best. They never had the time that I see my daughter's teachers taking. I can only use my daughter as an example. Her teachers have time to talk to an individual child and understand what his or her problems are. Our teachers never had that time. They had time to deal out corporal punishment; I can tell you that. But they had very little time to deal with problems and give us holistic education.

You really have to talk in the terms of whole-school education. You have to teach children to cope with life. You have to inculcate lots of life skills in it. You have to make them become part of the real world. The one flaw that I can tell you about in my education was that I missed the real world being played to me when I was a kid, right up to university. The real world was something very different than what I was seeing. Whereas my white counterparts knew about business from a very early stage, I didn't. For me, business was a little shop on the corner where the person or the owner didn't even know what a bank looks like. I didn't even know how to save money because it was never part of normal life. You have to have money to save it. I never related the things I learned to life because they were abstract to me.

Kgomotso Moroka

Kgomotso Moroka, to whom Dolly Mokgatle refers in the preceding excerpt, was born Kgomotso Motlana, in Sophiatown, Johannesburg, in 1954. Her father was not only a prominent physician, but was also a political activist and close associate of Nelson Mandela.

∞ My father was a doctor and my mother was a schoolteacher. She left teaching in 1954 in a defiance campaign against apartheid, and she has never gone back to teaching. My father practiced medicine in Soweto. He had gone to medical school at the University of the Witwatersrand. He first went to Fort Hare and then to Wits. Before 1954, you could go to Wits. Then Bantu education came in, and they transferred all their medical students to the University of Natal. My father is Tswana; my mother is Pedi. We spoke Tswana and English at home.

We left Sophiatown before the removals [see chap. 1]. We went to Soweto, to Orlando East, where my parents started working. When I was born, my father was doing housemanship [medical internship]. We moved to Soweto when he began his practice. I lived there until I got married in 1979.

I started school in Lesotho. My mother had left teaching when Bantu education was introduced, and it followed that we were not going to go to a Bantu education school. So, age five, I was on a bus to Lesotho to go and attend school there. My parents didn't have passports because they were both banned, so I was on this trip on my own. Actually, I had family with me on that first trip. Later on they used to hire a driver to take me to Lesotho and Swaziland.

My parents were banned because they were activists. They were members of the ANC. My father was a member of the Youth League and all sorts of things. They remained active although they are not active members of the ANC. They are active in community-based things. When their bank balances looked healthier, they moved to Dube, which was an area in Soweto where Africans who could afford it could build their own houses. My father continued to practice until about two years ago. He is now in full-time business.

[Ntatho Motlana is now chairperson of New Africa Investments, Ltd. (NAIL), the first black-controlled company on the Johannesburg Stock

Exchange. Dikgang Moseneke (see chap. 6) is Executive Deputy Chairman of the company. NAIL and its affiliated companies were formed in an attempt to bring blacks into the previously all-white financial South African financial community.]

I went to missionary schools in Lesotho and Swaziland. The missionary schools in South Africa had been closed down by the apartheid regime. The missionary schools that I went to were good. The school I went to was Roman Catholic. I am a Roman Catholic product although I am not a Roman Catholic. They accepted a lot of students from South Africa. There was this huge exodus of South African children to Lesotho and Swaziland. There was a high discipline in the schools, but there wasn't the kind of discipline that you found in South African schools—corporal punishment and that sort of thing. You didn't get that.

I did all of my grade school and high school up to matric in Lesotho and in Swaziland. When I came back to do matric, I was in Soweto, in the famous school, Morris Isaacson. That was in 1972. Bantu education is Bantu education. But I must tell you, I had a group of very wonderful teachers. It was amazing. Morris Isaacson High School used to produce such good results because the teachers, given the circumstances and the syllabuses, were just dedicated teachers. All of the teachers were black. They did a great job under the circumstances. You can't compare the quality of the white schools in town and the black schools in Soweto, even now. And you couldn't compare the school in Soweto to the schools in Swaziland. There were more students per teacher. Some of the things they were doing in Soweto, I had done long before I got there.

Lucy Mailula

Lucy Mailula was born in 1958. She practiced as an advocate in Johannesburg and is now a judge of the High Court.

∞ I studied in Northern Sotho until standard 6, and only when I went to high school did I have to use other languages, English or Afrikaans. I went to Hwiti High School, which is next to the University of the North, for my junior secondary school education as well as high school education.

The problem we had at Hwiti was that each year we would not have a teacher for one subject or another, sometimes even two or three subjects, and we had to teach ourselves. I remember we were to do a repetition of standard 6 in a different medium of instruction, in English [as opposed to Afrikaans]. Our English teacher left during the course of the year so we had to go through the syllabus ourselves and somebody would come in just to make sure that we followed the syllabus and then set an exam. I remember when I was in junior certificate level, we didn't have a permanent English teacher. They would get someone to come and help us for a while, and then the next term they would get somebody for us. When we did matric, we didn't have a maths teacher. He taught us in standard 9 but he was no longer there in standard 10 and we had to rely on university students to take us through the syllabus. When we did matric in standard 9, we had to do biology in Afrikaans. I don't know why the teacher was made to teach in Afrikaans because she had problems with Afrikaans herself. She was black—we never had a white teacher. So, when we did matric, standard 10, we switched over to English and we had to do the syllabus all over again. We managed anyway.

The high school was physically next to the University of the North [a black university], and the students who studied teaching at the university would come and do practical studies at the high school. We kept a relationship with those we thought were good teachers and we went back to them. They had their own work to do, but afternoons they would come and take us through whatever was giving us problems. It was a very difficult time, I must say, but maybe that was a good basis for hard work. You learned that you have to exert yourself in order to make it. Nothing is going to come on a silver plate.

Timothy Bruinders

Timothy Bruinders described his family situation in chapter 3. Here he talks about his early education. As a Coloured, his schooling was quite different from that of his black African contemporaries.

∽ I went to Harold Cressy High School, standard 6 to 10. Although it was a government school, it was quite elitist. You had to take an exam to get into the school. It was a stiff exam; they controlled the amount of kids per class. It was a Coloured and Indian school, but it was middle class. There were a lot of Muslims at the school and quite a few Indians. Trevor Manuel, the present minister of finance, went to that school. He was a couple of years ahead of me. The school was very different from my primary school. The school was one of the feeder schools for the University of Cape Town and it was a school that was very academically driven and almost spurned sport and the lesser pursuits.

I got to the school purely by chance. My best friend at primary school's brothers and sisters had all gone to the school. He followed them and I wanted to hang out with him. Initially, I couldn't get in because they said that they had filled the quota of people that they took for exams. It was a small school, never more than 600 students. They took only so many applications to write the exam. If a place opened up, as it did for me, you could write the examination and they would grade it and decide whether you should be admitted. It was a darned good school; that is all I can say.

It was a school which was very influenced by what was known as the Non-European Unity Movement [NEUM]. It was a movement in the Cape, particularly among Coloureds and Africans, but predominantly Coloured people: intellectuals, school teachers, lawyers, and so on who had a philosophy of nonracialism. They were very influenced by things European, and by that I mean European as opposed to British ideas. They were influenced by European socialism or Marxism. A lot of them weren't Marxist or socialist, but they were certainly influenced by those philosophies. They were the forerunner of SACOS [the South African Council of Sport], the people who got the Sports Boycott going: "No normal sport in an abnormal society."

They espoused nonracialism, so their credo was almost to deny racial characteristics. That's where I learned that racial features were something that you just didn't take into account at all. The pursuit of ideas was what life was all about. Ideas were color blind. That was the philosophy of the school. At least a lot of teachers at the school espoused that philosophy and were members of the NEUM or its teachers' organization, which was called Teachers' League of South Africa [TLSA]. They were middle-class Coloured people, who were from an intellectual segment of society. Also it was unashamedly elitist; it was unashamedly a meritocracy. If you weren't good enough, you ought not to be there. Affirmative action did not exist in that school.

The curriculum was very heavily science and literature. It de-emphasized the American. It had a distinct bent towards the European: Sartre, Merleau-Ponty, André Malraux. When you went into class in standard 9 or 10, teachers would list the books they thought we should read and those they would not prescribe. Stick to all these authors on the board. It was not compulsory, but they thought that if you couldn't do that, you ought not to be in that school. For example, it's not at that school that I learned about Faulkner or Sinclair Lewis. It was Eurocentric—James Joyce. So that was what we learned in literature, but it was a school very heavily oriented to science, physics, and maths.

People from that school would go on to university in very high numbers. They would go to the University of Cape Town generally rather than the University of the Western Cape [a university for Coloureds begun during the era of Bantu education]. Another point about the Unity Movement was that they frowned upon the University of the Western Cape as a bush college. It was a creation of apartheid, and it was a symbol of lesser status. They told us that we were elite and so we should go to a university with elitist status. In fact, a lot of the Unity Movement's struggles were against the University of the Western Cape when it was established in 1959 or 1960. Those Unity Movement teachers fought against the establishment of a bush college for Coloureds. Their attitude was that everybody had to go to the University of Cape Town. That university was not to be reserved for whites. There was a very heavy counterreaction towards that policy in the late 1970s, when the University of the Western Cape became a hotbed of radicalism and student activism.

5

♎

UNIVERSITY YEARS

A DISCUSSION of the university education of black lawyers should be divided into three time periods.

(1) Before the late 1950s, a few blacks were admitted to the white universities, especially the great English-language institutions, the University of Cape Town and the University of the Witwatersrand. The blacks who attended those schools were not discriminated against academically. However, they did have to deal with the pervasive racial segregation of the time and very clear, although usually unwritten, limitations on their social contacts with their white fellow students.

(2) A few years after the implementation of the Bantu education scheme discussed in chapter 4, the government turned its attention to tertiary education. The Extension of University Education Act of 1959 extended the policies of Bantu education to the university levels. Blacks were now even more limited in their ability to attend white institutions than before. Six new institutions, known colloquially as bush colleges, were set up under this program: four for black Africans (University of the North, University of Zululand, University of the Transkei, and University of Bophuthatswana), one for Coloureds (University of the Western Cape), and

one for Indians (University of Durban-Westville). The University of Fort Hare, which had provided a decent educational experience for blacks in the days of Nelson Mandela, Oliver Tambo, and Godfrey Pitje, was transformed by the government into another bush college. Instead of serving the black population as a whole, as it had previously, Fort Hare was limited to enrolling mostly Xhosa-speaking students. A predominantly white, Afrikaans-speaking faculty replaced the former teachers.[1]

The education provided by the black universities was distinctly inferior. The teaching was almost always poor. Library, classroom, and living facilities were woefully inadequate. Students invariably faced appalling overcrowding in the classroom and a faculty that cared little for them as individuals or for the possibility of their success as professionals. They also frequently encountered—and often fomented—a chaotic and unstable situation resulting from strikes, boycotts, and other politically generated disruptions.

Most of the black lawyers now practicing in South Africa obtained at least part of their education at one of these black institutions. Many also received at least a part of their education at the enormous correspondence institution, the University of South Africa (UNISA). As we shall see later, the availability of quality correspondence education such as offered by UNISA was both essential and frequently used by individuals who were in prison or under a banning order.

(3) Some of the restrictions on black attendance at white universities softened in the 1980s, either through government laxity or through the efforts of white academics to circumvent the restrictions. Again, the numbers were very small throughout all but the last few years that preceded the Mandela administration. Furthermore, even if their school elected to treat them equally, the apartheid government placed limitations on their lifestyle through devices such as the Group Areas Acts.

Phase One: The Years before Bantu Education

Ismail Mahomed

Chief Justice Mahomed described his background and early childhood in chapter 2.

∞ Although both my parents had had no education and there had been no real education in any of my ancestry that I knew of, I was determined to get some education. The university in my town was Pretoria University. It was a university almost exclusively attended by white people of Afrikaner descent. It was quite out of the question for me to gain access to that university although it was very close to my home and would have been very convenient to do so. The nearest university that was accessible to me was Witwatersrand University, in Johannesburg, and I got to that university in 1951.

Until then, I don't think that I had met white people except in terms of inequality. They were either officials who would visit our premises from time to time requiring explanations under the various laws which regulated our lives, or they would be salesmen selling goods to my father, who was a shopkeeper. Although that was the situation, and although I was segregated throughout my education and in my living, I was acutely aware intellectually of the fact that this was unnatural, it was unjust, it was unfair, it was irrational. I had been substantially influenced in this thinking by the publicity that had been given in the newspapers to the freedom struggle in India for its own liberation and to the tremendous impact which the life of Gandhi and Nehru had made on progressive opinion all over the world. I was also alive to the resistance of blacks in South Africa to racial injustice. Therefore, when I entered the university I had come from a segregated, but not from a servile, background.

The number of nonwhite students at Wits was infinitesimal. I would say it was not more than two percent or one and one-half percent. We stuck out. Wits was not only white but substantially Jewish in those days. There was a fair distribution of English and Afrikaans minorities, but basically it was white.

I still remember a very revealing thing which happened on my very first day. I will never forget it. We were all first-year students trying to get registration. We were queuing and we were all equally bewildered by the occasion. A young white student of Jewish extraction, with whom I later became very friendly, turned around to me in a state of confusion and bewilderment and tried to ask me something about what she should say on the form which we had been given. My reaction was immediately one of extreme protest, and very unnaturally so. I said, "Look here, you mustn't try to dominate me wherever you go. I am entitled to be at this university.

I am entitled to stand in this queue and I am entitled to stand behind you." She wasn't doing anything of the sort, but I had become sensitive to the fact that white people simply sought to dominate and oppress you and order you around. My mind couldn't imagine that she, a member of the privileged race, was actually seeking assistance from me.

I registered for Political Science as a first degree. I did so because I was acutely conscious of the irrationality of the South African legal system, which denied me the vote in the land of my birth, which made arbitrary laws restricting my movement, my occupation, my life, and my living without ever consulting me. I was grossly interested in how the evolution of political society had taken place. What attempts had been made by other societies, by other countries at other times, to comply with the demands of justice and equity? What socialist experiments were there? What limitations were there in the capitalist free market? All those things profoundly interested me. I had a nodding acquaintance with Marxist writings. I am not sure that I would have done Political Science on its own merit, but at the University of the Witwatersrand, before you could do an LL.B. you needed to do a B.A. It had to be in nonlegal subjects.

The small percentage of nonwhite people at the university was very important psychologically. Many things arose from that. Although I went to a university which at that stage did not discriminate on the grounds of color, I was acutely conscious that I was in a very tiny and invisible minority. My skin was visibly darker than 98 percent of my fellow students'. I was acutely conscious of the fact that I came from an impoverished background, that my school was not as good as the schools they had come from, that their parents were better educated than mine, that their parents were Jewish doctors and lawyers and intellectuals and my parents were from a class of semiliterate shopkeepers and housewives. I was acutely aware of the fact that I had a culturally deprived background.

That consciousness had many results. One was that I worked twice as hard as my fellow students. When they went to dances and sports, I sat in the library. Secondly, I became terribly achievement orientated. It was not good enough to pass. It was important to get distinctions. Thirdly, I became very assertive. I was not prepared to accept the state of simply being tolerated as a student. I became active in the student movement and in protests against racial laws. I stood for office in the Student Representative Council; I participated actively in student politics; I articulated various ideological positions on human affairs. I remember articulating all kinds of positions: the Russian occupation of Hungary, capital punishment, all sorts of things. Indeed, I remember talking about capital punishment in those days with great vigor and passion, little believing that one day the day would arrive when I would write the judgment on it.[2] But those things manifested themselves: an assertiveness, articulated political conscious, and tremendous diligence and hard work.

The other thing, of course, was that the normal avenues of enjoyment for students were denied to me. This great liberal university, in those days from 1951 to 1956 when I was there, prided itself in what was regarded as a very liberal and radical slogan: "academic nonsegregation" —not integration but nonsegregation, a negative. But secondly, the emphasis was on *academic*—the idea being you could study with us as equals, but surely you are not suggesting that you can be our social equals. Don't think you can dance with us and that you can play sports with us. So academic nonsegregation was the slogan of the time, and I never went to dances and I never went to parties, partly I think because I wanted to be a very serious student but because it was just not on [not possible].

Anyway, it was in many ways a very satisfactory time in my life. I did well academically; I did well in student politics and became an executive member of the Student Representative Council. I became an editor of the student magazine, which wrote flaming editorials of all kinds of political issues. I thought that the world revolved on what our views were on Hungary and Czechoslovakia, not realizing that these issues had little to do with us. But it was a great and stimulating time for me. But it had to end. Before it ended, however, I got so intensely involved in political science that I took an honors degree and registered for a master's degree. I flirted briefly with the idea of becoming an academic in political science, but it was a brief flirtation which was not really practical. In those days there was no academic at Wits who was black. There were only white teachers, other than in the faculty of African languages.

Fikile Bam

Judge Bam described his background and early education in chapter 2. Bam began at the University of Cape Town full-time in 1958. He was one of seven blacks out of a student body of over 500. The university had strict entrance requirements, examination scores that were beyond the reach of virtually all blacks. Bam faced the same kind of social discrimination at the University of Cape Town that Mahomed met at Wits—blacks would be admitted to academic activities but to no other aspects of university life.

∽ Most black people went to Fort Hare during those years. A number of the other people who were my contemporaries either finished at Fort Hare or did a first degree there and then went over to Rhodes University or to the University of Cape Town for a second degree. But few people could meet the standards for those universities.

There were hardly any black teachers at the University of Cape Town then. Professor A. C. Jordan, the father of Pallo Jordan [a minister in the Mandela government], was there. He was a senior lecturer in African languages. There was another senior lecturer, Dan Kunene, also in African languages. But all of the other faculty members were white.

I couldn't live in a residence when I started at Cape Town. I lived with the Jordans. The second year I found my own digs in Athlone. I also spent another year in District Six. I moved from one place to another until my arrest in 1963. I was at the point of finishing my second degree, the LL.B., in 1963 when I got arrested [see chap. 7]. So I never quite finished the year. The law degree took me another eleven years.

I was active politically as a student, but I hadn't joined any of the big national organizations. I hadn't joined the African National Congress. But when I got to the university I joined a student organization called the Cape Peninsula Students Union [CPSU]. The initials coincided with the Communist Party of the Soviet Union, but that was just a coincidence. It was affiliated with what was called the Unity Movement in Cape Town, of which a lot of intellectuals were members. The Unity Movement was predominantly a socialist political organization although it described itself as having national aspirations. So we were linked to them in a way, but primarily we were a student organization, and we kept ourselves busy with student politics.

We had an area demarcated as Freedom Square at the University of Cape Town, where we assembled between classes and lectures and talked and read politics. We demonstrated, boycotted, pamphleteered, and did

all sorts of things that students do. The CPSU had predominantly
Coloured, Indian, and African membership, with a sprinkling of white
students. This activity continued throughout my time at Cape Town,
from 1957 through 1963. I even became an executive member, general
secretary of the CPSU at the end.

After I got my B.A. in 1960, I became a part-time teacher at the university. If you had done particularly well in a particular course, you could
assist in teaching that course the following year. They called us demon-
strators in those days. I lectured in language, which was SeSotho, and also
in what was called Comparative African Government and Law.

My first degree was mixed in languages, law, and history. I had
already decided that I wanted to become a lawyer based upon my contact
with Oliver Tambo and Nelson Mandela back in 1955.

Justice Poswa

Justice (his name, not his title) Poswa was born to Xhosa-speaking parents in 1939. He is now an advocate in Durban and serves as president of
the Black Lawyers Association of South Africa.

ℂ I did matric in 1957 and came to the University of Natal. When I
came to the university, there was a medical school which was only black,
in the sense that it had only African and some so-called Indians. That was
a separate section. Then there was the other section for law, science, and
that kind of thing. Now in that part, there was also what was called a non-
European section. We were in this block of so-called non-European students.

The segregation was not quite complete because part-time white students were allowed to study with us. We were given part-time hours to
accommodate white part-timers. We were full time, but we would sit
there all day and only attend in the morning and in the evenings. The rest
of the day we would just stay there and couldn't move because they were
providing for white working students to come and join us. The section
was located in a factory that the university had bought, away from the
main campus. They had emptied everything in the building and had put
haversacks on the wall to avoid the echo. The building was not painted.

The walls were as they had been. They had unashamedly put us in those rooms. The lecturers were the same as at the main university. We had the same principal. There was a separate library for us at the old factory. Looking back, I think that the level of the library was for high school kids. The library wasn't what you have now, but it was quite all right.

Phase Two: Universities at the Height of Bantu Education —Education and Political Struggle

George Maluleke

George Maluleke is now a successful attorney and businessman in Johannesburg. He also chairs the board of directors of the Black Lawyers Association–Centre for Legal Education. He was born in 1940.

∞ In 1962 I went to the University of the North. There was a limited range of professions that one could think about in those days. You could either become a priest or a teacher, mostly a teacher. I wanted to become a teacher, not only because I had no other role models to think about, but I think also because there were attractive offers which were available to people who wanted to follow a career in teaching. You would get a bursary [scholarship] a lot easier if you were following a teaching career. Otherwise, your parents would have to pay, and there was no way that my parents would have been able to pay even a portion of the university fees. So I registered for a teacher's course.

I finished my degree in 1964 and then did a teacher's diploma in 1965. I was able to get more bursaries, and my dad thought maybe I was too young to teach. So I went back to university with no clear thought of what I really wanted to do except that I had these bursaries. I then registered to do an honors degree in English. It was supposed to be a two-year degree. Somehow in the middle of the year, I became involved in student politics and I just lost interest. I served in the Student Representative Council, and that led to a lot of confrontations with the university principals.

The issues we faced would seem very small now. For instance, we thought that the university was run more like a high school. The rules were very cumbersome. You would have lady students sitting on the one side of the dining hall and male students sitting on the other side, and in the middle the lecturers sat eating . . . things like that. But then there were more serious issues. There was very tight control over universities by the Nationalist Party [the political party that had promoted the apartheid policy]. All the university appointees, including those at the University of the North, were dogmatic, well-selected people, who had very strong Nationalist, Broederbond [a far right-wing and secret Afrikaner organization] connections. They were all white people and all Afrikaans-speaking. They would have been thoroughly checked.

The real confrontation between the rector and me came in 1965 when we, the Student Representative Council [SRC], arranged a meeting with the SRC group at the University of the Witwatersrand, to come to our university. The dominant student movement at that time was NUSAS [National Union of South African Students], which was basically composed of white students. The group at Wits was affiliated with NUSAS. At the same time, we had arranged for the SRC group at the University of Zululand to meet with us at our university. I was the secretary of the Student Representative Council at the time. The rector, on his own, canceled the meeting with Wits. He sent a telegram to them to say it was not convenient for them to come on that particular weekend. He then gave an instruction that it would not be tolerated in this university to have both a black university and a white university visiting the campus at the same time. We were very angry.

I drafted the motion in the SRC which said that we thought his behavior was most paradoxical, that he would cancel one meeting and not the other. He should have canceled both if he thought it was within his powers. So it led to a confrontation. He tried to single me out from the SRC. I had moved the motion and didn't want to back out of it. But once it was passed, it was a motion of the council. It wasn't mine, and I don't see why I should have been held accountable for it. But he did not dismiss me. What he did was to take away other privileges. As a senior student, you were in charge in certain dormitories. It gave you an allowance, which I sorely needed because of my financial situation. He took that away. I just decided then to leave the university. I didn't go back.

After leaving the University of North, Maluleke took a job as a clerk with an attorney in Johannesburg. He began to study law through the correspondence courses of the University of South Africa. He eventually turned his clerkship into the articles necessary to qualify as an attorney.

Justice Moloto

Justice Moloto was born in 1944. His mother and father were teachers.[3] Justice is now both his first name and his title. He now serves as a judge of the South African Land Claims Court.

In this excerpt, Moloto describes incidents at the University of Fort Hare, noting that although it is located in what was then the homeland of the Ciskei, it was run by whites. In fact, all the black universities were in the so-called homelands and all were administered by whites.

∽ The homeland policy formed the very foundation of the scheme known as Grand Apartheid. Black Africans, or Bantus, as they were called by whites throughout much of the era, were to live apart from other South Africans. The scheme envisioned all blacks as citizens of independent homelands, or Bantustans, based upon tribal groups. Once a Bantustan achieved independence, the members of the tribe based in it would officially become citizens of the homeland rather than citizens of the Republic of South Africa. Four homelands were made independent: Transkei, Ciskei, Venda, and Bophuthatswana. Others resisted independence and the scheme eventually faltered.

Although nominally independent from white South Africa, whites performed important functions within the homelands, including running universities and serving as judges of their supreme courts.

After high school, I attended the University of Fort Hare. Although there was no Student Representative Council at Fort Hare, there were student meetings. I got myself into the unfortunate position of always being elected chairman of student meetings. Therefore, I was seen by the authorities as a big instigator.

On one occasion, after I had presented the demands of students to him, the rector of the university asked me if I would call a meeting of the students where he would also be present. The rector was a white chap in this all black university in the homeland of the Ciskei. Tensions were very high between the students and the authorities at that time. The rector came to that meeting. After the students had elected me to chair the meeting, the rector decided to close the meeting. I then addressed the students and said that I, and only I, was going to close the meeting and the rector must subject himself to the ruling of the chairman. As this meeting was legally constituted under the university regulations, the rector had no right to close it. I said to the students, "You sit down until I close this meeting." I said this while the rector was still at the meeting.

After he had left, I said to the students that they were making a fool of me. How could I effectively make demands on the rector if he could come in and close our meeting? "You've got to decide now, in the light of what the rector said, what you want me to do and what are you deciding to do as students." And then the students, of course, decided to carry on with their strike. They were striking about any number of issues: the whole question of government and the fact that there was no proper SRC, the lack of facilities, poor food in the hostel, and a whole number of little things that niggle students at university.

Anyway, the fact that I had made those statements within the rector's earshot earned me an expulsion at the end of that year. He couldn't really expel me immediately, but at the end of the year, without giving me any good reason for it, he just said, Don't come for the year of 1967. If you want to come back to Fort Hare, apply for 1968.

Moloto was out of university for the whole of 1967. He taught at high schools in Soweto and Mafikeng, in the homeland of Bophuthatswana.

෴ In 1968 I went back to Fort Hare. The campus was in chaos, the students were still fighting, and there was a sit-in demonstration. The sit-in was part of a running battle between the authorities and the students. Part of it involved the lack of a proper student governing body and the fact that at times you would find unjustified expulsion of students or unjustified punishment of some students. But I think the sit-in had more to do with the status of students on campus and with police harassment of students. The police harassed us for things we thought we had the right to do as citizens. I remember we wanted to belong to national student bodies like NUSAS, and the university wouldn't allow it. They set the police on us to sneak around and find out what we did and what we didn't do. Therefore, we did some of our activities in a very clandestine manner.

We went to complain to the university authorities. We told them we were being harassed by the police. We said that the police just came onto the campus and picked us up, took us for interrogation, and beat us up. You could be arrested and the university would be told of your arrest two or three days later. I remember being picked up by the police and being interrogated and the university didn't even know—they didn't even care to know. We said to the university authorities, "Look, we need your protection. You are in loco parentis."

They said, "No. You are adults. We can't be in loco parentis. You are over twenty-one."

But we said, "Why do you discipline us like we are young children? You won't let us drink. If a boy was found on the girls' side, he could be expelled."

So the students had a sit-in because they were demanding that the authorities do something to protect them against the police. We said when the police came on campus, they had to report to the administration. They had to tell the administration that they wanted to interview a certain person, and the authorities had to know that they had taken that person, and they had to expect the police to return him. The university authorities said they were not prepared to do this and so we had a sit-in.

The entire governing body of the university was in white hands. The white lecturers were members of the University Council. It was almost all white, and the few blacks that were there were either lackeys of the system or were outvoted. Of course, the policemen were also white.

As a result of the sit-in, twenty-one of us were expelled. Now this time, it was for good. They said, "Justice, we don't want to see you or the others back here. Not only are you being expelled from Fort Hare, but you will be barred from attending any university in South Africa." That seemed to mean the end of our education unless we left the country.

There was an organization in Johannesburg called ASSECA [Association for the Educational and Cultural Development of the African People]. ASSECA was an association that was composed of adults and youth. I remember my mother was a member. I was also a member. The adult wing of the association decided to take this matter up on our behalf. They argued on our behalf: we understand that you say these students are troublesome at universities. However, at least there is one university here, UNISA [the University of South Africa], which is not a residential university and, therefore, their behavior doesn't matter much. They can study and work at the same time. Their argument was successful and dispensation was made so that we could study at UNISA. I did the rest of my studies with UNISA. If these arguments had not been successful, if I could have found the means to do so, I would have probably gone out of the country so that I could finish my studies.

In fact, very few black lawyers were able to go abroad for their education. Of the twenty-seven lawyers interviewed for this book, only one, Christine Qunta, did her university education outside South Africa. Travel abroad was prohibitively expensive. Even where funding was available, government permission to travel had to be obtained. The government often placed severe travel limitations on its citizens, especially activist blacks. Thus, for most blacks, an education abroad was not a realistic path to undertake unless the individual was willing to risk probable permanent exile.

Selby Baqwa

In chapter 3, Baqwa described his family's attempt to buy a home in a white area. In this excerpt, he mentions the influence of Steve Biko and his philosophy of black consciousness on him and his contemporaries. Biko's organizational skills, writings, and martyrdom deeply affected many South Africans, especially those who were students at the height of Biko's activities, the 1970s. Some of the lawyers whose stories appear here, such as Justice Moloto and Selby Baqwa, knew him well. Others knew enough about him to recognize his importance to the lives of black South Africans.

Biko was murdered in 1977 while in police custody. Recent revelations before the South African Truth and Reconciliation Commission clearly place the blame for his death on the then South African government.[4]

∽ I went to the University of Fort Hare in 1969. The South African Students Organisation [SASO], Steve Biko's organization, was born at St.

Francis College in Mariannhill, where I had been in high school, the year that I completed matric. It then caught on like wildfire in all tertiary institutions. Biko's philosophy called upon black students to liberate themselves psychologically and mentally and to stop looking upon whites as valuable, and degrading themselves. The movement really flourished. Sooner or later it caused great panic within white government circles because they realized that now there were subjugated people getting rid of their subjugation. Obviously what would follow thereafter was not too hard to see.

So I got very active, and now I can look back with pride at what happened at the University of Fort Hare. Just as I completed my junior degree and registered for the LL.B. degree, I was expelled for my activities in South African Students Organisation. I was charged with trespass (even though I was a student), put into detention and then expelled. But I can't regret that scrape with the law.

There were a number of grievances that we had as students against the authorities. These included mundane things like the kind of diet that was supplied. It was far from the kind of food that we expected to be eating at university. But there were other grievances. For instance, we were concerned about the kind of treatment that was accorded to students, even in the lecture rooms. We found that the lecturers, the people who came from Afrikaner institutions like Stellenbosch or Potchefstroom, people who could hardly communicate properly with you in the English language, would fail you. You would wonder exactly why they had failed you and whether it was to further other policies.

But there was a wide range of grievances that we had against the authorities then. The attitude of the then rector, a certain Professor de Wet, was one of *kragdadigheid,* if I can use an Afrikaans word [literally, efficiency or vigor]: however reasonable your grievances were and however possible the solutions, the idea was never yield to the black person. You could see that he was taking his orders directly from Pretoria because he had only one reaction: call in the police, call in the dogs, get them out of university. We did not go to lectures. We protested and occupied the administration building. It was a nonviolent protest. We were not burning anything; we were not breaking any windows. We would just sit. We demanded that the rector come and explain things to us and talk to us and convince us, and we would try and talk back and see whether we could get solutions. He would never come. After a couple of days, he brought out the police. He brought out the dogs, and we were chased and we ran into our rooms. He issued an ultimatum demanding that we should go back to lectures, which we didn't do and then he fired [expelled] us.

While we were away, we were called back by a radio broadcast. We were told that the students of Fort Hare should come back and make fresh applications for admission to the university. Based on this call, which had been issued to everyone, we went back. We did not intend to give up our strike. Our intention was, as soon as we got to the university, to call another meeting and advise the students not to reapply because that was a sure way to be excluded. What was going to happen was that some of us were going to be readmitted on the basis of whatever the informers had told them, and others would be excluded.

The police vans and dogs came when we were at our meeting. We were rounded up and bundled into the vans and taken to what was then the Great Hall. We were given a lecture by the police chief about how mischievous we were and why we shouldn't be doing the things that we were doing. After the lecture, most of the students were released to go back to their rooms, but myself and another fellow, who is also a lawyer now in the Transkei, Pumzile Majaga, were detained. We were told that we should not have been at the university even though the radio broadcast had called everyone back. We were known to be the people who were addressing the meeting when we were dispatched by the police.

Majaga and I were then detained for about two weeks and they formulated charges against us for trespassing. Our defense was that it could not have been trespassing because we had not been fired as students. We were there as students, bona fide students, and we had been called back to the university, all of us. But appearing before the magistrate then, there was no way you could escape. They got the message that we had to be convicted. You could see how well the system was working. We were indeed convicted and fined. We then tried to come back to the university. We were ordered to appear before the disciplinary committee, where we were duly expelled. We knew that was going to happen even before we appeared before the committee. So that's how that saga ended.

Ismael Semenya

Although incidents of confrontation with school authorities and expulsion were common in this era, not all the confrontations resulted in the student leaving school. Sometimes, creative devices were found for the students to engage in political activism while maintaining their status as students. For example, Ismael Semenya, now a well-regarded advocate in Johannesburg,[5] describes one such ruse while he was a student at the University of the North:

> ∾ I was involved in various organizations at the university. Obviously, a student organization did not take the complete profile of a national organization because all of them were banned. The SRC [Student Representative Council] was the principal organization. But there were things like the Sovenga Soccer League. We used sports in a very uncharacteristic fashion—as a front for our political activities. The administration of the university was able to spare some money towards sport, which we would use for the purpose of holding a series of meetings. There would be legitimate football played as well, but if you wanted to meet the SRC of another campus, the best way to do it was to organize a formal football game with that other university. Outside the hours of play, you could interchange ideas with your counterparts on the other side.

Phineas Mojapelo

Others, such as Phineas Mojapelo, found it possible to be active in the student politics of the day and yet remain in school to complete his LL.B. degree in the prescribed six years. Mojapelo, the former herd boy (see chap. 2), had perhaps a different view of even the modest amenities of the University of the North:

> ∾ Every time we were on strike, I had to be there with the strikers. I had to find time to read because the lecturers warned us that, strike or no strike, we were going to be tested on the whole syllabus. We had to write exams at the end of the year on the entire syllabus. I remember the norm

then for B.Proc., which was the degree I did, was that one had to take four subjects. If you felt you could manage, it was recommended that you should take five so as to lessen the load in later years. I had advised all the people who were financing my study loans and bursaries that I was taking five subjects and I had to make sure that I passed the five during the first year. Thank God I did! Other students managed to pass only one or two subjects. But I had the pressure of knowing that, if I could not pass all five, this was the end of my learning.

I studied very hard. At least at that stage I had one pair of shoes! It wasn't that hard. I had running water at school and I could switch on lights. The University of the North wasn't that bad. The library, I only found out later, was very poor, especially for a law library. But compared to where I had come from, this was a little heaven.

My schooling was interrupted, but I always stayed on track. It wasn't easy. It meant taking your law books with you wherever you went and reading all the time.

Mojapelo's LL.B. work was financed in part by his work as a part-time lecturer at the university and partly through assistance from the Association of Law Societies, the group governing attorneys' practice. The law societies' money was from the Attorney's Fidelity Fund, a fund consisting of interest earned on trust accounts kept by attorneys. Lawyers in the United States and Canada will be familiar with similar schemes in those countries.

Phase Three: Return to the White Universities

Kgomotso Moroka

In chapter 4, Moroka, the daughter of a prominent physician and businessman, described her early education in Swaziland and Lesotho. She then attended the University of the North. Surviving a series of strikes without being expelled, she ultimately completed her B.Proc. in 1977.

∾ Then I applied to Wits to do an LL.B. In the good old days you needed a permit, and they refused me a permit. My parents approached Helen Suzman for help. [For many years, Suzman was the only anti-apartheid member of the South African parliament.] They knew her through politics. I wasn't prepared to go back to Turfloop. I'd had enough of it. So I was sitting at home basically saying I was ready to do articles, but Helen Suzman raised hell in Parliament and I got a permit in May 1978. Although everybody else had started in February, I had to start in May. But at least I got in.

My LL.B. was supposed to take two years, but because I had started long after the other students had started, they refused to let me register for all the courses. So I had to do an extra year to catch up on those courses that I didn't do in my first year.

My time at Wits was difficult. As a white person, have you ever walked into a room that was full of just black people and every one of them was looking at you from the moment you got into the room until you sat down at your desk? For two full years, they just never got used to me. I'd be the only different person in that room. There were Indian students in the B.A. (Law) program, but no black Africans. In my first and second year, I think there were no other black African students in the LL.B. program. I was the only one. There were some others in my third year. I eventually developed friendships with some of the other students, but that first year was very difficult. I had a car, and so I traveled by car from home to university. If I hadn't lived at home, I could have lived in a student residence in Diepkloof, in Soweto, where black students used to live.

My relationship with the faculty was cold. Certainly, there were a lot of students. But nobody went out of their way to say here is a child from a different background, different from all the other students, and she must probably be feeling very alienated and maybe we should try and see if she needs help. They didn't say, You need a shoulder to cry on, we are here for you. None of those people did, except Professor Carmen Nathan. I only went there once or twice, but at least she offered.

My academic studies were fine. If you got 50 percent it was fine. I aimed for an A, but I coped! I never dropped a subject or anything like that.

Dolly Mokgatle

In chapter 2, Mokgatle described her background and the efforts of her mother to feed her children. In chapter 4 she told about her early schooling under Bantu education.

She began her university education at the University of the North. She was dismissed from the university in 1977 for one year, after participating in a strike called to commemorate the first anniversary of the Soweto uprising. After struggling to find work for a year, Mokgatle returned to Turfloop in 1978 to complete the last two years of her B.Proc. She found that her one-year expulsion had cost her her scholarship, or bursary, although she could still get loans to finance her education.

∞ In my last year of B.Proc., 1979, I was recruited by John Dugard and Ramarumo Moname at the Centre for Applied Legal Studies [CALS] at the University of the Witwatersrand. The center was doing a study of pass courts, the pass laws of the country. They wanted a student to come and sit in the pass law courts to observe the trends: the numbers of arrests, why people were arrested, and whatever. So I got a job with CALS in December 1979, after I had written my final B.Proc. at the University of the North.

My work at CALS made me realize what I had been missing. I had to use the law library at Wits to do my research for CALS. I discovered what I had been missing in my life all along. I found that the Wits law library had about eight copies of one volume of the law reports. Where I studied for the B.Proc., at Turfloop, we battled for one volume. Sometimes by the time you got to the library shelf, the volume would have the relevant pages missing because someone hadn't had money to photocopy the case. Another student would have torn off the case from the book and gone to his or her room to study, to the detriment of all other students. On the other hand, there was a wealth of knowledge in the Wits library.

I wanted to study in that institution. I wanted to be part of that institution. I wanted the opportunity and I knew that I would get it, and I did. I could have done my LL.B. at Turfloop; most people did. But I had now had exposure to Wits. By then, Kgomotso Moroka was at Wits. She was a year above me. I was also determined that I was going to Wits. It was not impossible.

I went to John Dugard and I said, "I want to study there next year. I am not going to go back to the University of the North." So he helped me apply. In those days you had to file a motivation to be admitted to a white university. You had to file this form unless you were doing dentistry or engineering or some other degree that was not offered in a black university. That was true even in medicine because you had Natal, which was a black medical school. At that time, three universities—Turfloop, Zululand, and Fort Hare—had law, so I would have had no excuse to study at Wits. The minister of interior needed a motivation to tell him why I had to study in a white university.

I told him all sorts of things. I told him that I was ill, my mother was ill, and that I couldn't leave, and it is too far. I just wanted to study, and I didn't care what I said so long as I was given permission. I beat them at their own game. I got permission to study, but only part-time. At that time, they were giving the opportunity to part-time law students who were, for example, doing articles with a B. Proc. or a B.A. (Law) or B.Iuris, who wanted to do an LL.B. So I attended part-time classes.

The minister initially wanted me to produce proof that I was employed while studying part-time. If I was attending part-time in a white university, I must have been working somewhere. I said I was still marketing [looking for a job]. I had no intention of looking for a job. I wanted to be a full-time student. In addition, I used to leave home in the afternoon to start the part-time lectures, which began at four. It was totally ridiculous. I finished my last lecture at half past eight at night and had to hop into the train from Braamfontein to Springs. Springs is the last train stop. It was half past ten every night, and my mother said, "It is not worth it, whatever it is you are doing." But I was determined to stay at Wits, and I did.

In June I went to Professor David Zeffertt, who was then the dean of the Faculty of Law, and I said to him, "Look, I have been attending part-time classes for six months now. I want to be a full-time student next year. What are the requirements?"

He said to me, "Well, you can go to full-time lectures even now. You have registered as a part-time student. No lecturer is going to tell the minister that you are attending full-time lectures."

And that made a lot of sense to me. So after the winter holidays, I started going to full-time classes. Then I felt like a student for the first time because I can't tell you what I was before then. I don't know what I was.

When the minister had given me permission to do LL.B. work part-

time, there was a limit to the number of courses you could do—four subjects per annum. I did four subjects, although I had the capacity to do
more. I could have done six. So I then still had quite a number of subjects
to do, which I couldn't do all in one year. Professor Zeffertt advised me to
write to the minister again. He supported my application by saying he
was happy with me as a student. I was then allowed to study full-time in
the second year.

Thus, in the second year I did the most subjects, six law subjects.
Nevertheless, because of the limitations on subjects my first year, my
LL.B. work was stretched over three years instead of the ordinary two
years.

Also, from October of the previous year, I had managed to get into
Glyn Thomas residence, in Baragwanath, in Soweto. At that time, because
of the Group Areas Act, you couldn't have black students living on campus at Wits. We all stayed at Glyn Thomas. I fought to be admitted there.
I eventually got in and now for the first time I really felt like a full-time
student. Not only did I attend full-time lectures, but I also lived close to
the university instead of going all the way to Springs by train every day.
[Baragwanath is roughly ten miles from the Wits campus; Springs is over
thirty-five miles.] My life was much easier. I had reverted to student life.
In my third year, I was only left with four subjects, which I again did part-
time.

There were very few black students at Wits when I was there. There
were three, just three of us, in my class at the law school. One, Post
Moloto, went to the University of Zimbabwe after his first year. The
other, Moposho, stayed. We had been classmates at Turfloop. When we
did second year, there were other black students from various universities,
but the numbers were still quite few. Life wasn't easy. We tried to be students as much as we could. We tried to have a normal life as students. But
there clearly were divisions. I specifically felt that the white students were
one up on us in various respects. First of all, they had facilities at home to
be able to study there. Their homes were in close proximity to the university if they couldn't afford to stay at a university residence. I had to get
bursaries all the time to include residence because there was no way I
would be able to travel by train every day and still do a good job of being
a student.

In addition, it might have been a wrong perception, but the white students seemed to have these contacts. They seemed to know the people that mattered. Some of them were on a first name basis with lecturers, that kind of thing. And for me the whole thing was so far away. I battled throughout my studies, and I always held the lecturers and the professors in great awe. Most of the time I wasn't sure about myself, but I worked very hard, and I tried as much as possible to get assimilated into the university. But I was very constantly aware of the divisions between the black student body and the white student body. I believe things got much better afterwards when the numbers increased and it was becoming common for blacks to study at white universities. It became better, but it was very difficult in my days to assimilate. The three of us hung together closely.

I made a few white friends. I am a very open human being, so I didn't feel there was a gap in terms of friendship. So I had a few girls I would sit next to in class, and we exchanged notes and there was no problem there. But I felt there was this very serious division.

One of the things that actually got to irritate me was a suggested change in policy at the law school. A new dean made the suggestion that the school must create an LL.B. I and LL.B. II, two streams of LL.B. The LL.B. I was to be the LL.B. as we know it, and the LL.B. II would be for those students who come from so-called disadvantaged universities. It would be a second-grade LL.B. I hated the person who made that proposal from that day on. That person thought we were not capable of passing the LL.B., so there must be two streams. But we managed to overcome the proposal. Those kind of people—nowadays you just look and shake your head.

Pansy Tlakula

Pansy Tlakula was born in 1957 to a Tswana-speaking father and a Xhosa-speaking mother, both of whom were teachers. She is now a member of the Human Rights Commission. Tlakula attended the University of the North in Turfloop and, like Mokgatle, was expelled in 1977. Again like Mokgatle, she eventually finished her B.Proc. in Turfloop but went to the University of the Witwatersrand for her LL.B.

∽ I came to Wits in 1982 and 1983 to study for my LL.B. It was during the days of noncollaboration. There was an organization called Black Students Fight on campus. The mission of the organization was to tell black students at Wits to just come to study, that's it. Don't participate in sports or anything else. It was lectures and out. We had very little interaction with white students because we never used to mix with them socially. There were very few black students. We were less than ten in the whole year LL.B. class, out of about two hundred.

We were the first group to live on campus. It was 1982. Before then, the Group Areas law did not allow black students to live on campus. I was one of the very first to live on campus, which was very strange. I remember we never used to interact at any level. We used the same dining room, but it was a them and us kind of thing. I remember down the passage from my room was a bathroom that no white girl ever used. It was mine for the two years, which was beautiful! I was the only black law student in the dormitory. There were a couple of medical students. Even in class we never used to sit together. The white students used to sit together and we had our own corner where all of us sat. It was very strange.

The quality of education at Wits was quite good. Of course some lecturers were better than others. Professor Boberg, who died a couple of years ago, was one of the most outstanding. At that time, I did not realize it. Most of the time I didn't understand what he was saying because I would look in the text book and try to find the things that he used to teach us, and I would never find them. I later went to Harvard, and I was able to compare between Wits and Harvard. I could see that, among the lecturers at Wits, Boberg was the one who had attained that international level. He was one of the ones who was very analytical in his approach. Others also took a keen interest in what they were doing, and the standard was quite high, I must say. But as long as you worked hard you passed.

One strange thing that happened involved a course we did with one of the senior professors. Shortly before the examination, you would find white students being in possession of a set of notes. You would never know where they got them from. They would say that if you had those notes, you would do well in the course. If you had white friends, they would then make copies for you.

There were no black faculty members at Wits when I was there. As a result, I had no real mentors.

Pingla Hemraj

Pingla Hemraj was born in 1958 to parents of Indian descent. Several years before the end of apartheid, she became the first black woman prosecutor in South Africa. She is now a successful advocate in Durban.

She began her university education at the University of Durban-Westville, theoretically the only university open to her racial group.

∽ When I finished, I wasn't wild about the University of Durban-Westville. There were boycotts going on about various things. I thought the lecturers were people that they didn't want anywhere else and they just dumped them there. We had Professor Budwell Ramchad, who is very well known in parliamentary circles. He was our dean at the time, and he was the only one who sort of traveled overseas and stuff like that. The rest were pretty local chaps. They were Indian, except for two or three white guys. Whereas, when we looked at the faculty of the University of Natal, there were people like Professor [David] McQuoid-Mason, Tony Matthews, the guys who had written the textbooks. I thought, well, that's what I want to do. I want to talk to them. Natal University was totally white. In 1977 I applied to the minister of education to get in. The way to get in was to say that you wanted to do a course that was not offered at the University of Durban-Westville. So I applied, saying that I wanted to do forensic medicine. I did three years at Durban-Westville and then went to Natal in 1978.

My time at Natal—that was something! It was like walking from the darkness into absolute daylight. You had all these very eminent professors and lecturers, and you were suddenly exposed to the whole world. That's what it seemed like to me. There was so much more going on. You weren't spoon fed. You were encouraged to think for yourself, encouraged to take part in student activities. I must say for the student population, it was great. It was a surprise having Indian students there who, when the first test results came out, came out top of the class. So that was something for them to get used to. There were just two Indian students in the first-year

class. There had been one Indian student before, a lady who had been a
year ahead of me.

Things were awkward for me socially. It was awkward on both sides.
We had had no experience relating to each other. Then I met this wonderful girl called Margaret. She is a blonde who is six foot something with
long blonde hair. She was born in Kenya of British parents. She and I
clicked immediately, and we have been friends ever since. We began this
exchange of cultures and ideas. She taught me all the things Western, like
how to lay a table, and I taught her how to cook curry, how to make rotis,
and how to meditate. She taught me how to differentiate between wines
and things like that, and then it became so much more enjoyable. She had
a lot to do with things improving socially for me.

My studies went well at Natal. I finished LL.B. and I graduated in
1980.

Timothy Bruinders

As Pingla Hemraj's comments illustrate, not all black students struggled
in the white universities. A few, such as Timothy Bruinders, who described
his intellectually challenging days at a Coloured high school in Cape Town
in chapter 4, were able to fit into their new settings without particular difficulty.

↝ Those first couple of years at the University of Cape Town were actually one of the most enjoyable periods of my life. I spent a lot of time
reading in the library and a lot of time talking to students, the majority of
whom initially were black or Coloured, Muslim, Indian, or whatever. But
progressively there were a lot more white students that one came across
who were not racist and had similar ideas. The longer I was there, I had a
lot of friends on campus who were both black and white.

I didn't have any difficulty with the faculty. Because I had been at a
school that was a feeder school to the University of Cape Town, Cressy,
we were a lot better educated than most of our white counterparts. We
had read more. I never had the feeling that I came from an inferior background or that my education was inferior. In fact it was superior to a lot
of the white students.

Vincent Maleka

By the late 1980s, the percentage of black students at some of the universities increased dramatically. Vincent Maleka, now a promising young advocate in Johannesburg, reports that there were twenty-five or thirty blacks in a class of eighty at the University of Natal (Durban) when he began his LL.B. work in 1987.

∽ The first year I stayed at Alan Taylor, the black residence [approximately thirty kilometers away from the university]. It was a dilapidated old police barracks on which the university had done some repair work. In those days of the Group Areas Act, it was difficult for the university, I suppose, to get residences for blacks within the residential areas designated as white residential areas.

The second year I lived right within the university. My residence was twenty meters away from the library. The barriers were relaxed by then. The university was involved in a sheer exercise of disobeying the law. It was quite clear that the Group Areas Act was one of the laws which was on the statute book but had no real effect in practice, at least at the university.

I actually didn't study as much for my LL.B. courses at Natal as I did for my B.Proc. at Zululand. Zululand, like any other black university, was notorious for its failure rate. You had to study. You had to aim at 90 to 100 percent to make sure that you passed. There were many black guys who did not make it, not because of their lack of ability, but because of sheer discrimination and victimization. The university had a high failure rate, which could not be explained except by victimization. You would have a class of, say, eighty black students, and only ten would pass. The failure rate was bad, really bad. You had Afrikaner teachers there who were not good enough to be other places. A number of them had to leave because at the point when students took the failure rate seriously, those lecturers could not explain their conduct.

When I went to Natal, it was funny because the pass rate was very high. These were people who were failing at Zululand. I can tell you that students who did B.Proc. for six years at Zululand did their LL.B. at Natal within two years and passed it with ease.

At Natal there were clashes now and then because of cultural differences. We were politically orientated. Our white colleagues might have seen something wrong in our staging a protest. We had our Sharpeville Days, our 21 March [the anniversary of the Sharpeville massacre, in which sixty-nine blacks were shot by the police, 21 March 1960], and black students would stage some sort of commemoration. That would obviously affect academic programs. We would spend the day in commemoration, while the white students wanted to study. So there was a clash.

Students would complain about accommodations. That was not an issue insofar as many white students were concerned. Black students would spend a whole week debating and staging all sorts of protests about that issue. They would go and disrupt classes. The white students would say, "If you guys want to demonstrate, go outside the university." But there were white students who took the black students' cause seriously, so it was not a typically racially divided issue. There were white guys who were very active and who wanted to make sure that the university authorities attended to the issue of accommodation.

Speaking for myself, I had good relations with the law lecturers. I was quite active in activities, arranging seminars, debating political issues, and I got to know David McQuoid-Mason [dean of the University of Natal (Durban) law school]. In fact, after I passed my LL.B., he wanted to arrange a scholarship for me to go and study at a program at Georgetown University in the United States. I said, "To hell with you! [laughing]. I am going to work now; I need the money."

DIKGANG MOSENEKE

Prisoner, Attorney, Advocate, Judge, Entrepreneur

I INTERVIEWED Dikgang Ernest Moseneke at his expensively carpeted and tastefully furnished office in the formerly all-white Johannesburg suburb of Bryanston. He presently serves as deputy director and deputy chairman of New Africa Investments, Ltd., a self-described emerging black giant, dedicated to achieving real economic power in South Africa. In his forty-nine years, Moseneke has been a political prisoner, one of the most successful black lawyers in the country, a judge, a draftsman of the new South African constitution, and, most recently, an entrepreneur.

Like the histories of Godfrey Pitje (chap. 1) and Dullah Omar (chap. 12), Moseneke's narrative is so compelling, and in many ways so unique, that it deserves to be told in its entirety. Some of the things he talks about, including his practice as an attorney and then an advocate and his role in the formation of the new South Africa, anticipate subjects that are treated in more detail later in the book. I include his descriptions of such events here as background for the stories of other lawyers told in subsequent chapters.

CHAPTER 6

The Trial of a High School Student

Moseneke was born in 1947 near Pretoria. In 1960 he began his secondary schooling at Kilnerton Training College, a Methodist church school in Pretoria where many other future black leaders trained. His father was one of the teachers at the school. The school was closed after Moseneke's second year there. The land was expropriated under the Group Areas Act and became part of a white suburb.

∽ In 1963, within months of my departure from Kilnerton, I was arrested. I was fifteen years, two months old. I was charged with conspiracy to overthrow the government by violent means. No acts of violence were proven. I think the truth of the matter was that we were a group of many people who sought to change apartheid and to transform the state. The conviction was based on a wide variety of utterances at meetings, and the court found that those utterances constituted a manifest intention to overthrow the state. I had said such things such as: Apartheid is bad; it is unjust; It must be wiped off the face of the earth; We are soldiers of good and they are the defenders of evil. Statements of that order. Most of the statements were inspired by the policies of the Pan Africanist Congress [PAC, a black political organization second only to the African National Congress (ANC) in size and influence].[1]

Other people were arrested at the same time. Mandela was tried in the same year . . . many other people. In fact, it was a national clamp down on political organizations, both ANC and PAC. It was a national swoop by the police to clamp down on what they saw as escalating political resistance. What followed were a large number of trials across the country, including the Rivonia trial. [Nelson Mandela and others were convicted at a trial that took place in the Johannesburg suburb of Rivonia.] Mandela was the known national figure and therefore there was more written about him. But together with him were thousands and thousands of people who were charged and incarcerated on Robben Island. There were eighteen people tried with me. I went to Robben Island, so did Mr. Mandela, so did Mr. Sisulu [Walter Sisulu, an ANC leader and close associate of Nelson Mandela, was released from prison in

1989, a few months before Mandela], so did many people, so did a whole range of South African leadership.

I appeared before the Supreme Court in July after awaiting trial in prison for six months or so. I was kept in Pretoria Central Prison. We were many, we were hundreds of political prisoners, and that was the saving grace. The atmosphere was therefore rarefied. There were no possibilities of physical attack or sexual attack or other sort of attack because we had political prisoners all together. We were kept together in the same cells and we were people with ideals who were joined together. We never mixed with criminals, never ever, and it was the biggest mistake the Nats [the Nationalist Party, the ruling party under the apartheid regime] made. They never mixed political prisoners with criminals. They thought it would pollute the whole criminal community, which in turn might become soldiers for revolution. They were dead scared of that and that, amazingly, ironically, helped us a lot. We could set up structures that were reflective of the society we came from, and that's what really saved all of us in many ways.

The passages at Pretoria Central Prison were normally very clean, abnormally clean, with all the brass knobs shining and shining. But it had cells with bloody dirty blankets. The food was awful, I mean you couldn't feed on it. I remember that by the time I went on trial, I had lost tremendous weight. I just couldn't eat that food. Fortunately, you were not totally limited to that food if you were awaiting trial. You were entitled to receive food from your family twice a week, or something when they came and visited you.

Political prisoners gave each other moral support. You had an opportunity to talk through the case you were going to face and what it was likely to mean to you. Therefore the levels of preparedness and mutual reinforcement were quite high. Because you know, at fifteen, you needed a lot of strength to go through the period of awaiting trial in jail. You come from a regular family, where you had a reasonably good way of living, a good bath and school clothing, three meals a day, reasonable access to reading and studying, and suddenly you're a prisoner. "Sorry, you said too much about us and you have to go to jail." And it's not like you blew up something. Most people were arrested for being members of the ANC or the PAC. They were arrested for saying things. My teacher, Stanley Mogoba, was one of them. Many teachers were arrested together with us. My father was arrested for a brief period and released. Anybody who they thought may have exercised influence over other people was a target for arrest, harassment, torture, and incarceration.

Godfrey Pitje was my instructing attorney. The first day I emerged from underneath the courtroom to get into the dock, I looked and Godfrey Pitje was the instructing attorney. I knew him; he was my father's friend. They were of the same age. So he would go to Godfrey and say, "My son is arrested. Provide defense," which Godfrey did provide in the early stages of the proceedings. It was the Supreme Court, and Godfrey engaged Sydney Kentridge to appear as my counsel. [Because of the South African split legal profession, Godfrey Pitje, as an attorney, could not appear before the Supreme Court, where this trial was to be held. Only an advocate, such as Kentridge, could act as counsel in that court.] It was dangerous then to be counsel to terrorists because you'd get marked immediately; you'd get tainted immediately yourself. But Godfrey was there for us. He was there when it mattered most. Remembering Godfrey at that moment in part gives an answer to the question, What made you want to become a lawyer?

Sydney Kentridge, who appeared for us as counsel in July 1963, came and applied for a postponement. He wanted the matter to stand adjourned so that he could prepare properly. The police had four or five months of preparation to get their testimony right. They tortured, extracted, forced confessions from people. He and Godfrey tried to take statements over the weekend, but it didn't work. It was clear that they weren't going to manage. They went back to court. This judge didn't want to postpone the trial. Sydney's position was that he would be totally embarrassed to appear for eighteen accused to whom he could not talk. He could not adequately defend and put their case across, and for that reason he withdrew from the trial in protest. Of course that meant we were left without counsel. He had perfectly valid points.

We then got Jack Unterhalter, who came and asked for a postponement, but the judge wouldn't grant it. The judge's name was Cilliers. He wouldn't grant a postponement. The case was adjourned again one day to allow Unterhalter to prepare. He said, "I can't prepare the eighteen people in one day. I need one day for each one of them. Adjourn the trial for three weeks, then we can prepare properly." He [the judge] wouldn't. Lawyer after lawyer came, five of them, and asked for postponement.

At the end of the fifth lawyer's withdrawal, the judge said, "Trial will continue. First witness." And the first witness was called. I had to do my own cross-examination at the age of fifteen. I conducted my own defense in a case that lasted for over three months. All of us conducted our own defenses. There was no counsel available, not because they weren't willing, but because they just did not have the time to prepare. You can't act for eighteen people if you don't know what their case is. So after three months the trial went on, and there were over forty witnesses. I cross-examined most of them in my own defense.

And when it came to sentencing, Judge Cilliers said, "Ja, you small little one." He used the fact that I cross-examined so well to my detriment. He said, "It shows you knew clearly what you were doing. I must attribute full mens rea [criminal intent] to you. And, having heard you talk in this court, I am satisfied that you have said these things that the witnesses alleged you said. I don't think there is any embellishment to what the witnesses say. I find you guilty of having conspired to try and overthrow the state by violence. Ten years in imprisonment."

So I picked up ten years in prison at the age of fifteen. And it was done.

Imprisonment

∞ I went to Robben Island in 1963—for ten years. I used the time quite well. I finished my standard 8 through correspondence. I did matric through correspondence in one year. I wrote the same exam as other matric students. I just had far more time than the average student. I had twice, three times the time they had. I had every single Saturday and Sunday; I had every single evening.

As a prisoner you work up to about 5 P.M. We did gardening. We worked at the quarry to break big slabs of quarry stones to extract them out of a bloody quarry dungeon, a quarry hole. We also crushed the big stones, and sometimes we cut them up with chisels into mid-size stones. Then some of the stones you had to crush into small stones, like for concrete and gravel. You would get the stones to concrete size, and then some of the stones were crushed into powder. So you had a whole process of converting large boulders of stone into powder, and I think quite often they just created nasty jobs for prisoners: crush stones and cut stones and use fourteen-pound hammers. I would work all day and would come home and study. I would take a shower at about five and then have time from five until they switched off the lights at about 11 P.M. Six hours.

At the beginning, the warders would beat you up. They would chase you down passages. That stopped when one or more prisoners actually beat the warders up. "You have no right to touch my body. I'm going to touch your body in a painful way." The warders had to make choices. There normally would be eight to ten of them with guns, but they were looking after hundreds of prisoners. So they could fire a couple of shots, but, in fact, I think they understood that they would die. There was a counterbalance in force because they would probably shoot a good few prisoners, but in the end the prisoners would get to them. So there was that ever present deterrent that was there. They did hit us when they said, "Come on move, move, come on," almost like dealing with cattle.

I also had a bit of fun. I was short. I was a boy, a growing boy. It was quite often that the warders had their sticks and pick handles up in the air. I was sufficiently short to be able to duck underneath the armpits of most of the adults and to run in between them. I would stand there and when the warders hit, they'd hit the heads of all the tall guys. I'd see the guys get hit and see blood coming out. My size helped me hide amongst all these tall guys.

But we were a collective body of political prisoners, and the sense of dignity was a very important one. The sense of who we were and our being was very important. And therefore, we wouldn't allow warders to abuse us. For instance, there was a move to resist warders stripping prisoners just anywhere randomly. I still had a right to privacy even though I was a prisoner. They demanded all sorts of crazy, sometimes racist, forms of address and we said, "You are mad! You want me to call you master or baas; you are mad in your head. Your job is to guard me, and I am a prisoner trying to overthrow your government, and you don't have any right to try and force anything on me." Very quickly there was mutual respect between warders and political prisoners, and that went a long way. So this barbaric rubbish of a few initial years stopped. My last seven years, there was no abuse.

The food was bad. They just said, "I can't do anything. The legislature has prescribed this food." There was a nice standoff, a healthy standoff. You do your job and let me serve my term, and you leave me alone. Mr. Mandela, of course, helped to cool down relations between prisoners and warders quite a lot. He was well known even then and well respected. He was the leader of the ANC and also the leader of the prisoners. It was generally accepted by everybody that he was the leader of everybody who was there.

I finished matric and got a B.A. in English and political science through UNISA [University of South Africa]. My family provided me with money. They would pay directly to UNISA, and UNISA would register me. I received books from the library. Once you were a registered student, you were entitled to order books from the library. So they would post the books from Pretoria to Robben Island. It took fourteen days, sometimes twenty-one days, for a book to come. But you got pretty used to that very soon. I would register in December with UNISA.

I would order the material in December, when everybody was starting to have fun at home. It's no fun in prison; there is no Christmas, I mean the food is exactly the same. So I would order my books and start getting them the third week of December or first week of January, and I would start working through my assignments. But I had a lot of time, if I think about it, and so I would read through all these text books and wade through the materials. If there were one or two of the guys who were doing the same course, we would have a little study group together.

I remember when I was doing Latin. Stanley Mogoba taught me. The Reverend Bishop Mogoba taught me Latin.[2] I used to push the wheelbarrow with him at the quarry. My father had been my teacher, and he took my dad's place. He taught me *amo, amas, amat, amamus, amatis, amant*— I love, you love, she loves, it loves, they love—the conjugation of Latin verbs. When conjugating and pushing the wheelbarrow with him, he would also teach me nouns: *mensa, mensam* . . . .

Once I passed matric, I started teaching other guys who were doing matric. I would read their work and analyze it jointly with them. They would write tests and I would mark their tests. So I became a teacher and a student at the same time. If you passed something, you would teach the other guys in the next level. Minister Steve Tshwete, minister of safety and security [in the Mandela administration], I taught him. He was in my English class. There were many other eminent people. I taught Mr. Sisulu English, old man Sisulu. People like Klaas Moshishi [another ANC leader], guys who came there as graduates, they taught me a lot of things. I chose English and political science because Klaas Moshishi had done English and political science as majors.

We had reading schools, drama schools. I remember clearly us performing *The Merchant of Venice,* and I was Shylock. We did *Hamlet.*

We had choir competitions—male-voice choirs. I remember clearly I was one of the guys in the choir which did the *Messiah,* Handel's "Hallelujah Chorus," "Unto Us a Child Is Born." The only source of paper on Robben Island was the paper that contained cement. We would smuggle that into the cells. You would rip off the outside. The inside was khaki color. You would knit it into a big chart and one guy would sit down and write out Handel's *Messiah* in tonic solfège. He would write it out in all the parts: soprano, alto, tenor, and bass. He would write them out like that and guys at five o'clock or weekends, they would start. We would have competitions. Cell 1 competing against Cell 6, 7, 8, 9, and 10 in the communal hall and the guys would sing Handel's *Messiah.* And it came out quite well because people didn't have lots of things to do, so they tended to focus on voice training.

There was a dance club. One, two, one, two. You would go dancing at arms length, and then you actually did ballroom dancing. You learned the basics.

There was a chess club and chess championships. There were soccer championships on Robben Island, and I remember quite clearly I was the chairman of the soccer association on Robben Island. English Naidoo, from the ANC, was the secretary of the soccer association. The two of us ran eight teams. We had a league and we arranged for the guys to buy their own soccer kit [gear]. So Saturday, you would look forward to it. You got out of your prison clothes and you put on your soccer clothes. There was a rugby league, and Steve Tshwete was the chairman of the rugby club.

The strategy was somehow to beat the prison authorities at their own

game. It was a battle of the minds. The physical incarceration you adapted
to very quickly. You got used to the fact that you had shorts on, you
walked barefooted, and that you had to cut your hair to nothing, as prisoners do. You would have a cold shower every morning, even in winter,
and have a shower in the afternoon when you came from work whether
you liked it or not. That's the way of prison and that you can overcome.
You just get used to the fact that what food there was was bad, no snacks
in between meals. The human body adjusts to that. We were all very
healthy, I must say—thin, no baggage, no cellulite.

I did my second degree which was in law. I did a B.Iuris degree—that
is, a three-year degree. I had done a B.A. in political science and English,
and I then did a B.Iuris, which is a purely legal degree. B.Iuris was enough
to permit you to practice as an attorney but not enough to practice as an
advocate. The only reason why I did a B.Iuris was the warders did not, at
this stage, allow us to do any postgraduate work. You had to do another
junior degree. Some people did four or five junior degrees. They said had
you studied enough, you could not do honors or postgraduate work. They
agreed to let us do postgraduate work the very year I was going to leave
prison. So the last year in prison I registered for third-year LL.B. from
UNISA. LL.B. is normally over four years. With the credits I got from
B.Iuris, I could to do an LL.B. in two years because I would get all those
credits which, really, normally would constitute the first and second year.

A Banning Order and the Beginning of a Career in Law

∞ Ten years were now gone. I had used up my ten years fully. I was
twenty-five years old, and I walked out of Pretoria Central Prison. They
transferred me from Robben Island to Pretoria just for release. The security cops were waiting there for me when I was released and they slapped
me with a banning order.

"I do hereby order you, Dikgang Ernest Moseneke, not to leave or
absent yourself from the residential premises being no. 29 Boleko Street,
Atteridgeville, Pretoria, any time during the hours 6 P.M. to 6 A.M. of any
day whatsoever and any time between 12 hours to 12 hours [noon to
midnight] of any Saturday and any Sunday. I hereby order you and pro-
hibit you from entering any institution at which you are provided with

any tuition, training, learning, technical, academic, or otherwise. I pro-
hibit you . . ."

I virtually know it by heart. A banning order was an order which the
minister of justice could give to any person in South Africa prohibiting
that person from leaving certain premises at certain times or from entering certain premises at any time, from conversing with any persons specified, from traveling to or entering any country, land, place, or institution
without the minister's permission, from consulting any doctor other than
the doctor specified in such a document, from consulting any attorney
other than the attorney specified.

When I came out they said, "Who is your attorney?" I said, "What?
Do I need one?"

They said, "Well, we have to specify it in the order. We will leave
those blank."

In fact you are under house arrest.

So for five years after Robben Island, I could never be outside of my
home between 6 P.M. and 6 A.M. I lived with my parents in Atteridgeville.
I couldn't leave my parents' home any time on Saturday. On Sunday I
could leave only between the hours of nine and twelve, exclusively for
purposes of attending a bona fide religious service. They specified a
church. You can't go to church A or Z; you have to go to that church!
They asked me, "Where do you go to church?"[3]

I said, "What?" I had just come out of jail. I said: "Leave me alone. I
served ten years. What's wrong with you?"

Then, of course, apartheid was in full swing. This was in 1974. It was
in full swing. It was nowhere near collapse or anything. It was to take
another almost twenty years for it to go. So I came out after ten years, and
it looked like I had done nothing. The situation was worse. They knew I
was coming out, and I was immediately locked up.

I continued my studies and finished my LL.B. from UNISA while I
was under the banning order. I also obtained permission to do articles, an
apprenticeship as a lawyer. A magistrate amended my order only sufficiently to allow me to travel to the city. I still wasn't allowed to leave the
magisterial district of Pretoria. Each time I wanted to go and do any work
related to the law firm where I was training, I had to apply for leave from
the local magistrate. "I want to go to Sandton [a Johannesburg suburb]. I

have to interview a client there." And he would say, Which client? And then he would say, Okay, I'll come back to you, and then he told the security guard. The primary function of that was to get information as to where you wanted to go so they could follow you. The magistrate had to ask for the recommendation of a security cop before he made the decision. If they said no, he would just refuse and say, Sorry, I cannot give you the permission.

So I finished my studies, then did articles. When I completed my articles in 1977, I moved for my admission to the Supreme Court. The Law Society opposed the application. Those proceedings are recorded in our law books. *Ex parte Moseneke,* 1979 (4) SA Rep. 884.

Moseneke's application to be admitted as an attorney presented two problems. First was the fact that he had been found guilty of "sabotage" and sentenced to ten years' imprisonment. Second, he had ceased to be a South African citizen. Moseneke and his family were Tswana-speaking. When the homeland of Bophuthatswana gained its "independence" in 1977, all Tswana-speaking people technically lost their South African citizenship and became citizens of Bophuthatswana, regardless of their physical presence within the Republic of South Africa.

With regard to his conviction, the court concluded that, although his offense was the equivalent of high treason, it was satisfied that there had been a "permanent reformation" and that Moseneke was a "fit and proper person to be admitted as an attorney."

The court also held that, although Moseneke was no longer a South African citizen, he was a resident of South Africa and had been admitted as an articled clerk before Bophuthatswana became independent. He was therefore entitled to retain benefits and privileges, other than citizenship, that he had had prior to independence. Those rights included the right to continue his articles and to be admitted as an attorney.

∞ My admission to practice was my green light. Willie Seriti, George Maluleke, and myself came together and said, We're going to set up a strong black firm that's going to go for it, boys. And we put it together. The name of the firm was Maluleke, Seriti, and Moseneke, in the order of our admission as attorneys. We emblazoned it, put up boards on brass

plates and everywhere, and we told the world, We're here, we're here! And
we took off like thunder. We really did. Our offices were in Pretoria.

We got into offices and then we got a notice from the Group Areas
inspector to say that we were occupying white premises and therefore we
were contravening the Group Areas Act. We were in the central business
district. It was a white area and it was an offense for blacks to have an
office there.

The inspector said, "I give you notice to vacate the premises forth-
with . . . Certainly not later than such and such a date."

And Willie and George and I had this one big one smile. I said,
"Boys, this is the best thing that has happened to us. There will be this
case of ours (which was all over in the papers). Even if we stop practicing,
our problem will be, How do you stop people from coming to us? There
will be a hell of a case. It will be all over in the papers: New Black Law
Firm Resists the Group Areas Act. What more fun can you have than
that?" In the end, they didn't charge us. For some reason they just backed
off from charging us. And we were dying to be charged.

We had a revolt in 1976 [the Soweto uprising], and that uprising
stands in very close association with the start of our firm in 1978. The
whole country had a new wave of resistance. They started again to arrest
people. But the Civil Rights Movement was beginning to gain tremendous momentum again.

People get scared for only a while. They had locked us up, bashed us,
and had given us ten years, twenty, life imprisonment. They sentenced a
good few people to death they didn't like. By 1974, all the organizations
appeared to be crushed. There was no talk of the ANC. It was unlawful to
say anything about the ANC, so too about the PAC. It was dead. When I
came out of jail you couldn't say A N without getting into trouble, even
without the C. It was dangerous. And the media never reported about
anybody. Nelson Mandela was dead, so to speak.

But in 1976 there was an uprising of the kids. They were the age I
had been when I was arrested and sent to prison. I saw them, and I had
just one hell of a big smile on my face. I felt totally vindicated. These kids
took to the streets and said, "You go to hell. There is no way you can keep
us under this system. Forget it." They put up barricades. They set police
stations alight. They used to stone police and the police shot them dead—

shot many dead. In some ways the kids were playing a game, but the cops didn't play the game the kids were playing. They were actually killing them. That led to a major migration of young people from South Africa who went out of the country to go into exile. They joined liberation movements, the armies, MK [Umkhonto weSizwe, the military wing of the ANC], APLA [the Azanian People's Liberation Army, the military wing of the Pan Africanist Congress]. They joined and became soldiers and they said, "We are going to go back there." The view was, You are not going to arrest me for ten years, like Nelson Mandela. He was then thirteen years in jail.

From 1976 though to 1986 there was no peace in this country. Young people never could take it lying down. There were waves of challenges, rioting, fighting the police, trying to burn down government buildings.

So I went into practice in this chaos. We did a lot administrative law cases; these abounded. There were challenges against executive orders of a wide variety, challenges against government decrees, challenges against directives which emanated from provincial authorities and councils. I did a lot of civil applications to court to challenge the wide variety of governmental action.

I would sometimes argue that a particular act was outside the law as it stands; it was wider than what the law provided and was therefore invalid as ultra vires. If the superintendent chucked somebody out of their house, because most of the houses were rented houses owned by the local authorities, I would go and review that in the Supreme Court.

Afrikaners had this formalistic sense of justice. If the superintendent did not comply with minor, nonsensical prerequisites, they would in fact set aside the order. They were not liberal judges, but their sense was that rule of law was important. I used to exploit this. I used to sit down and laugh at the government draftsmanship, which was always quite poor.

They would arrest people for passes. I would come in and apply for their bail.

The magistrate would say, "There is no bail here."

And I would say, "What? There is no bail here?"

He would say, "People arrested for passes never get bail. Go to the Supreme Court."

And that's what I did. I said to the court, "Have you heard of this nonsense? They say you could in fact arrest a person ad infinitum because if there is no bail, it means he or she could be kept as long as some officer wished."

The Supreme Court would say, "What? Obnoxious! There must be bail. You can't say there is no bail." So it was simple.

One case involved Richard Ramadipe, a black attorney. Richard got detained in 1979 or '80. He was believed by the local security police to be giving support to young activists. They put him away under State of Emergency laws. I was instructed by Richard's family to apply for his release on any grounds available, whatever the crime might be. His family didn't know why he was arrested. The police were not obliged to give you reasons and his family had no right of access to him. They were only obliged to tell you where he was detained and under what law he was detained. I put an application before the Supreme Court seeking Richard's release from detention under emergency regulations, on the ground that his detention was irregular.

The warrant of arrest, which was signed by the minister of justice and which authorized Richard's detention under the emergency laws, directed that he should be kept in a police station in Potgietersrus [a small town north of Pretoria]. He was in fact being kept in a prison—a regular prison, not a police lockup.

I said, "A warrant such as this is an instrument which limits liberty and must therefore be restrictively interpreted in favor of the individual."

All of those principles were still there in South African law. They never removed them. I argued that the policeman must detain the person at the place where the warrant directs. Otherwise he may detain this guy on his farm, in the boot of his car, at his friend's home, in a shebeen [a township tavern], maybe in a brothel. The judge bought that argument—again, this Afrikaner mentality. The point I'm really making was that we were doing a lot of challenges against the exercise of executive power and the exercise of secondary legislative authority.

We also had a fairly large matrimonial practice. Mos Mavundla came in as our next partner. Mos did that work, a matrimonial practice such as Godfrey Pitje had. This always abounds in all societies. You find lots of people want to get divorced, and that was a ready-made service to provide. So too amongst black people.

The third kind of practice was a very limited amount of commercial work. It was limited as there were few black business people. I represented many of the black businesses, all of them small businesses. I represented them in various negotiations or when the business was under attack by some rule or other and the authorities wouldn't want to issue a license. When there was no real valid reason for denial of the license, where it was a matter of law, I would challenge the denial in court. Licenses had to be renewed annually. In contrast, now you need no license to do any business. But then, every single year you had to go and plead for a license. In that way they used to compromise a lot of business people, get them to be informants. "Just tell us if you see something, someone unusual comes into your shop who looks suspicious might be a terrorist." Things like that. They increasingly gave licenses to people who had rendered some service to government. This was a form of thank you to people. This led ultimately to a tension between black business people and the community. Shops were set alight in retaliation for what they perceived to be a collaboration between small businesses and the regime.

There was a division in the firm. George did a lot of deeds and third-party cases [automobile negligence cases]. Willie did very much third-party cases too. We also hired three or four other young attorneys out of law school. We had this formidable firm of about eight qualified lawyers, four of whom were partners.

There was a whole pool of people who were regularly arraigned and indicted for political offenses. When that happened, all of us would put back whatever we were doing. We had divisions of responsibility, but we would put them aside to go in defense of people who were charged. We saw that as our role, as our contribution. We linked up with various American donors. The Lawyers Committee for Civil Rights in Washington put up a fund which would support litigation and provide defense for political defendants. Essentially the source of funds was the U.S. and London. We got funds from Germany and the Scandinavian countries, but those were so suspicious that they were channeled through London. There was nonpolitical business being done with the U.S. and the U.K., so the security cops were less likely to open the envelopes. But when you tried to clear a check, particularly against a U.S. bank, you always had to come in and say what the check was about. You had to fill in a declaration and we would enter, "services rendered."

The legal relationship we evolved was that Lawyers for Civil Rights appointed us as their agent to provide legal services to persons who we could identify as falling in certain categories predetermined by them. The authorities tried to stop that practice and I had a challenge in court. I argued that they could not stop legitimate business activity between the U.S. and South Africa. The court agreed. The government couldn't stop money coming as fees for services duly rendered by us as attorneys. It was like a lot of other business between Washington and South Africa, which was not political or terroristic. So the legal answer, the trick, was to go for broad principled positions that the court had to follow. You had to categorize your activity within a protected principle and you would fly. So we won cases ad nauseam. I just found it real fun. I could trick the system all the time and advance everybody's struggle at the same time.

Remuneration was not enormous. It was higher than average workers in South Africa, but it was not palatial. You dealt with people who had no money of their own. You dealt with donor communities essentially and a few criminals who would have had a bit of money of their own, but it never would be a lot. There was limited corporate work for any number of reasons, including the fact that my firm had this image of being involved in human rights. Corporate captains of industry don't like to be messed up with political battles. They stay out of that.

We debated the question of whether we should work within the system this way quite thoroughly both at Robben Island, that veritable college of ideas, and at home. You could make use of the courts provided the objectives remained quite focused. You had to remain committed to transform society. The upside exceeded the downside. The upside was that we were giving support to victims of apartheid, who would feel sufficiently fortified to want to continue fighting. There was no respite, no political defense, no support for the families of the detainees, no bursaries for children of people who were in jail, no support, either financial or moral, for the children of people in exile. So clearly, we played a very important ambulance role, where we had to deal with the casualties as they occurred. We were the emergency services.

Moving to the Bar

∞ I stayed with this firm for five years, until 1982. Then I went to the bar. [He became an advocate.] I had accomplished what was necessary as an attorney. The firm was strong and solid, had made a name for itself, and I had met most of my basic needs. I had a good car. I built a house, I got married, I had two little boys. Some of the more basic things were in place. There was no hunger at the door, and it was a time to make a move. I thought I had done reasonably well with litigation in my earlier days as an attorney. I wanted to actually argue most of the cases myself before the Supreme Court. My experience doing the cross-examination during my own trial influenced my decision as well.

I think that was the primary reason. Had I waited, I probably would have made quite a reasonably good corporate lawyer. If I had stayed in the firm as an attorney, there would have been enough work. [Advocates may not join together in firms, either with attorneys or with each other. They work independently, usually in a chambers, or group of advocates, whose only association is the sharing of office expenses.] The work was beginning to flow as more black people had a little more and started doing things. But I had a strong urge to be a trial lawyer, which is what an advocate is. You can handle big-time trial work and opinion work. You give opinions on a whole range of matters. You write up briefs, and you go to court and defend what you say in the briefs. That's really what an advocate's work is in this country. And I thought, ja.

I thought about people like Joe Slovo [head of the South African Communist Party; a close associate of Nelson Mandela, Slovo served as minister of housing in the Mandela administration until his death in 1995], people like Arthur Chaskalson, and Sydney Kentridge [both prominent antiapartheid advocates]. All these were very outstanding advocates who did a lot of hard work. So there were quite ready-made models to look at and to say, Well, I want to do like those guys. I had been an attorney for a short while; five years was it. I'd turned thirty. I had done my bit.

I started out as an advocate with chambers in Johannesburg. Legwai Pitje and I were the only black counsel there. Ismail Mahomed was also there, in all fairness to him. He was a black guy and he was there, but he was already so senior and there was a big gap between us. He had been at the bar then for twenty years or something when I got there. He was a senior counsel, probably the first black person that I knew as a senior counsel. He had enormous talent and he was litigating left, right, and center with ample energy.

It was easier for me to go to Johannesburg because the Pretoria bar was in the process of changing its admission rules. They had never had a black guy in Pretoria. In fact, their constitution expressly forbade black people from joining the bar when I applied in 1981. As a consequence of my application to the bar, they moved ahead to change the rules, and, believe you me, they had quite a fight in persuading each other that they should amend the constitution. They needed two-thirds majority to do so. I was quite happy to contribute to breaking down the edifice of the past by making the application. But I wasn't going to make it my daily bother to become an advocate, and so I went to Johannesburg and did pupillage there. After a year in Jo'burg, when Pretoria looked like it was settled down with its racial problems, then I moved to Pretoria.

I did pupillage in Johannesburg under the able leadership of Ernie Wentzel and Guy Hoffman. Wentzel was a senior counsel. I did a lot of work for Ernie and Hoffman in my early days. Remember, I had first been an attorney. I wasn't green by any measure. I then had a wife and family, which meant I had pressures to pass the exam and get on with a practice. I couldn't mess around. There were few black advocates, and this was a terrain to conquer.

I felt that it was the right place to be. Jo'burg at the time was really seen to be the center of excellence in law practice and in court litigation. At the time I got there, all the outstanding names and personalities were still there: Kentridge, Arthur Chaskalson, George Bizos, Mahomed. So there I joined what was clearly a very illustrious bar, well respected in the country. It failed in one respect, however. It failed in that it didn't produce any judges. The Afrikaner government was not really prepared to appoint any of these very bright lawyers who generally were deeply opposed to apartheid. They were seen to be dangerous liberals, and I went in to join them. I saw them to be fairly moderate from where I came from. My demands were much more strident than what they wanted in society. I wanted much more.

After writing the exams to become an advocate, to my total amazement when the results were announced, I was told I was one of the best candidates for all the exams. I had the highest marks for that particular year. I also had had the second highest marks for attorneys' admission exams.

I was then ready to practice. I had deep fears that I might never be able to quite make it. The bar would be hostile. There weren't enough black attorneys to support me, and it was a financial and career risk. But day one, Mathews Phosa, who today is the premier of Mpumalanga Province [no longer the premier], and Phineas Mojapelo sent a local attorney who came pushing a wheelbarrow full of briefs. Day one! This guy said, "Congratulations, brother." A wheelbarrow full of briefs. I had twenty cases lined up. What a pleasant surprise! George Maluleke came and he probably sent me ten matters; all these were civil trials. Willie Seriti sent me just as many. These were my former partners. And it never stopped.

And there I was, in business. I was never so busy in my life. I made three or four times the money I had made as an attorney almost instantly. By the end of the first twelve months, I really felt like I had been working very hard. In addition, most of the senior counsel—remember that we're talking about a fairly racist South Africa fifteen years ago—were very happy to invite me to be their junior to work with them. In the short time I was in Jo'burg, I had the rare privilege to work with George Bizos. I became junior to Arthur Chaskalson. I did work with Denis Kuny, an outstanding senior counsel of the Jo'burg bar. I did a junior brief with Lewis Skweyiya. Just name them. I don't know who I didn't have an opportunity to have a shot with. I worked with Jack Unterhalter, and I worked against Jack Unterhalter in one of my first cases. The first six months, I came before Judge Leveson in a case against Jack Unterhalter, who was senior counsel. I was quite lucky. It was clearly luck and I won. I was very excited, and I walked up to him and he was most pleasant and very supportive, I must tell you. I just felt like a fish in water.

There was a whole range of very fascinating cases. One involved Zwelakhe Sisulu, the son of Walter Sisulu, who was at Robben Island. Zwelakhe is now [no longer] CEO of SABC [South African Broadcasting Corporation]. At the time, 1980, Zwelakhe was writing for the *World,* now the *Sowetan.* As a journalist, Zwelakhe came to know a number of guys who had skipped the country. He wrote an article which appeared in the front page of the newspaper about people leaving the country to go for military training. The cops subpoenaed him under Section 189 of the Criminal Procedure Act to compel him to disclose whatever information he knew. You could subpoena any person to appear before any judicial officer. After being sworn in, that person would be obliged to divulge whatever he or she knew about any matter which was relevant to the commission of any offense. He refused to divulge anything and he was immediately arrested. We challenged the arrest on a number of grounds. The magistrate convicted him summarily for refusing to disclose his source. We then went before the Supreme Court to argue that the magistrate could not actually convict you summarily. He had to in fact engage you in a whole process of seeking to make you speak. He had to direct questions to you which would clearly indicate that you refused to speak. Once he got to that point, then and only then could he commit you. Our argument was upheld by the appellate division and his three-year sentence was set aside. It was an important case because he was a major, high-profile journalist.

In 1980 or thereabouts, there was a guy called Zolo Mahobe who fell in love with a young lady who was a cashier in a bank. She was working in the ledger division of the bank. She transferred a total of R11 million [in 1996 about $2.5 million] to him. It was a lot of money, particularly fifteen years ago. You can multiply the value of the money by three. His girlfriend was a very pretty young lady. Zolo was married and this was his mistress. Zolo was quite something. He had bought a professional soccer club called Mamelodi Sundowners. I had written up all the contracts and things for him to buy the club. I didn't know he was buying it with stolen money. He bought racehorses; he bought homes out at the coast and here, and this was actually all stolen money.

When the charges were made, he ran to Botswana and disappeared. I went to Botswana to persuade him that he had to come back and face trial. He probably hates me, wherever he is. I assured him that I would do my best. My best was to deal with the facts as they were, not to lie about any of the facts. He picked up fifteen years imprisonment. His girlfriend got twelve years imprisonment. Zolo's estate was sequestrated. He lost virtually everything he had. It was a long, protracted trial, lasting for six months. It was heavily covered by the media, almost like the Winnie Mandela divorce or the O.J. Simpson case. It intrigued the black community in particular how a young woman could bypass the computer system of the bank and over three years steal money of that quantity and transfer it into her lover's account. This perceived happily married wealthy man suddenly turned out to have been a beneficiary of a love affair. There was a book written about all this which made quite a lot of money. I didn't make the money; I was just a counsel in the matter.

I represented Winnie Mandela in connection with the Stompie matter in 1991, just after Mr. Mandela had come out of jail. [The now former wife of President Nelson Mandela, Winnie Madikizela-Mandela, was charged with participation in the 1989 slaying of fourteen-year-old political activist Stompie Seipei. She was ultimately convicted of kidnapping and being an accessory to assault. She was sentenced to six months in prison. On appeal, the sentence was suspended and she was fined R15,000 (about $2,800). These events were also the subject of a 1997 hearing before the Truth and Reconciliation Commission.] I was George Bizos's junior in the case. The trial went on for six months. The government sought to embarrass Mandela and to reduce his esteem in the community. The task of representing her fell to George Bizos and myself. I spent six months defending Winnie.

I did any number of third-party claims. They were basically the bread and butter of the practice. The cash flow issues basically were covered by those claims. I did a whole number of civil claims for bodily injuries arising out of shooting by police. Claims for widows for death in detention, applications for challenges for detention. I did a whole range of cases involving exercise of executive power.

As for political trials, it was like a national duty. Whether or not you were a criminal lawyer, you were obliged to have your quota of defending boys on the border or the guys who were in combat and were arrested when they came back into the country. I have done as many of those trials as you would like to think about.

We truly and fully exploited the prim and proper rule-of-law approach that the Afrikaners have always had. It was always an enigma. They were vicious oppressors and exploiters, but they also believed that they were part of some civilized world where there were civilized norms. As for the judges, they thought that, in fact, they could uphold the principles of the common law in the face of a basic statutory overlay that was going to trample each and every principle.

So you had a very strange thing—people who were very meticulous about rules, like most Calvinists all over the world. They were positivists; they believed that the law was sacred. What was law was sacred and had to be observed, even if the law was adopted for the wrong reasons.

So we consciously exploited what we saw as a weakness, the soft belly of a very tough animal. And we stabbed it just in one place, the soft belly. And we very cautiously strategized about these things and argued principles to their very limits. Time without count I had clients who were in business who were refused licenses by some bureaucrat sitting somewhere in the licensing offices, and you could rely on the fact that he would not have properly done his work. You would drag them to court and say, Justify your conduct. And the paperwork would not be good enough to meet the very high standards. They would throw out the refusal to grant a license. Most of the time we hoisted these guys on their own petards by using their own system.

This was summarized by a comrade of ours on Robben Island. He was very angry with a warder who was trying to assault him or to manhandle him. "Look here. Don't touch my body. I'm going to strike you before your own court, sue you in your own court, and win in your own bloody court." You know, that just about for me epitomizes the approach that most people had. It was their court; I had no control over it. I had no influence, but the system had rules and you pretended to be observing those rules. We made them play by those rules and I think it paid enormous dividends.

But ironically, on the other side, it made us addicted to fairness, to just dispensations, to an independent judiciary. Black lawyers in general honestly believe that the state must not be arbitrary. Executive power must be controlled by law enshrined in a constitution which must serve as supreme law, and the courts must be independent. We believe in democratic political institutions. Those issues were negotiated at Kempton Park [the deliberations that produced the 1993 interim constitution]. There was no debate about those issues because we were basically dealing with lawyers who, for the better part of their lives, had fought against the vicious system and had come to appreciate constitutional safeguards and constitutional democracy. There was not even a debate whether in fact we would have a bill of rights or whether we would have constitutional supremacy or whether in fact lawyers would have to play a very funda-mental important role. So out of that lawyering, there has emerged a very rich tradition of fairness, of judicial review, of rule of law, and, I think, of integrity. There are a lot of honest, good South Africans who would like to make the law supersede the whims and fancies of individuals in the executive arm of government. We made efforts to restrain the political power. Executive power is something that you find most lawyers of my tradition, my age, who have borne part of the struggle, don't trust. We want to limit power. That is the upside of that whole era.

After ten years at the bar, in 1992, Moseneke became senior counsel. He was the second black African and the fourth nonwhite lawyer to take this step.

Preparing for the New South Africa

∞ I had the rare privilege to be involved in drafting what became the interim constitution, the basis of the new constitution for South Africa. It came after I had spent two years leading the PAC; I was deputy head of the PAC from 1990 to 1992. During those two years, I did whatever I could to try to develop the PAC into another party which would work with the ANC. I did my damnedest to form a patriotic front between the PAC and the ANC. I hope I will be remembered for that. I tried as hard as I could. I tried to get them to put their votes together and run together. It was very uncertain how South Africans were going to vote after all the years of oppression and whether we were going to have enough votes or whether there would be enough people to register to vote. So it made more sense to go together. All that I did side by side with my practice. I never really left my practice. I just saw it as a support effort because I had no political aspirations.

At the beginning of the constitutional discussions, there was a lot of positioning. Inkatha left, we [the PAC] left, the National Party left, depending on what the issue was. If you didn't get what you wanted, you threw your tantrum. But we came back. You threw your toys out of the window, and people came and said please come back. So it is a South African thing; you walk out if you don't get your way. I didn't enjoy it. I was in the wrong terrain. You must be very power-orientated to be in the political setting. You need henchmen and support. Politics is quite something.

I didn't feel there was any vision on the part of the PAC. It was obviously useless to continue acts of violence, but there was still a contention by the PAC that we needed the threat of violence. So I resigned as deputy head. It was my whole mind-set as a lawyer, my training, and the way I fought the struggle for twenty years. I did not need all of that violence. [President] de Klerk had made very major concessions for the proposed new constitution. So I resigned, not from the party, but from the leadership. I don't like walking out completely, but it was important that I not be a leader. I haven't officially renewed my membership, but I have never formally resigned.

After my resignation from the PAC leadership, Mr. Mandela pushed me to serve on the constitutional committee which was going to write the constitution. I asked him who else would be there. He said Arthur Chaskalson would be involved, together with others, including a number of Afrikaners. So there we were. I was engaged as a lawyer who had done a lot of work with human rights and constitutional litigation. So it wasn't surprising that I would have been asked to come on into that role. Most people had faith in my ability to be neutral despite the political position I had taken in the PAC. I think most South Africans had accepted that I had a mind of my own and I could be independent. Initially the PAC was not even there, but it came into the process later. I divorced myself from them.

I just did my job, which was to record the agreements that people reached from time to time and to do research on a whole range of topics. We extensively studied the U.S. constitution, the Indian constitution, the German constitution, various systems in New Zealand and Australia. We looked at constitutional states right across the world. That gave me enormous opportunity to learn quite a lot about constitutional issues.

There were no real constitutional experts here in South Africa. There was no constitution to be an expert about. It was apartheid rubbish that there was real constitutional litigation. There was parliamentary supremacy. So all of us were novices. We were lawyers who basically had investigative skills, and our job was to put together what was negotiated.

We were the guys who wrote down the agreements as they emerged. So the constitution literally grew in our hands. Some of the texts I wrote in my study at home. I wrote the whole executive section. You'd do a draft beforehand, and your colleagues would criticize it and check the proposals. Sometimes we would put out four proposals.

Do you want an elected presidency or one arising from congress or Parliament? And we would put models. It was my function to put up models on the executive arm. I also wrote most of the sections on the ombudsman [a position which became the public protector under the new constitution and was ultimately filled by Selby Baqwa; see chap. 12].

We were basically the technical arm of the founding fathers and mothers of our constitution. We wrote it down for them. We showed them the options, and they were to exercise them. Often it was quite robust. They would come back and say, "We don't like this, Moseneke, we don't like it." We had to make presentations before this august gathering of women and men. And there were tough negotiations.

I remember tough negotiations around the issue of civil service. We would come and say these are the typical civil service provisions, ideal ones. And the Nats [the Nationalist Party] would say, This is the compromise we want: You must secure our pensions. We would write in the position of the police. We would change the name of the South African Defence Force. To give you an idea of the compromise, it became South African National Defence Force. It was the same and not the same—the South African Police or the South African Police Services.

We couldn't agree on the flag for a very long time. The flag has got all the colors that you can think of because they had everybody's color in there: Inkatha, the PAC, the ANC, the NP. And it ended up being a real bloody flag with so many colors. And then there was the anthem. The politicians had to go and broker a deal, and in the end they took the two anthems and fused them together and we wrote them into the constitution. Those were marks of the more visual compromises.

There was also a big debate about whether in fact the president should be the commander-in-chief of the armed forces. There was some suggestion that the commander-in-chief of the armed forces should be independent. They seemed to argue that an independent commander could make decisions about whether to enter into or declare war or some such rubbish. You find that in no constitution. You make someone president and then you give him the power.

But it was a seesaw like that. The game for those in power was to create as many independent institutions as possible and for those that were about to acquire power to have as many institutions as possible controlled by the political process. So it was a little seesaw but generally a very polite one.

The real power play would come very shortly with the elections. The provisions about the elections were quite important. Everyone was quite anxious about the elections. We worked very hard; we used to work eighteen hours a day. I clearly lost six months of my practice as senior counsel sitting there full-time working on the constitution. None of us had any illusions of grandeur. None of us thought that we would occupy any positions of importance afterwards. But we knew that the president came to us and asked us to do a particular job. So we would have his ear; at the best of times we would have his ear.

The constitution was done; there were big celebrations in the country. We started printing the constitution, disseminating it, having a major campaign to teach people about the new constitution. We started publicizing the new flag, and it appeared we were on our way to democracy. We finished the constitution in 1993 on around December 14 or 15. I packed my bags, took my family, and we went off to Kruger National Park and disappeared. I was tired. I was very exhausted, but I felt that I had done my duty to my countrymen and -women. I really went out with a deep sense of satisfaction.

Once in the Kruger National Park, I got a telephone call; it was a walkie-talkie sort of thing—a radio contact.

This guy comes to me and says, "I'm sorry, you have a telephone call."

I said, "You must be mad. Nobody knows I'm here. I told nobody except my brother Tiego where I would be."

I was tired and I had thought the bushveld was the best place to be. I said, "I won't take this call."

This ranger said, "I'm sorry, but a nice Mr. Mandela would like to talk to you."

And Mr. Mandela said to me, "Somebody must run the elections, lad."

I said to him, "But Mr. President" (we called him President even then), "Mr. President, I'm tired, I am really. You know how many times I have answered your calls."

When his wife was in trouble, I was there for six months of my practice. I set that aside to go and defend Winnie. When that was done, he asked me to go and do the constitution.

I said, "Do you know how hard I worked. I'm tired as a dog."

And he said, "Look, I'm your father's age. I think I'm going to announce in public tomorrow that I am tired. I'm going to resign. If young people like you can be so tired, I'm sure I must be twice as tired as you are. I respect what you are telling me, but it holds no water. I'm sorry. We've got to go and run the elections. You are not in politics. You are a well-liked lawyer, and you will have to go and run the elections."

I said, "But Mr. President, when is all this to happen?"

But I knew the dates. The date had been negotiated when I was there. It was 27 April. There were only four months left.

He said, "Ja, you know the IEC [Independent Electoral Commission] act. You're going to administer that act. Kriegler [Johann Kriegler, judge of the South Africa Supreme Court; now judge of the Constitutional Court] will be the chairman and you will be the deputy. We need representation there. De Klerk proposed Kriegler and I propose you. When the results are received, people will accept that you have done your damnedest."

And there I was. I moved away from the phone totally despondent.

I said to my wife, "I've just been honored to go and run the election."

My wife said, "Are you mad? Six months, we didn't bloody see you. You came home 3 A.M. every damn day and now you are going to run the elections? Did you agree?"

I said, "I agreed. I've just told him now. I've agreed. I'm sorry. And this means that we must cut our holiday short. He says to me that the first meeting of the IEC, of which you are now deputy chair, will be on 22 December."

This was around the 18 or 19th of December and I'm sitting in the Kruger National Park. I returned my keys, and we packed and went.

There we were uprooted out of our holiday in the bushveld and we packed and moved straight to Cape Town. At the Cape Town airport, I was rushed to the meeting place, and my kids and wife went out to go and find a place to stay.

At this meeting of the IEC, Gaye McDougall was there from the United States, a guy from Scandinavia; there was somebody from North

Africa, somebody from Canada, people from all over the world. Helen
Suzman was sitting there. There were five people from outside the country, and the rest was a panel of very good South Africans. It was a great
team of South Africans, and I had the privilege of being the No. 2 on this
team. We were told to set up machinery to run the elections. I was told in
no uncertain terms that, "You can't practice between now and the time
the elections are done. Sorry, Mr. Senior Counsel, forget about your cases.
This is your biggest case. If you argue this matter successfully, you will be
fine."

Just half a block from where our headquarters were in Jo'burg, bombs
went off. We sealed off the IEC office with the army. I went to Natal. I
was in charge of Natal ultimately. When I stayed in Natal, I was guarded
by paratroopers and sharpshooters as I went around my work. [Natal was,
and still is, the scene of bloody clashes between supporters of the ANC
and supporters of the Inkatha Freedom Party.] There was reason to believe
that the right-wingers wanted to polish off the leadership of the IEC and
in that way there would be no elections. I stayed more up in the air than
down. We used to fly most of the time with helicopters. It was quite a
thing. We met with Mr. Mandela and Mr. De Klerk, Kriegler and I, twice
a week. Twice a week we would meet to evaluate the situation and how
things were going and so on. It was the most enriching time of my life.
The last two months, I stayed away from home and we really went into
camp.

Then in April, I was seated with all the cameras right around the
world to announce the election results and to pronounce that Mr. Mandela would be the president. It was a rare privilege. I might just say that it
was a high point of my life. Here I was being a very key instrument of
burying apartheid. It tied in very well with what I had sworn to do as a
young person. It fell on me to help bury apartheid and I had that rare
privilege of being one of the guys who really ran elections in this country
and was right at the pinnacle of the process.

After the election I went on leave for about a month and a half.
That's how tired I was. When I emerged from that, I was appointed an
acting judge. I served as an acting judge for three months, from July to
October. I enjoyed that enormously. It was the height of irony. I sat as a

judge in the same court in which I was convicted—the Pretoria Supreme Court.

There I sat up on the pedestal high and mighty, and I was a Supreme Court judge. Wonderful! It vindicated something in me. If I was in any doubt about elections and the transformation, I was there. As an acting judge, I had at least three or four reported cases. I wrote some precedent-setting judgments.

Judge Cilliers, who had sentenced me in 1963, was still a judge of that court. He is still alive and well. He met me once when I was an acting judge. He said he remembered me.

Starting a New Career

∾ But I finally decided to leave the bench. Both the minister and the president wanted to shift me into the Constitutional Court, where I would have been for seven years. I withdrew my nomination on the last day. I know I might be lacking modesty, but it is reasonable to say that I would have made it to the Constitutional Court. I had more experience than the black candidates who were finally appointed. I had a personal restlessness. I just didn't think my contribution would end up there. In this country, the tradition is, once a judge always a judge. We have almost no examples of judges who leave the bench to do other things. One man left the bench to go into business. It was scoffed at; it was not a done thing. Also, I knew once I got in, I would probably be pushed up the fast track. I'd probably be pushed up very quickly, right up to the appellate division, or if I was on the Constitutional Court, I would be locked in there for seven years. I had not convinced myself—I was forty-six then—that I should be a judge at that particular point in time.

I spent three months with most of the gentlemen with whom I would serve as a judge. I found that it is a very cloistered life in this country. Most judges don't go out. In the old days judges would move around with security guards. So it was a very cloistered life, and I knew it would be the end of me. I knew I actually had to quit. Judges don't participate in public debate in this country. Judges don't sit down and write articles that express their mind. They keep it to themselves and shut up, except in their judgments and their opinions. And the tradition was not going to change. And I felt there were enough honest South Africans who could do the job well. There were a lot of people I trusted. There was a layer of people that I trusted who would do the job as honestly and well as I would have done it, with the same protection of rights as I would have done it. That doesn't go for the whole judiciary, but there are certain people in whom I had confidence.

But another reason was that I was just downright selfish. I just thought, I am not going to become a civil servant, not quite yet. I would try to make a little bit of money. I must be honest about that. I thought I could do more than what I had done. I worked long years and hours basically working to fight and change the regime.

The period ran for my appointment, and I was offered a permanent appointment. I refused and I went back to practice. The government started giving me quite a lot of work because I was a fairly experienced senior counsel, and so I started doing quite a lot of fascinating work. I acted for the provincial governments. I acted for the national government, for the minister of health, most of the ministries. When they looked around and they wanted to brief some senior counsel, I was selected. I got all of the juicy work.

Among his most famous clients as senior counsel, was, again, Winnie Mandela, this time in a dispute with her estranged husband, President Nelson Mandela.

∽ Winnie Mandela was fired as a cabinet minister by her husband, the president. I wrote up the full brief and appeared on her behalf to set aside the dismissal order. She was reinstated, albeit for forty-eight hours, and then she was fired again. This time the president had done everything prim and proper. In that case, I think his anger overfloweth. He had first fired her with a letter which was signed by him, but there was no seal of office on it. He had put no designation of his capacity when he signed the letter. He had not given her an opportunity to be able to deal with a whole range of matters which we had raised. The firing letter had at least eight or nine technical defects. It was not even on the official letterhead of the president, and he had therefore not spoken constitutionally. It could not have been a valid executive act. Before the court made a ruling, the president threw in the towel and Winnie was reinstated. I said to her, "You have got to resign, my dear, before your husband comes right back with everything done according to the textbook." She resigned a few hours before she was fired by the president. The president fired her anyway.

The Senior Counsel Becomes an Entrepreneur

∽ One day again, the president came and said, "We need somebody to fix Telkom [the national telephone company]." I had previously been approached by the minister of posts and telecommunications and I had refused. Then he got the president to call me and say, "We think Telkom is very vital and strategic. You must go there." I accepted that. I became the chairman of the board of Telkom. I thought I would do that side by side with my practice. I was wedded to my practice. It was agreed that I would be a nonexecutive chairman. I didn't have to be there all the time. I demanded a new set of board members. I had to find a new board which could do things together, unlike the old board. I had the right to choose the top executives from the company. In the end, it was agreed that I would have to spend at least 50 percent of all of my time at Telkom. It was a major job.

My practice started to suffer. Dr. Nthato Motlana, for whom I had acted as a lawyer, approached me and asked me to join his group. He said, "You are going to sink if you try and practice for half the time."

I learned very quickly that in fact it was not possible. For a year I had run Telkom and tried to go to court. I knew that I couldn't do both. The offer from Dr. Motlana was lucrative. It was exciting. I had new opportunities basically to use all of the little skills that I had developed over the years in making a major entry into business. Therefore, I joined New Africa Investments, Ltd., which is certainly the largest black business entity in this country. It is an infant in relation to other businesses. But majority shareholding is certainly in the hands of black people. We are going to expand.

Although firmly entrenched in the world of high finance, Dikgang

Moseneke is frequently mentioned in private both as a candidate for a high judicial post and for a high position in the executive branch of government.

Moseneke's description of both prison life and the practice of law in apartheid South Africa certainly paints a happier picture than that which might be provided by some others. Perhaps his ability to look at the bright side of horrendous circumstances can be attributed both to his personality and to the fact that he has ultimately become an enormously successful person by almost any standards.

But his descriptions are important in another respect. He describes the governing Afrikaner authorities as "positivists" who believed that the law was sacred, and who had a "prim and proper rule-of-law approach." He talks of exploiting their meticulousness about rules in order to win cases in their own courts. He calls their conviction "the soft belly of a very tough animal."

The problem was, of course, that the rules the white government was enforcing were oppressive. It was "positivism," or the rule of law, in the sense that rules established by the governing body, Parliament, were followed as literally as possible, sometimes even to the benefit of the oppressed people. However, it was not a rule of law in the sense of adherence to fundamental principles of human conduct.

Yet, even this adherence to a rule of law, as narrowly defined by the South African courts, has had a significant effect on the new South African government. Moseneke describes its importance in the drafting of the new constitution. Out of the lawyering that Moseneke and others experienced emerged "a very rich tradition of fairness, of judicial review, of rule of law, and . . . of integrity." Lawyers want to limit the power of the executive and enable the courts to restrain that power through the operation of the legal system. As Dikgang Moseneke says, "That is the upside of that whole era."

7

⚖

STRUGGLES—IMPRISONMENT, BANNING, AND EXILE

D IKGANG MOSENEKE certainly was not the only black lawyer to suffer greatly under the apartheid regime. Nelson Mandela spent twenty-seven years in prison, not to mention numerous prior detentions and arrests. Oliver Tambo spent a comparable time in exile. Godfrey Pitje was banned for twelve years.

The excerpts in this chapter relate the stories of other black lawyers who felt the sting of the South African authorities. Perhaps their descriptions also give some insight into the development of their character and background for the course of their futures as lawyers.

Fikile Bam

In chapter 2, Fikile Bam told of his background and early childhood in mission schools. In chapter 5, he described his time at the almost all-white University of Cape Town and the beginnings of his political involvement in student groups.

As he progressed as a student, Bam became increasingly involved as an activist. As he says, "student politics became a little bit too superficial for us." He and his fellow students began to identify more with what they saw as an armed struggle. They formed an underground organization called the National Liberation Front. The front was in the business of publishing information, including pamphlets originating in places like China, Cuba, and Algeria. The government caught up with the group in 1963 and Bam and his colleagues were arrested.

Eleven of them were tried in the Supreme Court in Cape Town under what was known as the Sabotage Act. There were seven men and four women; all were students or young teachers and all were black or Coloured. They were represented by white lawyers. Attempts to employ the only black advocate in practice in Cape Town at that time, Benny Kies, were unsuccessful. Kies declined to take the case for what Bam calls political reasons.

    ∽ The judge was van Heerden. The trial was pretty much what I subsequently got to know in our South African courts. It was very proper in terms of following procedures. Evidence was led; cross-examination was allowed. All of the prescribed steps were followed, so you couldn't fault the procedures. But quite clearly, at the end of the day, when it came to assessment of the evidence, there was a bias right from the outset that we were guilty. The police were seen to be speaking the truth and we were evading it. The trial took place at the same time as the Rivonia trial [at which Nelson Mandela and others were convicted]. It was a similar trial, except it was much smaller in terms of publicity, in terms of public perception. All of us were convicted. I was sentenced to ten years and sent to the Robben Island prison.

My years on Robben Island were very tough years, especially in the very beginning. The prison conditions had always been notorious for being very poor, very rough, and very brutal. We knew about this even before we ourselves went to prison. We came there in the winter of 1964, and it was very cold. The island was particularly cold that year, and we were dressed very scantily. We wore shorts and very thin canvas jackets and sandals.

You had to get up at half past five in the mornings to empty and wash your toilet bucket, be up in the yard at six o'clock, have your breakfast, and then be marched off to work at the quarry. We worked in hard labor most of the time, working in the quarry or digging stones. Some people crushed stones and others loaded them into wheelbarrows and packed them all along the beach front to reclaim land from the sea. Later on our group in the isolation section, led by Nelson Mandela, quarried lime—some people digging and others loading onto wheelbarrows and others pushing the wheelbarrows to deposit the lime onto a heap which would be fetched by trucks.

That's when I worked with the state president [Nelson Mandela]. We tended to work together, the two of us, because he was studying law and I was also a law student. And so what he read the previous night, he would want to come and relate it to me to hear commentary and also to test his memory. He was also studying for his LL.B., but for an English LL.B. from the University of Cambridge. I had been due to finish my LL.B. in Cape Town that year. It subsequently took me over ten years to finish because I wasn't allowed to register for a South African LL.B. During prison, I did some courses other than law courses. You could do commerce and languages, and I did that. But law, political science, and politics, all those sorts of subjects, were not allowed. You couldn't get permission to do them.

Apart from the work routine—that is, going to work and mining the quarry—initially we were not supposed to talk to each other at all. We weren't to communicate in any way, but it was obviously impractical to enforce that sort of rule. We just ignored it and defied it, and we started talking to each other. It became part and parcel of our existence, in fact, to be communicating with each other. It was a very instructive experience indeed just to get to know the group of about thirty in the isolation section, in which the state president and I were. Others who were there included Walter Sisulu, Govan Mbeki, later on Mac Maharaj, Ahmed Kathrada [all major figures in the leadership of the African National Congress as well as in the South African government that emerged after the end of apartheid].

Dikgang Moseneke was not with us. He was in the large section of the prison. We were in the isolation section. We were in single cells and kept apart in single cells. Moseneke was kept in the bigger section together with a group of younger people. He was very young. He was about sixteen and the rest of them who were about the same age group were kept together in a cell in a bigger section.

I was in the isolation section for the whole ten years. Most of the other people were there for much longer than that. The state president himself stayed in that section for much much longer.

The only permitted contact was with the prisoners in our own section, but we did communicate with the others. We found ways of communicating, but it was very difficult. Sometimes you could see them playing soccer through a window, a bathroom window, and sometimes you could even talk to some of them, but you had to make sure you were not caught when doing it. Notes did pass between us if there was a need for that, but it was all illegal and if you were caught you got into serious trouble. If the guys from the other side infringed one of the many prison rules and regulations and got punished, they were sent over to a part of the isolation section which served as punishment cells. While they were there, we were able to communicate with them after hours and find out what was happening on the other side. We saw them when we went out for exercise. It was limited to that.

When prisoners talked, we talked about everything. We talked about sex, women and children, politics, political trials, sports, news. We also talked about the particular study courses we were doing. If you were registered for an accounting course, you would probably talk accounting with whoever knew accounting, whoever was the expert around there. If you were doing history, you would go to another historian and share ideas with him, and so it went. The level of discussion and communication was very high indeed because we had the time.

We read a lot whenever we got hold of good books to read. Books were available in our section as early as 1965. We were lucky in a sense because before the prison sort of settled down to a routine, while we were being shifted around, the American Embassy in Cape Town just donated boxes and boxes of books to our section. The prison authorities didn't have time to censor these books and some of them were very good. Some were very political-orientated but others just very good literature.

There were lots of different things. There were just ordinary adventure stories—mostly about American life, of course. I remember one of the books I read and finished was *Gone with the Wind.* I had started to read it outside but never finished it because it went on and on. I think there were several copies of that book sent in by the Americans. But I also remember reading Tolstoy's *War and Peace,* and *Dr. Zhivago,* both of which I read to the end in prison. On the other hand, there were just ordinary storybooks, like *The Three Musketeers,* which were quite enjoyable when you have nothing else to read. I had read Kenneth Grahame's *Wind in the Willows* as a small boy, but I was able to reread it again and enjoyed it tremendously.

I didn't read any law books from the library itself. But Nelson used to get books that were donated to him by all sorts of lawyers from England, and I used to read his books eagerly. Then Alan Paton [author of *Cry, the Beloved Country* and other books describing and decrying apartheid South Africa] also managed to send me the *South African Law Journal* and *Tydskrif,* an Afrikaans journal, on a regular basis. He would also send me case reports, so I kept in touch with the law reading these reports. I also got the Annual Survey [of South African law], which was sent to me directly from publishers on a regular basis. So I was able to keep in touch. Unfortunately, Alan Paton died before I could go and see him and thank him for the service.

I talked about law all the time with Nelson, almost every day. He was actually allowed to continue his study. He had been given permission to study law through Cambridge University before such study was barred. He had gotten his permission to study in 1962, before the Rivonia trial, and they couldn't take it away from him after the privilege had already been given since this would have triggered legal action. He would talk mostly about English principles of law, but I think it worked out nicely for me. It gave me a broader appreciation of law. In turn, when there were interesting cases that I picked up from the law reports, I would convey those to him. He was for a while the only qualified lawyer in our section.

Much later, we were joined by a lawyer called Louis Mtshizana, who came from the Eastern Cape. Mac Maharaj had studied law up to a point. I don't think he had completed his studies, but he had a knowledge of law. He had taken legal courses in English universities. That was all, but if there was an interesting case, we would convey it to the whole group in our section because people were interested in what was going on outside. There were a number of cases, mostly political cases, going on outside that were reported.

As I couldn't study law at first, so I did commerce, I studied economics, and I studied accounting almost to the point where I could have gotten a degree in that. I studied languages: German, Afrikaans, and Dutch. At a certain stage, I was able to study law. Whenever a new officer started—they were always changing the officers around—you didn't let him know what was allowed and what was not allowed. If you quickly went and registered for jurisprudence or some other subject like that which didn't have the word *law* in it, you often got away with it. I did that quite successfully on a number of occasions. I did a bit of history too, just out of curiosity and enjoyment.

All of us did a lot of teaching of each other. For many years we ran a literacy and a numeracy course where we taught each other to read and write basic things. At every level people wanted to improve their standards, be it in English, be it in history. There was always someone there who had either taught the subject or had studied it. Neville Alexander, for instance, had a doctorate in German and a major in history. There would be people who wanted to do history and English at advanced levels. There was a full-blown school for that in our section. We kept ourselves very busy.

The other thing that kept us busy were games. We played chess, and much later we played card games. In the beginning there were no such privileges, but three or four years down the road conditions began to improve slightly. The Red Cross started to pay regular visits. Initially there were some very crude ways in which the authorities reacted to this. They would give us new clothes when the Red Cross visited or were about to come, and take them away after they left. But soon enough, if they gave you new clothes or new blankets because the Red Cross people were coming, you would be able to keep these.

It went on like that year after year. Sometimes you were able to study one year, and then you were not able to study because the privilege would be taken away. Sometimes the privilege would be taken away because they would say you were not cooperating. There was a very wide definition to the word *cooperation*. You never knew exactly what it was, except that if a new officer came and thought you were having too much of a good time and felt that the prison was being turned into a university, he would reverse the whole process and take away study privileges. He would say we should be treated more like prisoners, which was what we were there for.

But I was out in ten years, which was a relatively short time. Initially it seemed to be very long, but it actually went very quickly because of all this activity and good comradeship all around. There was never a dull moment, as it were. Initially we were subjected to a lot of assaults. I think the assaults on me personally were relatively slight. But I am still deaf in one ear because someone hit me with an open hand from the back and burst my eardrum. Also, because I was big, a lot of the warders just felt like having a go at me from time to time on the physical level. So I was beaten up on a couple of occasions, but not in a serious way. I never was knocked out or unconscious or anything like that. In fact, on quite a few occasions I had the better of warders, and the strange thing was that they never reported me for it. There was some psychological thing about a white warder going to the officers and saying that this prisoner had beaten him in a physical encounter So they shut up and I got away with that. But in a number of other cases when a tough prisoner repulsed a warder attack in public, it wasn't so easy. I know a lot of people who were literally attacked by a whole host of warders with batons and so on and beaten until they were unconscious. When for instance one of our own group, the burly Don Davis, got the better of a warder who had assaulted him, he was mobbed by at least fifteen warders with batons and boots while others pointed automatic rifles at the rest of us. He was heavily bruised and scarred and lost all of his teeth. He was handcuffed and manacled and summarily removed to isolation and a spare diet for several months. I have a friend, Andrew Masondo, who is now a general in the army, who was put in a hole in the ground and literally buried alive. He was covered with sand up to his neck and a warder urinated on him. The same happened to Johnson Mlambo, both at the hands of the brutal Kleynhans brothers, who were warders.

So a lot of terrible things happened in the early sixties, but that tended to become somewhat less as the years went on because we were fighting back. We were fighting back by making sure that the outside world got to know on a regular basis what was happening inside prison. As a result, certain of the more brutal warders were transferred to other areas. But the prison environment was never completely violence free. From time to time, dogs would be set on prisoners just to make them move faster. For all the time that I was there, searches and so on would always turn out to be violent in the end.

Towards the end of my stay there were certain improvements: improvements in diet, improvements in the clothing. I remember I got my first underpants and my first vest in my very last year. I was only able to wear them for about a week or two before I was released—and also my first pair of legally obtained shoes. I had usually worn sandals before that. One particular warder who liked me always made sure that I got a pair of shoes whenever my size could be found. But these would be taken away whenever the warder was not there. I would have to wait until he came back again.

Anyhow, I was out in May 1974, and the strange thing is that I actually felt very insecure leaving the island. I was looking forward to my release in a sense but with a lot of apprehension as to what it was going to mean. I remember feeling very emotional and hurt as the boat was receding from the island. I didn't know where I was going to from there. I was leaving what had become a home in a funny sort of way to me. The situation was one I could deal with, where I had picked up a lot of friends, and I was going into the unknown.

The unknown turned out to be a prison called Leeukop, near Johannesburg. Incidentally, I followed Dikgang Moseneke by a few weeks. When I got to Leeukop, I then heard stories of him having been there and fighting all the time against the brutality still being meted out to prisoners. I went to Leeukop to be released. Nobody was released, generally speaking, from Robben Island straight to their home or wherever they were going. You were released from the island to another prison. Leeukop (which means the head of a lion) was a very notorious prison. A lot of the Transvaal people were sent there before being released. You were sent there either because they wanted to make you forget messages which you might have been given on the Island, or, as some warders said, it was so that you should have a lasting memory of what prison really is. Leeukop hadn't changed very much in terms of treatment and conditions from what had been ten years back. We had been able to bring about improvements on the island. When we got to Leeukop, we found that we had literally to fight from the beginning to try and change conditions there.

From Leeukop, I should by rights have been released in Johannesburg, which is where my pass indicated that I should be. I had a permit to be in the Johannesburg area; I had a Johannesburg stamp. But in the meantime, my mother had retired to the Transkei. For that reason, the security police decided not to release me in Johannesburg, but to release me in Umtata, in the Transkei. I was at Leeukop for about two weeks and then spent another week traveling to Natal, and was then driven to Umtata. It took about a month after I had been on the Island for me to be home with my family. I was out the day before Easter in 1974.

I lived with my mother close to Umtata, in Tsolo. I was under house arrest and a banning order. All our group were subject to the same orders. But I was sent to the Transkei, and the Transkei was on the point of becoming independent. It was already being treated as if it were independent. So when I was taken to the Transkei I was subject to the Mantanzimas [the black leadership of the Transkei, beholden to the government of South Africa] more than to the South African government. That meant that my house arrest order was not effective in the Transkei itself because it had not been served on me by the Transkeian authorities. They merely said to me that I should know that they had their eyes and ears all over the Transkei, and if I still intended to be up to my old tricks again and instigated trouble, I would be inside again within no time. These were not empty threats and I was in fact detained by the Transkeian government on three separate occasions, each lasting for three months, between 1975 and 1979.

Fikile Bam, before being named to the Land Claims Court, practiced as an attorney and later an advocate in Umtata, the capital of the Transkei, a black homeland, as well as in Cape Town, Johannesburg, and Port Elizabeth.

Justice Moloto

In chapter 5, Justice Moloto described his politically active time at the University of Fort Hare as well as his two expulsions from that institution.

After his final expulsion, in 1968, Moloto continued his studies though the University of South Africa (UNISA). He also served two years as president of the University Christian Movement (UCM), a multiracial group formed by students and lecturers at white and black universities. The group's Christian identity protected it to some extent from the strictest government scrutiny. This limited immunity was enough to permit Steve Biko to form his South African Students Organization (SASO) in a symbiotic relationship with the UCM. White UCM members were permitted to solicit funds from abroad and they managed to raise money not only for the UCM, but for SASO as well. Moloto and Biko worked closely together to make sure that these funds in fact reached SASO.

∽ SASO had been founded on a black-consciousness philosophy. It presented an anomaly to outsiders that it was prepared to be in bed with UCM, which was multiracial. But UCM looked at the broad struggle of the black man in the country, beyond just student politics. Apart from this was the fact that SASO's livelihood really depended on UCM getting funding and then passing on the money. Of course, none of this relationship was public knowledge at the time.

The black-consciousness philosophy that we followed within SASO was based on a need for black people to take charge of their own lives in all spheres of life. A realization had come about that, for so long, we had belonged to multiracial organizations where the leadership was vested in white people. Even with the best of intentions, the white people very rarely knew exactly what the concerns of the black people were. Even when they came up with honest solutions to problems, they quite often did not address the problems of the black people the way the black people would have seen the problems addressed. So the philosophy was one of self-reliance, self-determination. Black man, you are on your own to liberate yourself. You've got to chart the struggle and see how you are going to go about it. You are going to prosecute that struggle in a way that you, as a black person, see the need arising. Hence, the philosophy was given all sorts of labels: black consciousness, whatever that meant, black power, and what have you, but all of which really meant that, without being anti-white, you were pro-black. You have to prosecute the black man's struggle and bring him out of the doldrums.

The first point that we felt was of the utmost importance was the whole question of psychological domination by Western culture, Western values. We felt that a black man must be psychologically liberated from his own hang-ups of inferiority. He must assert himself as an equal partner with all other races in the world. Once we had achieved that, we would then be in a position to mingle and to act freely, just like anybody else would, like a normal citizen in society. This was Steve Biko's philosophy; this was what he was preaching.

Steve Biko's death had a very serious impact on me as a friend and on me as a political ally.[1] Actually, Steve and I had been married to cousins. But quite apart from that, which was just purely by chance, we were very strong political allies and very good friends. His death came not only as a personal loss but also as a loss to the black cause in the country. It was after his death that, in fact, black consciousness as we had conceived of it at the time began to change.

Under Biko's philosophy, I didn't think we were necessarily saying that by being pro-black we were anti-white. We were just saying, White men, leave us alone. Let us do our job in the best way we think we can do it. We were not saying, We are anti-you. We were saying that, if you do want to give support to our program, the best way you can do it is to go to your fellow white men and make them understand why we have to behave the way we do. If you can do that, you will have done us a great favor. Don't come and try and meddle with us.

In later years, the philosophy moved from that position to a position that said if you were white, you were necessarily anti-me, and that is why I am also anti-you. This caused a little bit of tension in the races. I am not saying there were no tensions in our time. There were tensions, but they were things that we could sit around a table and talk about. It became increasingly difficult for various racial groups to talk about the tensions as they grew in later years. I am not saying that the black groups were entirely to blame for this radical position. The white groups themselves were progressively interpreting any black formation as a necessary anti-white statement and therefore assisting also in the exacerbation of the tension.

In 1971 I became the secretary general of the University Christian Movement, which was a full-time job. I was no longer the president but had a paid job as secretary general. The UCM had given me a bit of a salary because I was not at university full-time. I was spending most of my time as president in the office. It was really more of an honorarium than anything. But then when I became secretary general, I got a proper salary.

The activities of the UCM went from involvement in student politics to even more radical activities, such as literacy campaigns. In 1971, in the middle of a literacy campaign, the organization apparently finally crossed the line drawn by the government. Based on his involvement with the UCM, Moloto was banned and banished for three years to a small town, Mafikeng, in the then newly formed black homeland of Bophuthatswana.

∽ My banning order said that I could not be in the company of more than one person at any given time; I could not go into any place of learning, be it a school or a university or a college; I could not go into the premises of a factory; I could not address people at any gathering; I could not leave a particular magisterial district without permission.

They took me from Johannesburg and drove me to Mafikeng and dumped me there: Here's a little house. Stay there and we will find you work here.

They didn't actually find me work but just said that I must go to the Bophuthatswana government, which was still in its embryonic stage. I was offered a job at R50 a month, which was peanuts. I had to stay there for the ensuing three years. That was September 1971 to September 1974. I kept up my studies while I was in Mafikeng and by the end of 1974, I finished my exams.

I got married in 1972 while in Mafikeng under the banning order. My wife was then in Durban finishing her medical studies. By 1974 she had finished and was doing her internship. Although she had been in Tembisa [a town nearer Mafikeng than Durban] for the first half of the year in an attempt to be nearer to me, she had to go back to Durban for the second half because she was changing departments. She just couldn't get a hospital near enough to Mafikeng where she could do her internship for what she needed to do in the second half of the year. So when my banning order expired, she was in Durban. As soon as I finished my exams, I relocated to Durban, and I did my articles there.

Moloto practiced as an attorney in Durban and then served six years as director of the Black Lawyers Association–Legal Education Centre. He is now a judge of the Land Claims Court.

Matilda Masipa

Matilda Masipa was born in 1947 in Soweto. She graduated from the University of Zululand with a degree in social work. After some work in that field, she became a journalist with a black newspaper called the *World,* the predecessor of the *Sowetan* (now the principal black newspaper in the country).

∽ When the *World* was banned, members of the staff, including me, were arrested. They first detained our editor with a few other people and then banned the paper. Then we decided we were going to do a protest march, to go on a protest march through the center of Johannesburg— placards and everything. When you are younger it is very easy to do things like that. It was 1977 and we were shouting all sorts of things: Down with the government, Fascist regime, that kind of thing [laughs]. Obviously, those were the days where when you did that kind of thing, you knew exactly what would happen to you. They came for us in vans, they dragged us off, they thrashed us, and they put us into the van and off to John Vorster Square [the notorious headquarters of the South African police].

We were beaten. They pushed you and shoved you and didn't care whether you fell, that kind of thing. We were supposed to get out the same night, but what really happened I don't know. They usually have a way of saying: No, you can't get your bail tonight; try tomorrow morning. That kind of thing. I think they wanted us to taste what it was like inside.

The most frightening thing about being arrested was the fact that, for the first time, you realized that it was true that the police could do anything and get away with it. I think the reason why they didn't really kill us or do something like that was because we were journalists, and as journalists we attracted a lot of publicity, not only here in South Africa but in the whole world. It was after the Biko thing, and I remember one policeman saying, "Do you know Biko?" All I said was, "Well, I knew him but not personally," and he said, "Ja, vandag jy sal Biko sien" which [in Afrikaans] means, "Today you will see Biko." I mean he was dead then. It could only mean one thing [laughs]. Another policeman asked whether we had parachutes, because we were going to fly! If you didn't have a parachute, hard luck! [laughs] [There were numerous reports of deaths of people "falling" from the tenth floor of John Vorster Square.]

But anyway, the following day we went to court and we elected a leader, Zwelakhe Sisulu [the son of the then imprisoned ANC leader, Walter Sisulu].[2] He worked for the same paper. We refused to plead, and in those days that was something unheard of. You either pleaded guilty or not guilty. We told our lawyer that we were not going to plead because we did not recognize this court. It didn't help us much, except to make headlines in the newspapers. They fined us . . . I don't remember how many rands. We had violated, if I remember correctly, the Riotous Assemblies Act. There was a law like that. There were many such laws, all of them related.

Matilda Masipa worked for another black newspaper after the *World* was banned. The police continued to scrutinize her activities and, with considerable encouragement from her family, she embarked on study for another career, the law. Although suffering from periodic bouts with severe arthritis, she is now an advocate in Johannesburg and has been mentioned for appointment as a judge.

Yvonne Mokgoro

In chapter 4 Yvonne Mokgoro told about her early education at a Roman Catholic school after the onset of Bantu education. After a short period of study at the University of the North and an expulsion, she married and continued her studies through the University of South Africa (UNISA).

∞ My decision to go into law rather than teaching stemmed from an incident in 1974 or '75. I was working as a salesperson, living at home and studying through UNISA. I remember one day a friend had visited me when I came back from work. I walked her halfway home and I had my baby on my back.

During that time, every Friday evening, the police would patrol the townships, and they had what they called a sweep-up of undesirable elements. It was about sunset and we were just walking slowly. A police pickup van came at high speed in our direction. A young man was standing at the corner of the street, minding his own business. The van stopped abruptly right in front of this young man, who none of us knew. They simply picked him up and threw him into the back of the van. Just spontaneously. They didn't even think about it. I screamed at this policeman and told him that he had no right to do that.

"That man didn't do anything," I shouted.

The next thing I knew I was in the van, with this man. My friend later told me that when the policeman heard me, he came rushing at me, tore my baby off my back, picked me up and literally threw me into the van. I didn't even know what was happening. My friend took my baby, turned back home, and told my husband what happened.

It was sunset, about six o'clock on a summer evening. The police drove round and round the township until about 10 P.M., continuously packing people into their police van. I was the only woman in that van. All of us were squashed together. They had a cage between the driver's partition and the back part of the van where they kept a police dog. As they pushed people in and congested them into the van, the dog would growl and bark!

We were the first ones to get into the van, so we were squashed against the dog's cage. It went on for about four hours, driving round and round the township. That's what they usually did. When we reached the police station, they literally threw us out and then went back, picked up more people, came to the police station, and threw them out.

When we were at the police station, they started beating up these young men. That too was what they normally did. As they started beating them up, they ordered me to stand aside and I had to stand there and watch. These young men had not done anything. Nothing. Police just picked up people. They saw them as undesirable elements. They would drive past a beer hall and if they saw drunk people, they would just throw them into police vans. That's how the police conducted themselves generally. So they beat up these young men and they would beat them up thoroughly, kicked and punched. This was in Galeshewe township, in Kimberley—my hometown.

The police officers were both black and white. You have to understand the psychology and sociology of the police force if you want to
understand how blacks could do this to their own people. And so I was
made to stand there and watch how these guys were being beaten up.
That was probably my punishment. After that experience, they locked
me up.

That was on a Friday night. The following day was a Saturday and
therefore not a court day. When my husband came and asked if I could be
released on bail, which was perfectly permissible for minor offenses, they
simply refused. "We can't do it; she just has to spend the weekend in jail."
I understood that as sheer spitefulness. So I spent the whole weekend
in jail.

On Monday, I was charged with obstructing the ends of justice. My
husband had secured the legal assistance of Mr. Robert Sobukwe, then the
leader of the Pan Africanist Congress. Mr. Sobukwe had been banned and
confined to Kimberley. He had just been released from Robben Island.

So I appeared in court and he represented me. Naturally they withdrew the charge. We understood the thinking behind the whole saga perfectly well! But then I just thought to myself how lucky I was to have
somebody who was sufficiently informed to secure legal assistance for me.
I had legal representation. Other people were not lucky enough to find
themselves in that situation. I was lucky enough to actually get a lawyer.
Mr. Robert Sobukwe was one of only two black lawyers in Kimberley at
the time. The way he carried on his practice almost sounded like a social
welfare office. The man would just take cases and never charge people. He
took cases because, he used to say, he felt he had to do it. When we used
to scold him about it, he would simply say, "What else can I do? What do
you do when you find people in this situation? You don't even think about
money." And he had to maintain his office at the same time. He did that
with me too. My husband went to him, and I think he paid a deposit to
have the case taken and that was it. When we came back to pay him the
unnamed balance, he said no. I don't remember ever paying that man
finally. I think we paid about R3 to have the case taken [at today's
exchange rates, about fifty U.S. cents].

As we walked from the courtroom, I remarked to him—I guess I was thinking aloud—and I said to him, "You know what? I just wonder why you should be one of only two black lawyers in this town. The demand is so much. Can you imagine how many people probably go through this kind of experience without legal assistance? Can you imagine how many loads and loads of people were picked up on Friday? They are probably all in jail now. Some of them don't even get an opportunity to have a court appearance. I was probably made to appear in court because you were there. Where are all those people who I was picked up with on Friday? They are probably all sitting in jail. They will probably never get the kind of assistance I got."

Then I asked him, "I wonder why we don't have more men in Kimberley who study law. We need them so that they can start providing this kind of service to our people."

And then he looked at me and said in his soft-toned voice, "Yvonne, I should never ever hear you talk like that again. Who says women can't study law? You can do that too." Then we didn't have any woman lawyer in Kimberley. In fact I didn't know any woman lawyer at the time.

He then said, "Let's start with you! You can do that. I know that legal practice is a male domain and we sometimes see it as a male preserve, but women can do it too. Let's start with you."

When I went back to university the following year, instead of registering for a B.A. degree program, I registered for law. I've never looked back since. I've never regretted it.

Yvonne Mokgoro did become an attorney and then a law teacher at the University of Bophuthatswana, the University of the Western Cape, and the University of Pretoria. She is now a judge of the Constitutional Court.

Christine Qunta

Christine Qunta was born in 1952.

⇛ In 1973 I was a student activist at the University of the Western Cape. I became involved in SASO, the South African Students Organization, and the BPC, the Black People's Convention, which then were really the only organizations which were active in politics. Then students were seen

as subversive, and the university was closed for a time. Because of our dis-
agreement with the type of inferior education we were getting, we decided
to leave our campuses: UWC, Fort Hare, all the black campuses. Those
campuses were in upheaval.

I was the secretary of the BPC in Cape Town, and SASO for the
Western Cape region. Because of that, I was detained for a short while. It
is nothing to talk about, nothing to write home about. That was in the
beginning of 1975. I was detained for about a week. I wasn't beaten up. I
wasn't tortured. I was kept in solitary confinement, which I think is quite
awful, but it was nothing compared to what other people have gone
through. I was more concerned about my brothers coping without me
because my mother was not with them. She was in Johannesburg and we
were in Cape Town.

When I was released, we made decisions about whether we could be
effective operating above ground as we were all exposed and targeted. We
were considering an underground political organization. Steve [Biko] was
detained only much later, in 1977, but a lot of the important people in
the movement were banned and were in detention. Finally, as a group, we
decided to leave the country and go and get military training and come
back with guns ablaze, that sort of thing.

We left in 1975, but we didn't get any military training. I ended up
staying in Botswana for two years as an exile, and then I went to Australia
in 1977. When we got to Botswana, we tried to establish a new movement, different from the ANC and PAC. We felt that those were the older
movements, and we wanted something new. We wanted a continuation of
the black-consciousness movement. But that did not work out. Things
just didn't work out for military training. The people who were planning
it couldn't get their act together. People became demoralized. But I feel
you must always make something better of a situation.

We were very angry when we went into exile in 1975. That was
before 1976 [the Soweto uprising], and when 1976 happened, it made us
even more angry. But by then there was no prospect of going for military
training. The 1976 crowd just went to the different movements, they
went into the ANC or PAC, but my friends and I didn't want to do that.

So we felt that rather than just sit there and waste our time, we might
as well study. I got offered a scholarship in England and in Australia. Of

course, I would never live in England because of the weather. It was just too cold! I could just see myself being wrapped up in coats every day, and so I chose Australia. Under my scholarship, we were required to do solidarity work, antiapartheid work. It was given by the Australian Council of Churches.

Christine Qunta finished her law degree at the University of New South Wales in Australia. She practiced law in Australia, Botswana, and Zimbabwe before returning to South Africa after the end of apartheid. Qunta now heads a fledgling law firm in Cape Town, specializing in corporate work (see chap. 11).

Lewis Skweyiya

Lewis Skweyiya described his early boarding school education in chapter 2. By 1981, when the events he relates in the following excerpt occurred, he was a successful advocate in Durban. His practice also took him to the black homeland of the Transkei and its capital, Umtata.

After a political trial in the Transkei, where my clients were acquitted, I was followed by two security policemen as I was going to the robing room to change. I met Fikile Bam near the entrance and I said to him, "I suspect these chaps are up to something, I just have that feeling."

Fikile said to me, "That can't be so."

Indeed, I went to the robing room, and they followed me into the room and they said to me, "We are sorry, Sir. We have a warrant of detention for you."

I said, "No, you can't be serious."

They said, "Yes, we do have a warrant. You are being detained in terms of the Security Laws."

I said, "I have never been involved in Transkeian politics. I am not interested in getting involved in your homeland politics, and I can't see how there can be any reason to believe that I was engaged in anything."

I had been traveling with Justice Poswa, who was involved in some other case, and we had gone in my car to the Transkei. I said, "Let me then advise Poswa that I am being detained."

I sort of peeked into court and said to him, "Look, I am being detained." He couldn't believe it. There was confusion.

I said to these men, "Allow me to get in touch with the chief of Security Police because I am sure there must be a mistake." We went to the registrar of the court's offices for me to phone. When I phoned, I was told that the man who was responsible, who was instrumental in my detention, had gone to Port Elizabeth for the weekend, and nobody knew how to get in touch with him. It was a Friday afternoon.

I was then taken into a combi [minibus] with my clients. My clients had come from Queenstown, which is not far from the Transkei, and after being acquitted, the order of the magistrate was that they had to be taken from there right up to the South African border and left there. Even when my [instructing] attorney said, "I'll take them. Don't worry," the police insisted they would do it.

So when I was detained, I was taken and placed in the same combi with the clients who I had been defending and taken to the Security Police offices. My clients were now feeling sorry for me. "Oh, we're sorry, we're so sorry." That I also can't forget.

I was in detention for eleven or twelve days. I was released because there was pressure from the bar council and complaints. Ultimately, I was released because of pressure from people in Durban. I was quite convinced that it was a malicious detention. In those days, nobody believed that you could sue and succeed if you were detained in terms of the Security Laws because the act gave the police absolute power to detain you. All they had to say was, We believe something. I was quite adamant that I wouldn't let it just end there. I felt I could sue. So I kept on harassing Griffiths Mxenge,[3] who acted as my attorney, to bring suit. Ultimately we sent a letter of demand and issued summons. Andrew Wilson, who is now a judge, was my advocate in that case. He drafted the summons. And the government of the Transkei paid a settlement to me.

That was my only detention, but I was hounded virtually all of the time with threatening calls. I don't know if they were from the Security Police, but it must have been from those sources. They would say, "What has happened to so-and-so will happen to you. What happened to Mxenge is going to happen to you." So I just used to ignore them. Sometimes I was aggressive in my response when I got such a phone call and would not show that I was scared. I said, "You try it. You are a coward. You won't do it. You try it. We'll see who is able to shoot first"—that sort of thing.

The only other harassment was the question of my passport. I was getting lots of work from the Transkei. Because the Transkei was supposed to be an independent country, at one stage I was not allowed to go there to do cases. I appealed to the bar council in Durban and said, "Look here, I can't go and do my work." The council then arranged with the minister of police that I would be allowed to go there on a case. I had to say in advance what that case was, what date, and at which court. Each time, I would then be given an emergency travel document to go for that specific case.

As is illustrated by these excerpts, no one who opposed the government was immune from its retaliation—not journalists, not successful advocates. However, not everyone was imprisoned for long periods. The threat, the knowledge of the power of the state was thought to be enough.

Also, as in the case of Lewis Skweyiya, the power of the state extended beyond the borders of South Africa itself, certainly into the nominally independent black homelands. Sometimes the homeland authorities were even more zealous than the South African government itself in rooting out dissenters. Julius Chambers, former director of the NAACP Legal Defense Fund and now chancellor of North Carolina Central University, tells of his own detention by the Ciskei police in 1985. His fellow detainees included his wife, Vivian, and Judge Thelton E. Henderson of the United States District Court for the Northern District of California. All are African Americans. They were told that they were suspected of seeking to subvert the government of the Ciskei. Fortunately, in the case of these American lawyers, the detention lasted only a few hours.

Perhaps what is most remarkable about the excerpts in this chapter is not simply that these dedicated, often brilliant, people of integrity were mistreated by the apartheid government. Such mistreatment was commonplace and is historically unsurprising. Rather, what may be most significant is that after their liberty was more or less restored, these individuals were able to function effectively in the same country that had imprisoned or banned them. In most instances, they carried on with their lives without bitterness and without rancor.

For most, their return to a relatively normal life occurred prior to the change of government in 1994. The same government that had sent these individuals to jail, into exile, or placed them under house arrest ultimately acceded to the orders of courts, which refused to bar them from the practice of law. Some, like Pitje, Moseneke, and Fikile Bam, practiced law for nearly twenty years after their release, or the end of their ban and before the election of Nelson Mandela as president of South Africa. The fact they were able to do so is a testament both to the character of these individuals and the paradoxical society in which they lived.

8

⚖

STARTING INTO PRACTICE

AN ASPIRING South African lawyer has to decide whether to become an advocate or an attorney. In common usage, advocates constitute the bar, attorneys the side-bar. The paths are very different. Advocates, often called counsel, are the courtroom lawyers—traditionally the only lawyers permitted to practice in the Supreme Court,[1] which had jurisdiction over both the trial and appeal of more significant civil and criminal matters. Theoretically, an advocate does not deal directly with clients, but rather is briefed by an attorney. Attorneys do office work and appear in the magistrate courts—the lower courts. Attorneys serve a two-year apprenticeship, called articles; advocates do a four-month pupillage with a more senior advocate. Different examinations are given for each branch of the profession.

Until recently, almost all black lawyers in South Africa elected, at least initially, to become attorneys rather than advocates. Although the number of black advocates has increased dramatically over the past several years, the overwhelming majority of blacks still opt for the side-bar. There are several explanations for the career choice. Many blacks achieved only an undergraduate law degree, usually a B.Proc. An LL.B., a graduate degree, is required for the bar. In addition, because of the small number of black lawyers generally, black advocates have to depend, to a large extent, on white attorneys to brief them in cases. Attorneys can deal directly with clients. Furthermore, most black people who can pay for a lawyer have small matters requiring office work only or, at most, litigation in the magistrate courts.

Starting Out as an Attorney

Starting into practice, even as an attorney, has been far from an easy process for the typical black law graduate. Because there were few black attorneys, there were few people with whom aspiring blacks could become articled. The stories of Justice Moloto and Norman Abraham illustrate the struggle of most blacks.

Justice Moloto

In chapter 5, Justice Moloto described his turbulent university days. In chapter 7, he told of his political activism as a close associate of Steve Biko, and of his three-year banning and exile to Bophuthatswana. At the end of his banning order, he joined his wife, who was a physician in Durban. Here he describes his attempts to enter the attorney's profession.

    ✑ I looked for a principal to take me on for articles. I hadn't finished studies but was reading privately through UNISA. I could do my articles while I was still reading for my degree.

    I had applied to at least one firm of white lawyers, but I couldn't get my articles there. I didn't apply to others because I didn't anticipate they would help. When I first got to Durban in 1975, I went to Reggie Ngcobo, who had promised to take me on. But he was one of those guys who never knew what was happening in his firm. There was a limitation as to the number of clerks an attorney could take at any one given time. The maximum is three and he had said to me that he was prepared to take me, when in fact he already had a full complement of three. I worked for Ngcobo for a while and then, because of the limitation, went to another firm, another black guy.

    This black guy was in a position to article me, but when I tried to register my articles with the Law Society, the Law Society said they were not prepared to accept articles under him because they said he was not a fit and proper person to train lawyers. The Law Society had brought several disciplinary hearings against him.

The net result was that I wasted a whole year in these two situations. While I was with the second lawyer, I started looking elsewhere and even approached a white law firm. They wouldn't give me articles. I then went back to Ngcobo and said to him that I would come back to work for him and wait for one of the clerks to qualify. The first of the three was going to qualify in February of the following year. So the following year, 1976, I joined him again. The first of his clerks qualified on 28 February, and on 1 March I registered my articles. On 27 March, that same month, Reggie Ngcobo, my principal, died. There I was, back on the street.

Moloto finally found articles with a black lawyer named Frank Sithole.

ᴄᴐ During my articles, I did different kinds of work. I did a bit of conveyancing. I did civil and criminal litigation. I couldn't go to court because I was studying at the same time, and so I didn't have any right of appearance. But I could take down statements. I could do everything on the file up until the time when it was to go to court. The first time I ever went into court I was a qualified attorney. I found that unfortunate because I felt I could have learned a lot of things while I was doing articles, in terms of court procedure, but that's the way it went and I had to accept it.

I was paid R150 a month [about $25] as an articled clerk. I would imagine that clerks today would be paid R500 a month or more depending on which firm you are in. If you are in a poorer firm, I think it would be somewhere around R500. I think the richer firms would be able to pay R1,500 or something like that.

Moloto finished his articles with Sithole in 1978. He then set up a firm on his own. He practiced alone until April 1986, when he teamed up with four other black attorneys in a partnership. He practiced there until 1987, when he became director of the Black Lawyers Association–Legal Education Centre.

Norman Abraham

Norman Abraham was born in 1949 to Indian parents. He attended the university created for his racial group, the University of Durban-Westville. As an Indian, some doors in Durban were open to him that were not open to Justice Moloto, a black African. But many doors were also shut. His experience as an articled clerk in Durban was typical of young Indian attorneys.

∞ After I finished at the university I began my articles with a firm called G. S. Maharaj and Company in 1972. It was an Indian firm and had just one lawyer. At the time, it was very difficult to get articles with a firm that was so-called white. White firms would only give articles to so-called white people. I spent some months looking for articles in Natal and I got articles after someone had left this firm.

Maharaj did commercial work and criminal work to a large extent and, of course, motor vehicle insurance claims. This was a typical Indian firm and I think this still applies today. My practice, when I started off, was also on these lines. There is quite a noticeable body of Indian traders everywhere, even in small towns, and your civil work firstly revolved around debt collections because it was a steady source of income. Debt collection was and still is an industry in South Africa. You recovered your expenses fairly quickly with that work.

There is always criminal work for attorneys who were other than white. Maharaj did a lot of that. He did what we call MVA [Motor Vehicle Assurance] claims or third-party claims. There was litigation as well, much of this arising out of debt collections, or there were the delictual [tort] claims, damages concerning mainly auto vehicles. I think his practice probably would have been 10 percent Coloured, 60 percent Indian, and 30 percent African indigenous people. He probably could have had one or two white clients.

After I finished my articles, I immediately started practicing on my own. I had built up sufficient clientele to make it economically viable to do so. I know that was a difference between us and whites. A newly qualified white attorney would never make it on his own unless he came from some prominent family who would generate a lot of work for him. A non-white lawyer might make it on his own. I think the average Indian client is not necessarily faithful to a firm of attorneys. They are faithful to an individual, while whites worked to a large extent around corporate work and commercial concerns, and such concerns were faithful to a firm more than anything else.

We got the scraps. We did not get work from banks. We did not get work from the huge corporations, like insurance companies or listed companies. So the type of work we got was rather limited. Of course, we didn't get very much criminal work from whites.

Abraham practiced as an attorney in Durban for many years. He is now a staff attorney with the Legal Resources Centre, the public-interest law firm in Johannesburg.

Movement to the Bar

As the apartheid era began to wane and black attorneys gained better access to the courts and to clients, some black lawyers who started as attorneys became advocates. Fikile Bam, whose struggles in and out of prison are described in chapter 7, floated several times between practice as an attorney and as an advocate. Such movement is unusual, but explainable in part by Bam's need to set up residence in different places to avoid government restrictions and in part by some unusual job opportunities. Others who started as attorneys, like Dikgang Moseneke (chap. 6), moved to the bar to fulfill their ambition to be in the courtroom at the highest levels. The stories of Lewis Skweyiya and Justice Poswa are also illustrative of the movement to the bar.

Lewis Skweyiya

In chapter 2, Lewis Skweyiya described his early education. He told of his detention by the Transkei authorities in chapter 7.

∞ I served my articles in an attorney's office in Durban with a man called Nyembezi. He was a very busy practitioner, and one of the few black attorneys at that time. The bulk of the work was criminal work although there were some third-party cases, insurance cases, that sort of thing. There would be seven or eight cases on an average a day. I would do lots of criminal work. He used to like taking cases which would take him to the outlying areas and leave me to do the cases in Durban.

I just could not stand the injustice which I saw in the lower courts. In the first place, I was fairly young when I completed my LL.B., and there were hardly any young blacks in the profession. The magistrates would not believe that I was qualified to appear. When you had an LL.B. you had automatic right of appearance in court. You could handle cases in lower courts. On a few occasions when I went to some courts, they would tell me that I could not appear unless I could prove that I was qualified. As a result, the Law Society introduced a system where you were given a letter, which had their stamp, to say that you were in fact qualified. It was an age thing more than a race thing, but it was a combination of both: because you were black and you were this age, they thought you could not be qualified as a lawyer.

Skweyiya also tells of the same phenomenon described by Godfrey Pitje in chapter 1—the prosecutor's requirement that black lawyers remain in the courtroom to await cases being called. White lawyers were permitted to leave the courtroom and return at a set time. Often the black lawyer's case would not be called at all and the lawyer would have to come back another day. In a profession where time is money, the practice was costly indeed for the black lawyers.

      ✍ I also became concerned about the manner in which the unrepresented accused were treated by the magistrates and the prosecutor and the obvious collusion that was going on. That I could not stand. I decided that that was not for me. Based upon my experience in my articles, I didn't see myself practicing in the lower courts. So I came to the bar.

I also wanted to become an academic, so I applied to the University of Natal to do a master's degree in law. In those days, if you wanted to move from being an attorney to go to the bar, you had to have a quarantine period. You could not have anything to do with an attorney's office for a period of six months. So I then started at the University of Natal thinking that I would have more time to study and read, and I applied to be admitted as an advocate. I thought that if I was an advocate I would depend on getting briefs from an attorney. Therefore, I wouldn't get that much work. I would have time to teach, and I would be able to get some money as well.

I remember the desk and office furniture I had when I opened my chambers—the bare necessities—were bought by a lady who had been a classmate, an African lady who had a small café or shop and she brought those for me. But what happened was that, from the time that I started, I became busy. I got briefs. I got them from chaps like Justice Poswa. Justice was then an attorney and we were contemporaries. I started getting briefs even though there were few African attorneys then.

The bulk of my work was commercial work and it came from Indian attorneys. There were quite a number of Indian attorneys. I got lots of work from them. For some reason they had confidence in me. Quite early on, I did some briefs which attracted attention. I won one or two cases which were in the newspapers. One was a civil case against the city council of Durban. It was a claim for damages by someone who had been assaulted by the city police, against the city council as the employer. I did that case, despite the belief then in the African community that you couldn't win any case against organizations like the city council. I won the case against an experienced counsel. It started there, and some of the older Indian attorneys began briefing me, and I became quite busy.

Justice Poswa

In chapter 5, Justice Poswa described his education at the University of Natal in the late 1950s.

≈ I finished my LL.B. and did articles with R. A. V. Ngcobo [the same attorney with whom Justice Moloto began his articles]. My original intention had been to come straight to the bar. I had actually applied. I was going to be the second African advocate in Durban. But attorneys in Durban told me of the experience of a guy before me, a gentleman from Pretoria. They felt that, being Xhosa by origin, it would be risky for me to be one of the first African advocates in Natal. They thought I might not get work from local people, because they were all Zulu. So I abandoned the idea of becoming an advocate and opted to become an attorney.

I also would have had another problem being an advocate because I hadn't completed matric Afrikaans. I was among the first to be caught by the requirement of Afrikaans for admission for the bar. I did Afrikaans privately and I had my matric exam on it after I had finished articles of clerkship. I passed the examination, but I didn't bother about the application to the bar. I came to the side-bar and I had my own firm for seven years.

Ultimately, I decided to become an advocate rather than an attorney. The first reason was that I always wanted to go to the bar. The second was—now I have to say it—I always felt that we had mediocre black advocates. I thought that we needed black advocates who could stand there and do what we would like them to do in political cases. I saw myself in the courtroom arguing. I am not talking about ability, I am just talking about the tendency to debate things, but also I was one of the better students at university.

Blacks in White Law Firms

Occasionally, more frequently in recent years than earlier, a few blacks were able to practice law with white firms. Some had the opportunity to do articles with those firms. One of the earlier instances of such an opportunity was that of Tholie Madala.

Tholakele Hope Madala

Tholie Madala was born in 1937. He attended the University of Fort Hare and received an LL.B. from the University of Natal (Pietermaritzburg) in 1973.[2]

    I graduated from law school with an LL.B. and did my articles with Venn Nemeth and Oliver Hart in Pietermaritzburg. It was a white law firm. I did work there across the whole spectrum: criminal work, civil work, public law. I had an involvement in all departments. It was a liberal firm. It got me going. When I served my articles I was the only black at the firm. There were three other articled clerks. I must say that, of all the articled clerks in Pietermaritzburg at the time, I was the best paid, probably based on the fact that I was married. I needed the money.

Even when the firm had one or two Afrikaners, their attitude could not come out against me. There were five partners at that time. From the first partner to the bottom, they were all professionals. The secretary in the office had to know that she was not dealing with another black man.

She was dealing with a professional. After I completed my degree I had to do Afrikaans for purposes of admission. It so happened that, at the time, the principal partner, Oliver Hart, also needed to brush up his Afrikaans. So the firm had a policy that on certain days of the week, it was to be an Afrikaans-speaking day.

I would sit in my office and a white man would come, look at this black fellow and say, "I have this matter, but I think I need to see Mr. Hart." I would have been working on the file but he wasn't going to want to communicate with this black fellow sitting there. I would say, "Well, I've got the file here but if you want to go and see Mr. Hart, I'll call the secretary." I would go to the reception area and say, "Please, this gentleman would like to see Mr. Hart." Two minutes later, he would come back with Mr. Hart, who said, "This is Mr. Madala, who is handling your case. Take a seat. Good luck." And Mr. Hart pushed off. So that was generally the attitude of the firm.

Madala practiced first as an attorney and then as an advocate in Umtata, the capital of the Transkei homeland. He was appointed a judge of the Supreme Court in 1994 and later that same year was named to the Constitutional Court.

Sometimes a black lawyer would get a start in a white firm that had substantial business in the black community. George Maluleke had that experience.

George Maluleke

As described in chapter 5, George Maluleke left the University of the North in 1965 after a dispute with the administration of that institution. He began his studies through the University of South Africa and began his association with a white attorney, Henry Dolowitz.

∞ In the beginning the firm was called Stein and Dolowitz. But Nat Stein left when I was there and went to work for Anglo American in the property division.

There were very few black firms at the time. You wouldn't call them firms. They were struggling little things. They were around but they could hardly afford a clerk. All the attorneys then served articles in white firms, small white firms, and it would mostly be those firms which did black work. Stein and Dolowitz did almost exclusively black work. They had a black clientele. Firms that did work like conveyancing would hardly ever take a black clerk. This firm did criminal work, a lot of it. Nat Stein did a hell of a lot of it. They did personal injury claims, they did divorces, they did maybe some small time agreements, etc. There was almost no commercial activity among black people. It was mainly criminal work and personal injury and divorces. There were quite a lot of divorces actually, come to think of it.

There were just the two of them, Stein and Dolowitz, when I joined the firm, and myself as a clerk. Now and again they had, I think, a white clerk.

After Nat Stein left, we had less work. Stein was the one who had showed greater dynamism, and he was the one who had quite a bit of a white clientele because of his connections. I know at some stages we ran the firm, Dolowitz and I, without any secretary. That's how I learned to do the typing and switchboard and everything.

It was impossible to get decent training or articles of clerkship. You were almost restricted to small firms. My person, Henry [Dolowitz], tried to help me during my clerkship. He had a brother-in-law who did a little bit of corporate work and debt collection work in Roodepoort. I went to spend six months with him and it was a very great help to me. It was a break which was not generally available to black lawyers then. You would find that you came out with having had very restricted practical training. It was most frustrating. By the time you qualified and entered the profession you had these disadvantages built into the quality of lawyer training that you had. You learned nothing as a clerk. You really began to learn during the first two years after you qualified. That was when you began to become exposed daily to a variety of work.

During the course of his articles, Maluleke had the same sorts of problems that plagued Godfrey Pitje in his early days (see chap. 1). He had to be properly "influxed," that is, to obtain government permission to remain in Johannesburg. After several years, with Dolowitz's assistance, he finally convinced the bureaucracy to issue the necessary permit.

∞ After I was admitted in 1974, I had an offer to remain with Henry Dolowitz as a professional assistant [the equivalent of an associate in an American law firm]. By that time we had been together for at least eight or nine years. So we had really got used to each other. We talked about possible partnerships. It was unheard of then but we talked about those things. I remained with him about two and half years after qualifying, through 1976.

I still see a lot of Henry. We are still friends. He does a lot of my work in Johannesburg still. He is my corresponding attorney there.

After leaving his association with Henry Dolowitz, Maluleke worked with his father's growing grocery store business and opened a small law office not far from the store. In 1978 he, Dikgang Moseneke, and others started the law firm to which Moseneke referred in chapter 6. Although his brother is now the dominant partner in the family business, Maluleke remains active in its management. Both the grocery business and his law practice have grown in the ensuing years to the point that Maluleke is now both a leading businessperson and a prominent attorney in the Johannesburg area (see chap. 11).

George Maluleke's association with a lawyer who worked extensively in the black community was not particularly astonishing. Similarly, Tholie Madala's work with a small liberal firm in Pietermaritzburg seems relatively predictable. What is somewhat more surprising is that, beginning at least in the late 1970s, a few of the larger commercial firms in Johannesburg began to take one or two black clerks each year. These clerkships permitted a few aspiring young black lawyers to get exposure to a type of law practice totally out of the reach of the vast majority of their contemporaries. However, practice in large white law firms was not without its difficulties.

Phineas Mojapelo

Phineas Mojapelo, the former herd boy (chap. 2), finished his LL.B. at the University of the North in 1978 (chap. 5). Mojapelo met a senior partner at the Johannesburg firm of Webber Wentzel when he came to the city to receive a prize of R50 worth of law books awarded to him for academic excellence. He was first given a vacation job and was later selected as an articled clerk for the firm.

 confido I did clerkship with them for two years. It's a large white law firm, and gradually a new world was opened to me. There I was in the city in an all-white firm, a very big firm in which I was the only black professional. Indeed, the only other blacks in that firm were messengers and cleaners coming from Soweto. I was working with people who came from a completely different environment. I had never lived in a big city before, except for short periods when I went there during vacations. I came in contact with people who had only read about the lives of black people, and whose only contact with black people had been at the level of the maid and the gardener.

The most detracting level of experience at Webber Wentzel was with the typists and even certain law graduates. People refused to admit that a black person could be a lawyer, and typists would want to send you out on errands like a messenger. But it was an attitude, and you had to fight that attitude in such a way that you would convince them. The word amongst typists was that black education was different from white education. They believed that we had our own LL.B. It was not really like the LL.B. of Norman Barlow [the partner who had hired him] and other people, but it was an LL.B. for black people.

Webber Wentzel had a very good training program. The week prior to assuming articles of clerkship they would sit around with you, discuss your ambitions and your profile, and they would structure a program for you through the various departments in the firm, putting an emphasis on things you would eventually want to do. So by the time you started working, you would have a written program of how many months you were going to spend in which department through the twenty-four months of your articles. I did my first stint in estates, which is the drawing up of wills and administration of estates, administration of trusts, drawing of deeds of trust. I did basic estates for five months and from there I went on to the litigation department doing civil, commercial, and corporate litigation. It was predominantly in the Supreme Court, with a little bit in magistrate court. That took eight months. Thereafter, I went on to the conveyancing department and then to the commercial department.

My client contact depended on the principal with whom I worked. Some principals would basically keep you drawing up memos. You would work on files, and they would not involve you much in consultation with clients. Other principals would involve you in consultation from time to time. There were a few problems in dealing with white clients, but there were a few principals who were prepared to take the plunge. I remember Ken Douglas was exceedingly supportive and he would always check with clients in advance to see if they minded if I sat in consultation. Of course, they were servicing corporate clients, and I had no prospects of having any of them interested in me in the sense of keeping them as clients. But it was very good exposure.

They also had a very good internal education program. Articled clerks had to develop a written program of discussing all recent developments in the law on an ongoing basis. Articled clerks were obliged to attend sessions for articled clerks in their department, and also all education sessions for other departments as well. In terms of education, I treasure my time at Webber Wentzel.

After doing articles of clerkship with Webber Wentzel, I remained at the firm for a year as a professional assistant. I was the only black professional assistant. At that stage there were thirty-seven partners. On average, each one of them had at least two professional assistants, and then there would be candidate attorneys. It was a very big corporate atmosphere. There were more than a hundred lawyers. They had an overseas practice as well. I was the only black. I think at one stage another black came and did articles of clerkship. They did a good job, and allowed me an opportunity and access to those facilities.

I still have excellent relationships with Webber Wentzel and they are very supportive in my work. I did some work with them for a time, although I don't do much with them now. When I went on my own, certain senior partners at Webber Wentzel wanted to assist me and sold me secondhand furniture, which enabled me to start, and referred me to certain clients.

After leaving Webber Wentzel, Mojapelo opened a law office in the small northern city of Nelspruit. His partner was Mathews Phosa, now the premier of Mpumalanga, the province where Nelspruit is located. Phosa had also done his articles at a white firm in Johannesburg. They were the first black lawyers in the area. Although faced with the limitations of the Group Areas Act, with some help from their Johannesburg law firm connections and what, at the time, was a surprisingly supportive Nelspruit town council, they established an office in the white city. Their practice served blacks in the surrounding area. Town politics took a more conservative turn a few years later and, as Mojapelo says, "they started to wish us away, but it was too late."

Kgomotso Moroka

Kgomotso Moroka, the physician's daughter (chap. 4), described her experiences at the University of the Witwatersrand in chapter 5. After receiving her LL.B. in 1980, she did her articles at a prominent white firm, Bowman Gilfillan.

> ∞ It was a white firm; there were no black lawyers in it. They took one black articled clerk every two years. When I got to the firm, I was made to write an IQ test. None of the other articled clerks were made to do that. I went to an institute next to Wits where I wrote an IQ test. They never let you know if you failed, but I became an articled clerk. I suppose I should be grateful because all the other white firms had turned me down. Others didn't even bother to write me a letter of regret. I always tell a partner in one of the other firms about it. He says, Kgomotso, it was a big mistake. And I say, ja, a BIG mistake. And Bowman made me go and write an IQ test.
>
> One of my best friends at Wits also was at Bowman Gilfillan, Fiona McClachan. So it was okay and it was fun because in those good old days, blacks and whites just didn't have relationships. We would walk down the street sharing an apple in downtown Johannesburg and cause a stir. We used to love that. She helped in that sense because at least she made me feel it doesn't matter what all these others do or say, I have a friend. But it was still difficult there too.
>
> I don't know what I did at Bowman. I used to go begging for work. The white clerks used to get work. Kgomotso used to go begging for work. I eventually got to a state where I said to myself, I am going to sit and study for the board exams [the examinations taken to be admitted as an attorney], to hell with them, and that's exactly what I did. I wrote the exams in the first year. You are entitled to write any time after you finish your first year, and I did that. So when I did my second year, I already had

my board exams in the bag. I think I didn't get work because they didn't know what to expect of me. I suppose they expected me to do criminal work, which I didn't like. They then expected me to deal with their black clients. The white clients were theirs, you know.

After finishing her articles, Moroka joined her husband, who had a business in the Orange Free State. She was a magistrate there for four years and then spent some time with a white law firm before returning to Johannesburg to begin practice as an advocate (see chap. 11).

Dolly Mokgatle

Dolly Mokgatle, the child of a single mother (chap. 2), went to state schools for blacks (chap. 4). She received her LL.B. from the University of the Witwatersrand in 1982. She too was given an opportunity to do articles at Webber Wentzel.

∾ Webber Wentzel was not very sympathetic as a firm, but there were a few lawyers that saw the light in terms of being more liberal than they had been before. They had already had black clerks. Phineas Mojapelo had been a clerk there. There were at least two others before I came. I am not sure how many came after me, if they increased the numbers. But they had kept the numbers very small. In any one year, you would find either one black clerk or you would find a first-year black clerk and a final-year black clerk, not more.

It was also a fascinating period in my life. I am sure it is like most law firms, where you find secretaries being very resentful of clerks. They see clerks walk in, nose in the air, with university degrees. The secretaries in fact know more than you do. I always tell the story of one of the senior secretaries or paralegals meeting me one day in the ladies room. Webber Wentzel occupied three floors of the building: nine, ten, and eleven. On one side of the lift on the ninth floor was a ladies room and on the other side there was a gents room. When I started at the firm, someone showed me a door on the fire escape and said that is where I should go. I looked at it and I noted it, but every time I needed to use the ladies room, I would just go to one near the lift. What I didn't notice at first was that the sign to that ladies room was painted white. It meant that it was a whites-only room. Every other nonwhite member of staff had to go to that pit down the fire escape. I refused to go to the fire escape.

This white woman—this senior secretary who combed her hair in a way that it looked like a beehive—found me there one day washing my hands. She was an Afrikaner and spoke with a very heavy accent. She said: "Aren't you people supposed to have your own toilets somewhere else in the building?" I replied: "Well, I'd like to use this one. If you want to use that one be my guest." She went out and went straight to the manageress. She was a very British lady, always making women toe the line: You must wear stockings when you come to work, and so on. So the secretary went to the manageress and told her that I had been using the whites-only toilet, and that I leave the place in a mess. It was a very demeaning thing.

The next day I was asked to stay after work to have a meeting with a very senior partner. By then, I had been given a hint that the word was out that nobody should touch me. Nobody should make my life a misery. If the secretary couldn't toe the line then she would be the one who would have to leave. So, by the time I had the meeting with the senior partner I had a good indication that I was actually not in trouble. Quite the contrary. He told me he had heard the story. He had talked to the manageress and to the secretary. He told me that I was welcome to use any bathroom facility I wanted to. If there was any problem I was to see him.

You know, the way they handled the situation was not right, but at the end of the day it worked out okay. They could have made a statement. They could have given a message to the organization on policy. They didn't review the policy. They dealt with the individual. They didn't say stop this segregation; they didn't do that. They just solved the problem for someone they perceived to be quite assertive. Things didn't change for the rest of the black staff.

I was lucky in the sense that the people that I worked with as principals were good people. The thing I missed, and I think it wasn't only me but most of the clerks, was the bigger corporate work. The senior partners preferred to do the work themselves for the big clients: Anglo, JCI [large South African corporations], and similar companies. If you were a clerk you wouldn't do much in the corporate department. There wasn't much difference between black and white clerks in that regard. That's where you felt you were a clerk. A few white clerks did do corporate work. However, they were not happy, because they were only allowed to stay there for four months to six months at the most. They were never really allowed to do much work on the "big file," as we used to call it.

I had a good relationship with my colleagues. There were a few who thought they were bigger than others, but I think the entire workplace is like that. There were the obvious gaps between blacks and whites. You could see that the white clerks were more advantaged. Whether it was a question of perception, I don't know. There were a few incidents, yes, but I had a real good stay at Webber Wentzel. Although it was a very small thing, they did assist me. But they were sympathetic me without really changing their principles in a big way.

After leaving the Webber firm, Mokgatle worked at the Centre for Applied Legal Studies at the University of the Witwatersrand and then the Black Lawyers Association–Legal Education Centre. She ultimately joined the legal department of Eskom, the giant electric utility (see chap. 11).

Although the number of black articled clerks or professional assistants was limited and the circumstances often difficult, the fact that young black lawyers were part of this elite corporate law structure during the height of apartheid may have laid the foundation for more significant integration of these firms in the new South Africa. Prior to the civil rights revolution of the 1960s, very few comparable American law firms would have had an African-American associate or law clerk.

Some Unusual People

A few blacks had experiences very different from an attorney's office practice or the struggles of ordinary advocates.

Pingla Hemraj

Pingla Hemraj finished her LL.B. at the University of Natal (Durban) in 1980 (chap. 5). She did pupillage in order to become an advocate, joining a bar in which there were just three other women, two white and one Indian. She struggled for a short time as an advocate and then joined the staff of an insurance company as a legal advisor. Unhappy in that position, she applied to join the Justice Department as a prosecutor.

∞ When I got this prosecuting post, the Justice Department said to me, You can take it or leave it, but the only available post is in Scottburgh. Scottburgh is about forty minutes' drive from Durban, about halfway between Durban and Port Shepstone, along the South Coast. It is a beautiful little city, very Afrikaans, extremely conservative. I knew that at the time, but I needed the job and I said yes. It was a wonderful salary, I thought. I thought, This is where I am going to get the experience. I took myself off to Scottburgh.

The experience was an eye-opener. It was a totally white staff except for two Indian clerks and one black gentleman who was the messenger. There had been one Indian prosecutor before me, who stayed for a short while, but he grew up close to that town so he knew the guys. I was coming in from the outside, and it was not very nice. I didn't fit in socially. For example, they would have a Christmas party, and I couldn't understand why the senior prosecutor would say to me, "I think you can go home at two o'clock today." I wondered why. Ordinarily, I tried to leave at a quarter past four instead of half past four, and she really would come down on me. The next day I would come in and find glasses lying around and I knew they had had a party. I wasn't encouraged to have tea in their tearoom.

Work was also difficult. Initially the court orderly taught me how to draft the charge sheet, because nobody else would. You were left very much to sink or swim. I remember one magistrate, Du Plessis, sitting in court and saying to me that in this court we do half our cases in Afrikaans. He obviously thought that I couldn't speak Afrikaans because I am an Indian girl born in Natal. I thought to myself, well fine, I'll show you.

You are too scared because these are all very senior magistrates. You are the most junior prosecutor of the lot, and everybody looks so learned, and they absolutely know what they are doing. It was totally intimidating. I found learning how to do everything very stressful. Then I found one excellent magistrate, Chris Schoeman, and he basically took me under his wing and taught me everything I knew about prosecuting. He was excellent, very kind. He was a white magistrate, Afrikaans-speaking, but he taught me how to go about prosecuting. He sat down one day to write out questions for me, showing me how to lead a witness [in American parlance, direct examination]. And that's when it sort of turned around—after about six months of floundering. I was the prosecutor in Schoeman's court, and we developed an excellent working relationship. Then I started to read law reports and to read and read, and just generally to learn better what I was doing.

I couldn't prosecute white accuseds. I could prosecute Africans or people of other races, but I wasn't allowed to do any cases involving whites. I was the only one in that entire building with an LL.B. The others had worked their way up in the Justice Department with various diplomas. [Prosecutors would not necessarily be qualified attorneys or advocates.] The senior prosecutor said, "You are really one of these 'factory-trained' prosecutors who really doesn't know what to do in court." It was very antagonistic. We still never socialized, except for Chris Schoeman. The rest were chatty and that sort of thing, but there was always that distance, always.

I also spent some time in the Johannesburg regional court. They had a shortage of prosecutors in Johannesburg. They were looking for people to volunteer to go there, and just to get out of Scottburgh, I volunteered to go to Johannesburg. It was probably the best thing I did. It was a big city, a different mentality. Everybody helped everybody else. In Scottburgh I would never have ever seen the kind of cases I did in Johannesburg. I prosecuted in the police court, where only policemen were the accused. Later in my stay, I prosecuted attempted murders, people who would have an argument in the street about who overtook who and then they would shoot each other up, stuff like that. I did lots of shooting cases, which for me was new and very exciting. I had to learn pretty quickly. I would get eight dockets in the afternoon to prepare for trial the next day. You would be expected to do those trials, and run as many as you could as quickly as you could.

One had to learn fast, but it was an amazing learning experience. The people were wonderful, from the chief magistrate down to the clerks. It being Johannesburg, they just didn't have the problems that small-town people have. I was the first Indian to prosecute in the Transvaal. It got into the newspapers; I remember it in the *Star.* The lady in the cafeteria upstairs refused to serve me because she said it was a whites-only place, so I had the senior prosecutor take me up for tea. Silly things like that. They

said, Don't say anything about it in the interview with the press. It was a
wonderful learning experience.

After returning from Johannesburg, I decided I had had enough of
the district court—trespass, prosecuting trespass and pass offenses, and
people getting drunk and beating each other up. I decided that I wanted
to go to the Supreme Court to prosecute.

Hemraj then applied and, in 1986, after some difficulty, obtained a
transfer to the attorney general's office in Durban, where she began to prosecute more serious cases in the Supreme Court.

∽ The attorney general's office was also a wonderful place, a brilliant
office. The people were very highly qualified, very professional. It didn't
matter what color you were. Color just didn't matter for the first time
ever. It was good. I was the only black woman in the office. I was the first
black person, male or female, ever to prosecute in a South African
supreme court. I remember a book came out at the end of the year listing
all the people that had achieved firsts for that year and this was one of the
things—first black person to appear as a prosecutor in the Supreme
Court.

In that office we prosecuted gangs and murders and robberies—bank
robberies, shootings, and all sorts of things I thought terribly exciting. I
absolutely loved it. My brother was a police officer at the time, but he was
very junior—a constable. But because you work so closely with the police
as prosecutor, you get a very good idea of what was going on. The police
were very helpful. Certainly we worked a lot with the murder and robbery
unit when I was at the attorney general's office, and they were highly
skilled investigators. I learned a lot from them. I don't think my race mattered to anybody. You were there to do a job and you got on with the job
and did it. I have never had any adverse reaction, any adverse comment
from any judges. In fact they were mostly very kind. They told me when I
made a stupid submission and berated me for it and then, if it was good, I
got what I was looking for. But there was never any sense of unease or
anything like that.

I finally left the attorney general's office in Durban over the question
of prosecution of political cases. I was there for three and a half years. I

was very happy. I thought I would stay a long time, but it seemed at the time that the way to become a senior state advocate was to do these political cases. I remember the head of the office asking me to be his junior in a matter which was a result of a bombing in Amanzimtoti, and I said to him that I could not. Amanzimtoti is about twenty kilometers south of Durban. An ANC group had put a bomb in a trash can in a shopping center, and it was pretty bad.[3] My problem was that I couldn't prosecute that case, and live in the community that I lived in. I could never go into private practice.

Also, I determined that even if I stayed I wasn't going to get places. I guess there are only so many cases you can prosecute, after which it becomes just another murder. It sounds a bit blasé, but that's the way it felt at the time. I always felt that I wanted to come back and prove that I could make it at the bar, because I had left without making it. I wanted to do that, so the events kind of pushed me to make that kind of decision.

Hemraj left the attorney general's office in 1988 to open chambers as an advocate in Durban. She has become successful, devoting a large percentage of her practice to the defense of police officers charged with serious crimes, especially murder.

Ismail Mahomed

Perhaps the most remarkable beginning to a practice was that of Ismail Mahomed. Mahomed told of his background and early childhood in chapter 2, and his education at the University of the Witwatersrand in chapter 5. He began his practice as an advocate in 1957, at a time when there were almost no other nonwhite advocates. In just a few years, he established himself as one of the nation's outstanding lawyers. He did so under extraordinary circumstances.

∞ When I finished an LL.B. at Wits I immediately decided that I was going to the bar. My personality and my interest were such that I wanted to confront injustice in the courtroom. I didn't want to be buried in the bureaucracy of documents. I enjoyed confrontation, I enjoyed argument, I enjoyed disputation. I enjoyed visible conflict and engagement.

The problem arose, How do you go to the bar? The constitution of the bar of the city of Pretoria, from which I came, said in clear and expressed words that only white persons shall be members. I then went to Johannesburg and I asked the local bar there whether I could become an advocate.

They said, "Of course. There is nothing in our constitution that stops you from becoming a member. So, welcome. But there is a problem."

The problem was that advocates, unlike attorneys, have all got to be housed in the same building, in offices approved by the bar council.

I said, "Well, I suppose you have an office available."

He said, "Oh yes, we have. But the Group Areas Act says that no person who is not white can occupy chambers in an area proclaimed for white ownership and occupation, and the building in which we require all advocates to be is situated in an area proclaimed for white ownership and occupation."

I asked what I could do and he said I could apply for a permit. Well, a permit was not on [was not possible]. The policy of the state was that each race must practice in its own area. That would have been ridiculous. There was an Indian area proclaimed in Johannesburg, some twenty-five miles away, in the veld [the countryside]. No advocate in South African history had ever practiced, except fifty feet away from the Supreme Court building. It was just not on. What was I to do? I could either abandon the profession altogether or become an attorney and go in some area where Indians were allowed to occupy offices. Neither of those alternatives appealed to me.

What I then did for the next twelve years was quite an extraordinary thing. I traveled everyday from Pretoria to Johannesburg by train. In the building where advocates occupied chambers, there were approximately ten floors and each floor had one or two groups of advocates. You had to join a group which had a common telephonist, secretarial staff, and typists. I went to the sixth-floor group, which at that stage included Bram Fischer, who was subsequently convicted and sentenced to life imprisonment, Sydney Kentridge, Arthur Chaskalson, a considerable number of "left" people.

The following arrangement was made: every morning I would go to the telephonist and I would say, "Who is in court today?" and she would say, "Mr. Fischer has a case today." I would then go into his room. If the case lasted I was okay, but very often the case got settled by half past ten and Mr. Fischer would come back. I would then pack my bags and go back to the telephonist and say, "Is there anyone else who has got a case" and she would say, "Well, Mr. Chaskalson has gone on inspection in an accident case," and I would go there. That's how I practiced without a room for twelve years—from 1957 to 1969.

I built a big practice in that period, largely dominated by anti-apartheid work: defending people charged for political offenses, defending people being prosecuted under the Group Areas Act. Indeed I acquired a considerable expertise in that subject and wrote a textbook on the legal interpretation of the Group Areas Act, which became a standard work. But the practice grew, and I still had no fixed address. You wouldn't have found my name in the telephone book; you wouldn't have found me at any address. The word got around to the attorneys that, if they went to the sixth floor and went to the telephonist, she would direct them to the particular room which I was occupying for that hour, or she would call me and say, "There are people here." She would ask if I had a consultation that day.

I would say yes, and she would say, "Let me see if I can't find a room for you."

She would call one of the chaps and say, "You know, Mr. Mahomed has a consultation, are you going to be in your room for long?"

He would say, "Oh well, I am going for tea anyway so for the next forty-five minutes tell him to be my guest."

That's how I used to practice. But I don't want to now exaggerate just how tough that time was, and I don't want to become sentimental about it, but I want to illustrate just how difficult it was.

It also coincided with the time that outside that building there was no restaurant where I could go and have a cup of tea or have lunch. There were many restaurants but I was prohibited by law from "occupying" them. I brought sandwiches from home every day. Once or twice in those twelve years, maybe three times, I couldn't eat my sandwich anywhere except in the toilet. The bar council had a common room where advocates had tea in the morning, tea in the afternoon, and prepared hot meals at lunchtime. It would be peopled by as many as fifty, sixty, eighty people at lunchtime. I wasn't allowed to go into that room. I think a kind of insensitivity developed and the whole thing was regarded as normal. We would be working on a case—I would be junior to some silk or I would be leading in a case—and at one o'clock they would be hungry and they would say, "See you at two o'clock." Off they would go to the common room, and that all became accepted as being normal.

My office situation changed in 1969. I had a difficult case in which I was briefed as junior to a senior advocate who was generally believed to have considerable clout in government circles. He was perceived to be a friend of the government.

While we were working together he said to me, "If I need you tomorrow, where do I get you?"

I said, "Just ring the telephonist on the sixth floor."

He said, "Yes, but which is your room number?"

I said, "Just ring the telephonist, and she will tell you."

But he said, "Don't you know your room number?"

And I said, "No, I don't."

"What do you mean you don't, haven't you got a room?"

I said, "No, I will be in a room tomorrow which is not the same as it is today. I can't tell you now which room number it will be."

He said, "Why?"

I said, "Well, the law doesn't allow me."

He said, "There can't be a law like that," although he was a supporter of the government.

I said, "Yes, there is. This is a white area."

He said, "But that is outrageous."

I said, "Yes, well, I also think so."

He said, "Well, I am not prepared to accept that."

I don't know for a fact what happened, but my understanding is that he then phoned the then minister and said, "This is outrageous. The law was never meant for this kind of situation." He couldn't put up with the injustice. Eventually they gave me a permit to occupy a particular room in that building.

So after twelve years I got a room of my own and then for another five years I practiced in my own room. The permit didn't extend to attending the common room where they had their lunches and teas.

Seventeen years after my admission to the bar, I thought, and my colleagues thought, and the bar council thought that my practice was sufficiently substantial to justify applying for silk [become senior counsel]. Thus in 1974, seventeen years after my admission, I applied for silk. [It is common for advocates to take silk after ten or twelve years in practice.] My application was recommended by the bar council and by the judge president of the Supreme Court and then had to be approved by the minister of justice and the state president. The last was supposed to be a formality. There had never been senior counsel status for any person who wasn't white. My application was supported by the professional bodies on grounds of merit.

My application was held up for a considerable time, something like seventeen months, whereas normally it takes two months, or something like that. I never understood the true reason for that, but I think it would be unfair to say that it was held up only because of my color. I rather suspect there was also some security consideration, because I was not a friend of the government. That was manifest from my speeches and my writings in defense of antiapartheid activists. I was refused a passport for fifteen years. They weren't refusing passports as a matter of course to nonwhites. A lot of nonwhites traveled. People who had any kind of security risk, in their perception, were refused passports. This was because of my activism in antiapartheid litigation. Anyway, I eventually got that silk after seventeen months.

The situation in chambers became quite anomalous when I was about to be named senior counsel. All my juniors were going to be white, and I couldn't have tea with them. They could go and I couldn't go into the common room. Eventually there was some kind of informal meeting among advocates, who said that this was an intolerable situation. He's got a bloody office here, he has practiced here for the last seventeen years, why can't he have tea with us?

All this happened behind my back, but as I understand the story, a lot of liberal advocates got together with some of the perceived Afrikaner supporters of the government and said, "Look, we can't go on like this." And the liberal chaps then said to the Afrikaner chaps, who were supposed to be supporters of the government, "Look, you guys are responsible for the situation. You better go now and invite him because it is not our doing."

One day I got a call from a leading Afrikaans-speaking advocate and he said, "May I come and see you in your room?" By then I had had a room for the last five years. I said, "Certainly, come in." I didn't normally have much to do with him.

He said, "I would like to say something, but before I say it I want two promises. The first is that you allow me to speak for a minute without interrupting me and the second is that having done so, at the end of it you won't say, 'Fuck you.'"

I responded, "These are extraordinary conditions but I give you both." I didn't know what it was about.

He said, "Well, what I have come to tell you is that I am grossly ashamed of how we have treated you for seventeen years. I am terribly ashamed, very embarrassed, and I have now come to ask you whether you will do us the honor of coming to the common room today."

He had taken the words from me because I wanted to say, "Fuck you."

9

THE PRACTICE OF LAW
UNDER APARTHEID

MOST BLACK lawyers had, and to a large extent still have, very modest practices. They rely heavily on minor criminal cases, domestic relations matters, and motor vehicle work. During the days of apartheid, commercial work was virtually nonexistent, at least for black African lawyers. Lawyers of Indian descent, especially in the Durban area, would have handled small commercial cases, such as debt collections, brought to them by the nation's many Indian traders. Black African lawyers would seldom see such cases. A black lawyer of any ethnic background might be involved representing a defendant charged with serious crimes, but only on a *pro deo* (court appointed) basis, where a limited fee would be paid by the state.

Conflict with Liberal White Lawyers

Major human rights cases often went to liberal white lawyers who had developed an expertise in that area of law and who were known to the funding sources. Particularly beginning in the late 1980s, the selection of white lawyers to handle major civil and criminal cases critical to the struggle against apartheid became a significant sore spot for many black lawyers. Godfrey Pitje, who was director of the Black Lawyers Association–Legal Education Centre at that time, felt a keen sense of rivalry with liberal lawyers groups, especially the Legal Resources Centre (LRC). The LRC is a public interest law firm heavily involved in human rights work. During the apartheid era it received substantial funding from foreign (including American, British, and European) sources. Many of its lawyers were black, including Fikile Bam (chaps. 2, 5, 7), Mahomed Navsa (chaps. 3, 10), and Timothy Bruinders (chaps. 3, 4, 5, 9, 11). Indeed, Bam, Navsa, and Bruinders eloquently praise not only the outstanding legal work of the center, but also its role in providing high-quality training for black lawyers. Nevertheless, at least until very recent years, the leadership of the organization was white. Its leaders, such as its director, Arthur Chaskalson,[1] who is mentioned several times in this book and who served as one of Nelson Mandela's lawyers at his 1963 trial, were well respected, indeed universally admired, but white nonetheless. Thus, there was rivalry with black lawyers' groups, especially the Black Lawyers Association (BLA).

Pitje describes the concerns:

> The LRC became a very successful and powerful body. Politics caught up with us, particularly with the establishment of the United Democratic Front [the UDF, a political group formed in 1987. In effect, the UDF was a legal stand-in for the banned African National Congress]. The BLA didn't join the UDF. We were to suffer because all the political work, the representation of people involved in political cases, then went to people who were UDF, like the LRC. In some cases, a black attorney would have received instructions, gone to court, gotten a postponement and briefed an advocate. The next day, he would find that one of the liberal lawyers had been instructed and he was told to transfer the file to lawyer so-and-so. We starved for political work. That continued up to the end of the old government.

Whether or not Pitje's strongly held perception of the politics was correct or fair, a review of civil and criminal cases involving significant human rights issues reveals that a high percentage were handled by white rather than black lawyers.[2] Of course, one explanation was that there were many more white lawyers, even many more liberal white lawyers, than there were black lawyers. Furthermore, white lawyers almost always had the advantages of experience, a better education, and extensive contact with both the judicial and the administrative establishment of the country. The fact that they would be chosen by foreign funding sources to represent the antiapartheid cause may not have been the correct decision, but it was an unsurprising one.

Nevertheless, there were several black lawyers heavily and effectively involved in human rights work. Some were among the best-regarded advocates in the nation. In a racist nation bent on maintaining the dominance of the ruling group, these lawyers suffered more and risked more to represent their clients than their white counterparts.

Danger and Death

Pius Langa

One of the leading black lawyers doing human rights work was Pius Langa, who practiced as an advocate in Durban before being named to the Constitutional Court after the new government came to power. In 1982, Langa represented three individuals—Makubela (an attorney), Gaba, and Ncqwita—on treason charges. The government alleged that they were involved in limpet mine bombings and in the hoarding of weapons. They were ultimately convicted. All three now hold positions in the ANC government.

> ∞ Just before the trial started a friend of mine, Griffiths Mxenge, was killed. I was very close to him, not only workwise but also socially. Because of Griffiths's death, the attorney in the trial of these three young people was Griffiths's wife, Victoria. We would travel from Durban to Pietermaritzburg for the trial.
>
> The trial was traumatic in a number of aspects. The accused Makubela, the attorney, was my friend. He had served articles with Griffiths Mxenge. Some of the witnesses who were detained and produced in court to give evidence against these three were my friends as well.

One of those detainees, who was produced as a witness, was a man called Ululani Xgco. He is now the chief whip in the South African Senate. There also were a number of others who are in public office who were involved in that trial. But it was quite a thing to see this man Ululani Xgco, for instance, being brought up from solitary confinement, from detention, and produced in court by the security people. We were told that he was going to be a witness against his close friend Makubela. Ululani refused to testify, much to the relief of the defense team. That meant, of course, that Ululani was going to go to jail, which in itself was traumatic for me, being a friend of both Makubela and Xgco.

I was associated with Griffiths Mxenge from the time he served articles in Verulam [an Indian area near Durban] with George Sewpershad, who was president of the Natal Indian Congress. Griffiths was very active politically and in community life. We were always involved in trying to do something to raise the awareness of people with regard to their rights and what was happening there, and always involved in trying to assist people who were detained. It was the beginnings of the Release Mandela Committee. I think that is how Griffiths incurred the wrath of the government. He was always under surveillance, but he was a very great person and he worked well under those conditions.

Griffiths would brief me as an advocate on many occasions. There was community work as well. He was instrumental in supporting the beginning of what was called a joint rent association [JORAC], a movement which played a role in the townships in protesting high rents. There were many instances when the joint rent association had to go to court for this or that, and Griffiths and myself would represent them.

Everyone knew that the security police did not like Griffiths Mxenge. Well, they did not like many people actually. On the particular day that he was killed, I had been working with him. I was actually the last person known to see him alive. I handed over some papers to him just opposite his office outside in the road and I drove off.

About midnight, his wife phoned me to say that he had not arrived home. "Where is he?"

I said, "Well, I don't know. He should have come home."

I suggested that he might have thought of going somewhere else, but she was very worried and in fact it turned out that he had already been killed. His body was found the next morning. He was found with many wounds. He had been cut up—mutilated and so on. So that was Griffiths. No one was ever prosecuted. He died in November 1981.

An inquest was subsequently held. The fact that I had been the last person to see him was publicized. It was in the press, it was everywhere, but the police never asked me about it. We found that odd. There were many odd things. When the inquest was held, a lot of questions were left unanswered. It was quite clear that there had been no investigation at all.

His wife, Victoria, was killed some four or five years later under similar circumstances. She was hacked to death as she arrived at her house. That was tragic. One of her sons rushed her to hospital, but she died. No one has yet been prosecuted. At least there are suggestions that the people who killed Griffiths are known. I haven't heard anything about the killers of Victoria Mxenge. She was a very brave person as well. She had just carried on where Griffiths had left off. She was an amazing person, very capable as a lawyer and also as an administrator. She was very unpopular with the security police.

In 1997 a white former police captain and two black former policemen were found guilty of the murder of Griffiths Mxenge. Victoria Mxenge's murder is still unsolved. Ironically, amid the destructive rioting that followed her death, the former home of Mahatma Gandhi, outside Durban, was destroyed.

∞ I was concerned for my own safety a number of times, particularly when Griffiths died. My friends thought I might possibly be next because I had been very close to Griffiths. I should say I was concerned, but there was very little one could do. I could not isolate myself. I didn't know what precautions to take that would be effective, so eventually I just thought it was not even worthwhile to take precautions. There were threatening phone calls from time to time. These would come in waves. There were times when, over a three-month period, I would get them almost every day, in the middle of the night, scaring my wife. And then they would just vanish. This continued throughout the time of my practice.

CHAPTER 9

Timothy Bruinders

Fear of the government and the police was not confined to well-known human rights lawyers such as Langa and the Mxenges. Young lawyers could find themselves in frightening situations. Timothy Bruinders, who told of his background and education as a young Coloured person in the Cape Town area (see chaps. 3 and 4), began practice as a young advocate in Johannesburg in late 1989. Here he describes situations in the Northern Cape (a mining area several hundred miles southwest of Johannesburg) in which he was involved in 1990.

⌒ I had a case where a little boy, seven years old, had been killed. Riot police, together with sort of reservists and AWB [Afrikaner Weestandsbeweging, a far-right-wing, pro-apartheid organization]-type supporters riding shotgun, had shot at people who had demonstrated a few days before. At the time of the shooting, these people were not demonstrating but had collected and were dancing at a local shop where they had a disco on a Saturday evening. The police and the others rode by to warn these people to leave. When they didn't leave within a minute, the little boy was killed.

We were called in to participate in the inquest into this little boy's death, and to try and get people who had been jailed as a result of the activity arising out of his death off on bail and to deal with their cases.

We went into a place called Danielskuil, a small rural township, which is very close to one of the biggest diamond mines in the country, the De Beers Finch mine. I got there in the afternoon and started consulting with people in a four-room house with no ceiling. The house had metal doors. It was primitive housing. I was taking a statement of what had happened, just filling in the history of the matter so that the next morning I could approach the police to get people out on bail and plead their cases.

Because they knew that the lawyer from Johannesburg had come down, the entire township had queued up to tell me what they had seen and what they had heard. About nine o'clock, we were sitting there in this little house packed with people telling me what had happened, when suddenly I heard this incredible commotion. I heard something rain upon the metal doors and the roof and people started diving for cover.

I said, "What the hell is going on?"

They replied, "They're shooting at the house."

"Jesus," I said.

So I ducked under the table and I could hear this sound of things raining on the doors and windows and then it stopped. The door was kicked open by chaps clad in khaki and smoking, real Ku Klux Klan stuff. I got up, and my knees were knocking, and I was a bit nervous. I had been beaten up before.

I walk up to them and with my blue brief cover in my hand and said, "Good evening, sirs. I am an advocate from Johannesburg."

He said "What?"

I said: "I am the advocate from Johannesburg."

And he said, "Fuck you too, mate," and pushed me out of the way saying, "Where is so-and-so and so-and-so?"

I said, "You can't arrest these people now. I am consulting them."

They basically told me where to get off. I went outside, and there was a truckload of white males, some were policemen and some were reservists and clad in this AWB-type of uniform. There was really very little as a lawyer that I could do. I couldn't stop them from dragging off one or two people. All I could do was take their names and say, I'm going to be there.

I spent a couple of days there as well as in Kimberley [the largest city in the area] at that time. It was a vicious time, and a time where I realized that no matter how articulate and eloquent and erudite I was, when someone has a smoking gun, there is very little I could do.

At the same time, there was a lot happening in Kimberley, in Galeshewe, which was the black township. I spent a lot of time there and made some very enduring friendships there. I didn't see too many AWB there. I didn't see so many khaki-clad people as I had in Danielskuil, which is in a remote rural area. There was no media in the remote areas, nothing. You would go from day to day there not knowing who might be arrested, where they might be, what might happen to them. It didn't get into any newspaper. There were people living out there at the mercy of these fascists.

In Kimberley, one of the people that we worked with, Yusuf, was in a youth organization. He was quite important to my team because we acted for a large group of youths who were all charged with a similar offense. I can't remember what the charges were, but it was either public violence or public violence related. Yusuf did the leg work of coordination for us.

We got word one afternoon while in Kimberley that he had been arrested. We went into the township trying to get hold of him, tracing after these huge cop vans. The chap I was with spotted him. It was almost a surreal scene in this township where groups of children, young children holding hands, pretty much what I imagine Auschwitz must have been like. They were being marched like cattle into this truck. Yusuf was sitting in the truck with all these kids. He had already been marched into it. The kids ranged in age from ten or eleven to about sixteen. They were young, young kids, all holding hands. They were virtually being frog-marched up the ramp into this huge cattle truck, and they were all going to be taken off to the police station.

I went up to the police and said, "I'm the lawyer," and was quite confident and said, "I want that man in the truck there. He is assisting me."

They said, "Well, you can't have him actually. We've got him."

I said, "Well, I'm a lawyer," and again they paid no attention to me.

While I was talking, we were surrounded by police vans, again guns smoking. There had been a shooting just down the road. I was aware of what I thought was a huge pile of paint, red paint, lying in the street near where I was standing. I didn't take much notice and the chap who was with me stuck his finger in it and said to the policeman, "This is blood."

I said, "Are you sure that's blood?" and he said, "Ja, its hot."

And I felt it. It was this lump of red blood.

And we said, "Who does this belong to?"

The cop said, "Ah, there were two kids we shot dead and they ran into the house over there."

We dashed off into the house and people were crying and these kids had been shot and it was dreadful. One kid eventually died. They were twelve or thirteen years old.

I recall these incidents even more vividly perhaps because it was my first year at the bar. Despite my experience at the Legal Resources Centre and the Campus Law Clinic, for the first time I had a distinct feeling of powerlessness to prevent either injury, harm, or death to what really were children.

The Role of the Lawyer as Friend

As illustrated by Langa's and Bruinders's accounts, lawyers often faced risk similar to that of their clients. The threats to their personal safety did not deter them from providing both representation and support, usually with either no fee or very modest compensation. Their very presence, their willingness to withstand the racially charged atmosphere of a South African courtroom, at least alerted the government that it had to adhere to legal forms.

Furthermore, the lawyer was often the client's only friend at a time of great personal crisis. And, as will be further illustrated in the history of Dullah Omar (chap. 12), they were frequently the only line of communication between the accused and the outside world.

Justice Poswa

Justice Poswa, who described his education at the University of Natal in chapter 5 and his early days in law practice in chapter 8, became an advocate involved in significant human rights cases.

∽ Even for my clients who were convicted, the most important thing my representation gave them was dignity as accused persons. Those guys were brutalized by the police in many respects, even to the point of view of being humiliated. When their cases came up, they were taken to areas away from their own area. They were the only person there, with nobody else except their lawyer. So your presence firstly gave them dignity because the police could see that someone gave them a degree of respect. They also had someone to discuss the case with and someone to relate all the stories to.

It also gave them the hope of being acquitted. Quite a number of them were acquitted. Even the hope of being acquitted and seeing the police being cross-examined gave them something. It discouraged the police from just arresting people at random because they knew it was not the end of the matter. They had to be more careful. They had to prepare their cases.

In some cases, they would just detain people and release them. So our representation gave support to the accused person, respectability in court, and also it did tend to discourage the police from just randomly taking people to court, because there was no guarantee that there would not be a lawyer appearing in those cases. We were able to throw out a number of confessions that were improperly obtained.

It also sharpened us because those of us who did those cases became better lawyers generally. We had to do those tough cases where the judge was at his worst, the magistrate at his worst, the police were the roughest, the conditions were awful, and everything was said in Afrikaans. We improved everything—our understanding of Afrikaans, of procedure. It was really a very useful thing for us and the accused and their relatives as well. The relatives at least felt that their son was not just alone there. The organization has done something for him.

Some Important Cases

Before the South African Interim Constitution of 1993, which included a bill of rights and established a Constitutional Court to enforce it, the role that the law could play in changing the way the government operated was extremely limited. Parliament was supreme. There could be no *Brown v. Board of Education* declaring that segregated schools deny equal protection to black children. Even if the educational system had been declared invalid as contrary to the law of the land, the South African parliament would have been free to reestablish the same schools through the enactment of legislation.

Nevertheless, as described by Dikgang Moseneke in chapter 6, lawyers could often be successful in challenging governmental decisions based on the rule and procedure set up by the government itself. Despite their limited numbers, several black lawyers had enormous success in such cases.

Lewis Skweyiya

Certainly anyone knowledgeable about the South African legal scene would count Lewis Skweyiya among the nation's leading lawyers. He was the first black African to become senior counsel. Skweyiya told of his early education in chapter 2, his detention by the Transkei authorities in chapter

7, and his early days in practice in chapter 8. Here he tells of his involvement in the 1986 trial of Andrew Zondo in the Natal port city of Scottburgh, where Pingla Hemraj (chap. 8) had been a prosecutor.

⌇ Zondo had left this country as a sixteen- or seventeen-year-old, something like that, and went to the ANC camps. He trained and then he placed a bomb at a shopping center. I think three persons died and some others were injured. He was eighteen when he appeared before the judge.

This young man said, "Look, I acted contrary to the instructions of the ANC. I did this because on two occasions I had people who were friends of mine who died next me as a result of the raids which were conducted by the South African Defence Force."

The Defence Force would go into adjoining countries and abduct people or kill people. In Lesotho, people died in that fashion; in Mozambique, people died in that fashion. He said that a friend of his died next to him and he made up his mind he must act. Five days before he placed the bomb, there was the Lesotho raid by the South African Defence Force, where something like nine persons died, including Lesotho citizens.

I had gone there initially, not to appear at the trial, but because, at the beginning when the boy appeared, he said he wanted no defense, no lawyers. Then the bar council appointed a senior counsel and a junior counsel, who were both white persons, colleagues of mine. They went and represented him at the preliminary stages and wanted him to tell his story. He did not want them.

He said, "I don't want any defense."

Ultimately the parents of the boy then came to me. Judge Didcott [John Didcott, later a judge of the Constitutional Court] was presiding at that stage. He said, "It's a serious case. You need to get a lawyer."

Then the parents approached the attorney to approach me to go and speak to him because they believed that he would accept me, because he did not want to be represented by these two white colleagues. I had gone there to explain to him his rights to an attorney and to ask for a postponement. I ended up by being in the case.

The judge denied my application for a lengthy postponement, and gave me only two or three days to prepare. The judge did grant my request to have a senior counsel lead me in the case, Denis Kuny.

I did the trial of this case before Judge Leon. The court was arranged in such a way that the accused's box was behind my back. The witness box was on the right-hand side and the judge was in front. The prosecution presented the case in a very smart way, perhaps, from the point of view of influencing the feelings of the judge and the community. They asked to lead evidence of the injuries and introduce photographs of people who were injured there. I said I was prepared to accept that evidence [to stipulate to it]; they didn't have to lead it. They nevertheless insisted on bringing it out.

One of the victims who was brought in to testify was brought in in a wheelchair, and the wheelchair was pushed by his father. He had to push the chair behind my back. He would then let this wheelchair be stationary next to the witness box, and the evidence was given from there.

After the evidence was given, the father pushed the wheelchair again behind me. Each time he went past me, I had to turn to make sure that I was not in the way. As he was going past, he then lunged and hit at Zondo, my client. Then there was commotion in the court and one of the security police, sitting in the back, said, "Kill him."

The man went out into the passage outside, and I waited for the judge to comment. Nothing happened. He then asked: "What happened?"

I waited for my colleague, the prosecutor. He was on his feet and said, "Look, I didn't really see what happened."

Then I stood up and said, "Now look, this is what happened."

But nothing was done. The judge did not say anything. The whole thing was flushed in the newspapers that evening. The next day when we started proceedings, the judge started making a statement, "Look, you understand their emotions, people must not take the law into their own hands," and that sort of thing. He added, "Justice was seemed to be done."

That really made me lose faith. I can't believe that the judge didn't see what happened because he was sitting right there. But assuming that he had not seen what happened, the thing he could have done was to ask the orderly to call the man back and ask him what happened.

Zondo was convicted and was sentenced to hang. When we went to him, after being convicted and sentenced to hang, we told him that we wanted to appeal on the question of his sentence. He said "No, don't do it, don't do it. I accept that I did wrong. They won't understand why I did it, but I did it. I feel sad about it. Please don't. You must not make an application." We ignored that, of course. We did petition the chief justice, but we were not successful. He was hanged within the shortest possible space of time—within one month to six weeks.[3]

Selby Baqwa

Selby Baqwa, although not as senior as Skweyiya, Poswa, or Langa, was nevertheless involved in some significant human rights case. Baqwa was an attorney, and then an advocate in Durban from 1978 from 1995, when he was appointed as Public Protector of South Africa, an ombudsman position. He told of his childhood in chapter 3 and of his time at the University of Fort Hare in chapter 5. Here he describes his involvement in a 1989 case in Natal.

∽ The case involved the murder of school children in the Pietermaritzburg district, where there was very serious internecine violence between the United Democratic Front, which was ANC in disguise, and the IFP [Inkatha Freedom Party]. Because the children were from an area which was perceived as IFP, people who were perceived to belong to the ANC were charged with having perpetrated that crime. They denied it. I believe they had not committed the crimes. Their alibis were the kind that made me convinced that they were victimized because they were known to be ANC.

The incident had been reported in Parliament, and a reward of a quarter million rands was announced for anybody who would give evidence that would lead to the arrest of the perpetrators of the crime.

The crime itself was quite a gruesome one—it would really make your body turn. The children who were killed were the same ages as my children at that time. They were shot when they were on their way to school in uniform. When you saw the pictures of the killings, it really said a lot to you in terms of inhumanity of man to man.

While many people questioned why I defended those people, I had no qualms about defending them because I was convinced that what they told me held together as a story. Eleven people were alleged to have been involved in the massacre, but two were caught—these clients of mine. One was thirty-nine years old and the other a youth of about eighteen years old.

We were in a trial within a trial, which is the test that a statement or a confession has to go through in order to be used for conviction. The only evidence against the youth was a confession, nothing else. So if that confession was out, he was free and if it was in, he was found guilty.

What would often happen is that policemen would take you in, beat you up, and force you to make a confession. But, invariably, an array of policemen went into court, from the constable to the highest captain or major, to deny that they forced this youth to confess. This went on in this case for about two weeks. It indeed looked as if I was knocking my head against a wall, because each and every policeman came in and said, "No, we never touched him, we never touched him, he just came out freely on his own."

In the confession that the young man was alleged to have made, he gave names of the perpetrators. He gave the types and the kinds of weaponry that had been used—AK-47s, you name it. He had stated that the perpetrators wore army uniforms and he told how they moved around and so on. The confession was so detailed that, if all that had been said by the accused, he had to be convicted. Where could he have gotten all that information if he wasn't involved?

Just about the time the trial within a trial was about to end, a young constable was called to the stand. I remember that my cross-examination went something like this:[4]

Q: Why did you arrest my client?
A: Because I had certain information.
Q: Information about what?
A: Information about the vehicle that had been used during these murders.
Q: Where had you gotten this information?
A: From an informer.
Q: When did you get the information?
A: Two days before I arrested your client.
Q: Well, if the informer knew about the vehicle that had been used, he had to have all the other information about the crime?

A: Yes, he did.

Q: And so he knew about the perpetrators, the names of the perpetrators?

A: Yes, he knew them.

Q: And he knew about the guns that had been used?

A: Yes, he knew what guns had been used.

Q: He knew the clothes and the uniforms that had been used?

A: No, he didn't know that.

Q: Okay, that's fine. You knew that this was an important case which had been reported in Parliament and that a quarter of a million was on the table for a person who came with information about this crime?

A: I knew that, yes.

Q: So from the time that you heard about this information it must have been like a long distance between you and your high authorities to go and tell them that I have got the information?

A: No, it wasn't such a burning. I didn't have such a burning desire to go to my superiors.

Q: I can't understand. You had gold in your hands. You had a quarter of a million, even if not for yourself, for the informer?

A: No. I didn't have to report it.

Q. Why not?

A: The investigating officer was with me.

Q: Are you saying that the warrant officer was there at the time?

A: Yes. He was with me, so I wasn't going to be the one to run to the superiors. He was going to do that because he was the investigating officer.

At that point in time, it was out that they had been lying. The warrant officer had already testified that he never knew anything about the crime until after my client had confessed. Their argument was how could we have known all these Zulu names and so on before my client told them about them. And even the judge, Jan Combrinck, said, " Oh, it looks like Mr. Baqwa had been knocking his head against a wall for a period of about two weeks. But at the end of two weeks, it looks like he struck oil."

He went on to say, "We are going to see whether actually it was oil that is struck or whether it is water." And that sort of sent a chill down my spine. This was a judge that had been senior counsel representing the minister of police. He was a very pleasant fellow otherwise. Sometime before this case, he had told me that he had a problem about disabusing his mind of the fact that he had represented the minister of police when he was a practicing advocate.

I just thought, What does he mean? Strike oil or strike water? But when he adjourned that day, he said he was going to recall this policeman. Of course the judge, in terms of the Criminal Procedure Act, had the right to recall to clarify points or whatever. But to cut a long story short, I knew immediately that when Jan Combrinck said he was going to recall that man, he was going to recall him so that he could undo my cross-examination. Lo and behold, that's exactly what happened!

He recalled the young constable, who then changed his story. My clients were convicted. The oldest fellow of my two clients was sentenced to death, my only death sentence during my practice as an advocate. It was quite an unpleasant experience. He escaped the noose because of the abolishment of the death sentence.

Ismail Mahomed

Clearly, no lawyer—advocate or attorney, black or white—had more impact on human rights cases than Ismail Mahomed. He described his background and early childhood in chapter 2, his education at the university of the Witwatersrand in chapter 5, and his struggles as an advocate without an office in chapter 8. Here he tells of some of the cases with which he was involved during the course of his thirty-four-year career as an advocate.

∾ One of my earliest appearances was in an inquiry under the Group Areas Act. That was a statutory procedure which had to precede the declaration of an area as a group area for a particular racial group. Blacks of Indian origin who had lived and traded in the middle of the city for three generations would be subject to a proclamation that would throw them out into a veld, twenty or twenty-five miles away, where there was no civilization.

In 1957, my very first year in practice, I appeared in such an inquiry in Springs, where they said that blacks of Indian origin must move out. It was a charade because they clearly had made up their minds that people of color could not stay in that city. I appeared without a fee, as I very often did in this sort of matter, on behalf of the Transvaal Indian Congress.

I was sick in my stomach as I heard the story of how there was this magnificent piece of veld to which these Indians could go, and how it was fair and just that they do so. There was some requirement in the act which said that, in considering the suitability of an area, you had to look into its practicability.

I said in great anger, "Mr. Chairman, you mustn't assume that the mere printing of the *Government Gazette,* in which you are going to put this proclamation, is going to ensure the obedience of my clients." It was a rash thing to have said. What it really meant was that we might disobey the law.

The man who was appearing to support the expulsion stood up and said that he was greatly ashamed to call me a colleague because he thought the first requirement of a respectable colleague was to obey the law. I had stood up and had the absolute audacity to say that we were not going to obey such a law. He reported me to the bar council. I remember that my career almost got smashed before it began. I think it was about three months after I had come to the bar.

Fortunately, the complaint was dropped because I think they thought I was a brash young man with no experience. But the proclamation of the Group Areas Act came and the Indians were thrown out.

Among the political cases in which I appeared was a treason trial in Pietermaritzburg in 1985 which involved the whole leadership of the United Democratic Front. The state attempted to prove that the United Democratic Front was consciously an agent of the ANC, deliberately seeking to promote the objectives of the ANC in South Africa. Since the ANC, it was said, was dedicated to the overthrow of the state by violence, it followed that the UDF was also planning to overthrow the state by violence and therefore its leaders were guilty of treason. It was what I called "talk talk" treason as distinct from "do do" treason. It consisted of words and documents. There were no bombs, nobody had done anything. It was based on a political theory which was advanced by the state through an expert witness.

The whole case was centered around an expert who said that he had studied Marxism and communism. He said he had done a thorough study of the documents of the United Democratic Front and he was satisfied that the front was engaged in a deliberate campaign to further the objects of the ANC to overthrow the state by violence. There was a long cross-examination of the witness to show whether his theory was sound or not.

The first fallacy in his theory was that everybody who supported the objectives of the ANC in freeing South Africa from apartheid was also furthering the objective of overthrowing the state by violence. A lot of people who agreed that there should be no apartheid did not want to overthrow the state by violence. The expert's tenuous theory was that the United Democratic Front was a creation of the ANC.

Some of the accused were members of the Transvaal Indian Congress. The state had charged that the Transvaal Indian Congress had decided in 1962 to enter into a conspiracy with the ANC to overthrow the state by violence. Now this seemed to me to be quite remarkable because, by 1962, to my knowledge, the Transvaal Indian Congress had ceased to have any activity at all. How could it have possibly been then engaged in a conspiracy to overthrow the state by violence?

On cross-examination, I took him through the history of the Transvaal Indian Congress and the Natal Indian Congress. The Natal Indian Congress had been founded by Mahatma Gandhi in 1894. He was an apostle of nonviolence. A serious decision to depart from policies of non-violence and to conspire to overthrow the state by violence had to be authorized.

The cross-examination continued:[5]

Q: Who entered into this conspiracy on behalf of the Transvaal Indian Congress to overthrow the state by violence? This was a very serious decision to make.

A: Yusuf Dadoo entered into the conspiracy on behalf of the congress.

Q: Really! What was his authority to enter into such a very important conspiracy which is in conflict with the history of the congress?
[The witness responded that Dadoo was a leader, that he had esteem in the community.]

Q: You know of no authority?

A: No.

Q: Very well, tell us more about Yusuf Dadoo.
The witness had a little notebook and flicked it to his reference to Dadoo.

Q: Read it, tell us who he was.
He began to read Dadoo's history including the fact that he was a member of the Communist Party and had been indeed chairman of the Communist Party, and it ended, as he read in his own diary, with the words: "forced to resign from the Transvaal Indian Congress in 1955 by a banning order."

Q: If he resigned in 1955 from the Transvaal Indian Congress because of a banning order, what conceivable authority could he have had in 1962 to bind them into a conspiracy of such dimensions. He was not even a member.

A: I hadn't thought about all that. I know what I read. The whole United Democratic Front was in fact initiated by the ANC. On the 8th of January 1985, Oliver Tambo, in his address to the ANC, called for the formation of the United Democratic Front and on the 22nd of January, two weeks later, Allan Boesak launched a United Democratic Front in Cape Town. It is quite clear that one is the response to the other.

Q: Really? Have you got Tambo's speech?

A: Yes, it's in *Sechaba* [the journal of the ANC]. He called for the formation for the United Democratic Front.

Q: I see Tambo's speech in *Sechaba* called for the definition of "a united democratic front"?

A: Yes.

Q: Isn't there a difference?

A: No, it is between *the* and *a.*

Q: Don't you see a difference?

A: No.

Q: A united democratic front is a concept which was well known. For example in the Nazi resistance in Europe, you form a united democratic front against Nazi advance. The United Democratic Front is an organization.

A: I see it that way.

Q: In Tambo's speech, a united democratic front occurs in ordinary letters. In your reproduction of the speech, the Democratic Front is put in capital letters. Who did that?

A: That is mine.

Q: But Tambo didn't do it?

A: No.

Q: Did you say at the end of that quotation, my emphasis or my capital letters? What does that mean?

Court: As an academic, when you quote and you put an emphasis, do you not follow the practice of saying, my emphasis or my underlining or my capitals?

Witness: No.

Court: Very well, continue (in a voice that showed me that the man was down).

There were two massive satisfactions out of that case. The first was in the initial stages of the case. In those days, if the attorney general gave a certificate that he did not consider it in the interest of the security of the state on the maintenance of law and order, then the court was precluded from giving bail. You just waited in jail, even if in the end nothing happened to you. While the trial went on for a year or two, you stayed locked up. In that case, we attacked the validity of the certificate and we succeeded and we got bail. It was a very good thing to see the leaders of the United Front get out.

The other satisfactory thing was that, after the cross-examination of the expert and the way we managed to portray the trial, every accused was acquitted. That was very satisfying, very satisfying.

There were other cases, perhaps not so serious, but also very interesting. I used to defend Professor Fatima Meer, a friend of mine who was subject to banning orders. She is a writer of very considerable distinction, a sociologist by training. She in fact wrote the first biography of Mandela, called *Higher than Hope*. She has also written the book on Gandhi's presence in South Africa, upon which a film is based.[6]

The first time I defended her was when she was subjected to a banning order which said that she was precluded from attending "a social gathering." It was an intolerable order. Nobody who tried to obey the order could ever have managed. There was just no way in life that you wouldn't act contrary to the order in some way.

One day, she was invited by some fellow academics in Durban for dinner and she went. A lot of security policemen hid in the trees around that house. They must have tapped the telephone while these dinner arrangements were made. The guests had their first course of fish, and then the main course, and as they were bringing the sweets, these people jumped out of the trees, descended upon the house and charged her with attending a social gathering in contravention of her banning order. It was a ridiculous prosecution for what was truly no more than an innocent occasion.

We attacked the order itself, saying it was meaningless. We said we didn't understand what the order meant: "a social gathering—i.e., a gathering at which persons also have social intercourse with one another." We didn't know what other things people had to do apart from having a social intercourse. We didn't know what social intercourse meant. It was great fun. Indeed, these orders had been prevalent for some years. We actually succeeded in getting the order set aside in the Supreme Court in Durban, but the decision was reversed eventually in Bloemfontein [by the appellate division].

The next time she was prosecuted, it was even greater fun. One of the terms of her order was that she was not to leave the magisterial area of Durban. One day she found herself in the Phoenix settlement in Verulam, which had been Gandhi's settlement. They followed her and found her there, about ten to twelve miles from Durban. They prosecuted her and charged her with contravening her banning order by leaving the magisterial district of Durban and being in Verulam without permission of the state officer concerned.

I did a lot of elaborate preparation on what the magisterial district of Durban consisted of. The boundaries of the magisterial district of Durban were defined in the *Gazette*, which gave this kind of description: "from the middle of the Mgeni River to where the Indian Ocean has its high-water mark." We spent a lot of time with experts to show them that the middle of the river wasn't a constant condition, that it depended on floods, that it depended on the erosion of the banks, and that the high tide and the low tide in the Indian Ocean varied terribly. We argued that that made life intolerable to her because she wouldn't know where to swim on which day, that kind of a satiric argument. I didn't know if it had much prospect of success.

Anyway, we got to court, and I had all these geologists and so forth talking about the river and floods and erosion and geology. What else could we do? The prosecutor said to me that his first witness, a land surveyor who was going to tell us about these boundaries, was not available that day. He noted that I had come all the way from Johannesburg and was probably not charging a fee. He said, "I don't want to have to bring you back, but I will have to postpone this to get the land surveyor, unless you admit that these are the boundaries."

I was just not going to admit anything. I was just incensed that there should be a prosecution and just out of sheer bloody-mindedness, I said to him, "No, I don't admit that. Call him as a witness."

He responded, "Well, you will just have to come back from Johannesburg and you are not even charging her."

I said, "That is my story."

We got back the next time and the surveyor was there. As I walked in, the prosecutor calls me and says, "Oh, I've got a problem."

"Again? What's the problem? Is he not here?"

He said: "The surveyor is here, but I have a problem. You will soon discover my problem when you cross-examine him."

I scratched my head, I couldn't imagine what the problem was. Anyway, the guy came in and he started to delineate the boundaries of the magisterial area of Durban according to the plan he had in front of him. He plotted it and plotted it and then stopped. I said to him, "And then?"

A: Those are the boundaries.
Q: But the two haven't linked yet.
A: Yes.
Q: There's a gap. That means the magisterial district of Durban can be in Cairo!

A: Yes, there is a mistake in the gazette. The gazette doesn't link it sufficiently.

They [the surveyor and the prosecutor] suddenly discovered that Durban had no magisterial boundary. [The client was acquitted.]

In one of the last cases I had before I became a judge, I was briefed to appear for a fellow called Ebrahim Ismail Ebrahim, who is now a member of Parliament. He was an ANC operative who was kidnapped in Swaziland by members of the South African state police or defense forces. They kidnapped him, and brought him across the border, detained him here, and eventually charged him with all kinds of serious offenses. I appeared in the Supreme Court and among other things, I made the point that, since he was captured illegally and without warrant by the agents of the South African state, he was not liable to prosecution in South Africa. They quoted a wealth of authority from America, from the U.K., from Israel (including Eichmann [the reference is to the abduction of the Nazi Adolf Eichmann in Argentina by Israeli agents]), saying that this is not a valid argument. The judge agreed, and gave my client twenty years' imprisonment.

On appeal, I said we were dealing with Roman-Dutch law and, as I understood it, Roman-Dutch law has a doctrine that requires that whoever comes to court must come with clean hands. I said the state has not got clean hands here. They can't ask the court to exercise jurisdiction when they are not prepared to obey the law. The court bloody upheld that argument. Ebrahim, who had been sentenced for twenty years, was out. He sued the state for unlawful prosecution and detention and was paid hundreds of thousands of rands in damages.

But there was also frustration as well. So far I have told about the satisfactory moments. In the bloody Group Areas cases, never mind how many statistics we brought up of the devastation that would be caused to the Indian community, that trade would be lost, that businesses would be ruined, the tribunal would always in the end confirm that they must go out of the area. In a famous case called *Lockhart v. The Minister of Interior*, the court upheld the Group Areas Act, saying it was a great social experiment and hardships are inevitable.

But even apart from that kind of case, I still have some very very bitter memories of some of the political prosecutions. One of the prosecutions in respect to the armed struggle was in 1978 and concerned a man called Solomon Mahlangu, in whose name a college has now been set up in Tanzania. Solomon Mahlangu was a kid, a young lad of seventeen or eighteen, at school in Pretoria when the Soweto uprising of June 16, 1976, broke out and the school was closed. He was the son of a very humble woman of very meager means.

He went to the local railway station to sell apples when the school was closed. He was approached by a man who said, "What are you doing?" The man said, "The school is closed and we have to fight for the struggle." Until that stage, this young kid hadn't even been to Johannesburg. He was in Pretoria, which is thirty-six miles away, but he had never been to Johannesburg.

The next thing he did was to climb onto a train and go off to Swaziland. From Swaziland, he was sent to Angola to training camps, to lectures on dialectical materialism and political philosophy. [Swaziland, a small independent nation bordering South Africa, was a frequent transit stop on the way to ANC camps and bases outside the country.]

Some eighteen months later, he came back with two other friends. They went into Johannesburg, into Diagonal Street, where the stock exchange is. In those days, it was also the place where the black taxi rank was. If you wanted to take a taxi to Soweto, you had to go Diagonal Street. This was his first time in Johannesburg, notwithstanding his time in Angola or wherever else. He and his two colleagues had been given some armaments, one or two hand grenades and similar instruments. They had been told, when they reached Johannesburg, Take a taxi at Diagonal Street, go to Soweto, and deposit these things with a lady. Then don't do anything at all until one day you are called to do something. That was the limit of their instructions.

They went to the taxi rank and they had their goodies in a little plastic shopping bag. In those days, the job of black municipal policemen was to harass black people about their right to be in the area. This young bewildered lad, who has come for the first time to Johannesburg, was confronted by a municipal policeman who probably wanted to check his papers. He was not a security policeman or anything like that.

He said, "What have you got in that bag?"

Solomon and his colleagues panicked and ran. The three of them ran. One ran in one direction, and to this day I don't know what happened to him. He had the apt name of Lucky. Two, Solomon Mahlangu and a chap called Mondi, started running under the freeway bridge. They ran wildly. They didn't know where they were going, They went into a warehouse. Mondi ran to the first floor, where he saw two white men having tea. Solomon was on the ground floor under a bus, hiding, a little frightened kid. The white fellows stood up from their tea, surprised to see Mondi there. Mondi looked at them, took fright, shot, and a man was killed. Solomon was found about half an hour later.

Both of them were arrested and charged with murder. Mondi's defense was that he couldn't stand trial because he had been so badly hurt that he had lost his mind. He had a big gash on his head. Three psychiatrists examined him and agreed. He went free in the sense that he became a mental patient incarcerated at a state hospital. Solomon was charged with conspiracy to murder. The shooting was just something done ad hoc by Mondi. It was not part of the plan. Mahlangu wasn't aware of it, but he was charged with murder. Solomon Mahlangu was not only convicted of murder, but no extenuating circumstances were found and he was hanged. A young boy. Hanged.

I still remember it. It was a very frustrating case for me from every point of view—political, legal. We couldn't even get leave to appeal to go to Bloemfontein. Apart from legal problems and factual problems, there was also a problem of perception of human beings. The authorities saw what they called a terrorist. I saw a young lad selling apples. It was an awfully frustrating case and every time I think about it I almost weep.

What is especially remarkable about the excerpts in this chapter is not only that black lawyers like Lewis Skweyiya, Selby Baqwa, and Ismail Mahomed represented leaders of the struggle against apartheid and that they won some meaningful victories in the courts. The importance of these individuals and the many others whose contributions were less visible and dramatic is that they in fact had significant legal careers. By all rights, under the system as it existed, they should not have been in the courtroom at all— except as defendants in criminal cases.

The knowledge and experience of these lawyers cannot help but have laid the foundation for operation of a true rule of law in a new South Africa. The lawyers saw how the system worked. On occasion, as in some of the successes reported here, they learned the value of recourse to legal rights. On other occasions, they learned the value of a judiciary untarnished by racial bias simply by observing one that was not.

The South African system had legal processes that could provide a fair trial if the judges themselves would rise above their own prejudices and pressure from the executive and legislative branches of government. The lawyers who learned such lessons are now in positions of leadership in a new order. As Dikgang Moseneke suggested in chapter 6, the need for an independent and effective judicial system cannot have been lost on them.

10

⚖

NEW JUDGES AND
OTHER OFFICIALS

THE EMERGENCE of a new South Africa in 1994 as a constitutional democracy, founded on principles of nonracism, dramatically changed the lives and careers of black lawyers. Not only were they no longer concerned about such things as whether they could have an office in the central business district, but avenues such as judicial appointment and governmental service were now opened to them.

The Constitutional Court

The new South African Constitution established a Constitutional Court. Remember that, under the old government, Parliament was supreme. Now the constitution is supreme and the Constitutional Court is the final arbiter of its meaning and application. Cases may come to it directly or through the regular judicial process.

There are eleven justices of the court. Unlike other South African judges, who have life tenure, justices of the Constitutional Court have twelve-year, nonrenewable terms.[1] Retirement at age seventy is compulsory.

The first president of the court, selected directly by President Mandela, was Arthur Chaskalson, a distinguished white advocate, dedicated opponent of apartheid and former director of the Legal Resources Centre. Four others were chosen from the ranks of sitting judges. These selections

included two blacks, Ismail Mahomed and Tholie Madala. Mahomed, who
was named deputy president of the court,[2] had been named a Supreme
Court judge in 1991. Madala had taken silk in 1993 and had been appointed
to the Supreme Court in 1994.

Six others were chosen from among practicing lawyers. The Judicial
Service Commission, which is now responsible for the selection of judges
generally, interviewed twenty-five of the nation's most prominent lawyers.
Ten names were submitted to the president, who selected six to the court.
Two blacks, Pius Langa and Yvonne Mokgoro, were part of this group.

In the short period of its existence, the court has made its presence felt
in South African society. Its most visible opinion worldwide was a unanimous decision declaring that the death penalty was unconstitutional.[3]
Eleven separate opinions were written, each one thoroughly analyzing a
question that has plagued every modern society. Perhaps more significant
for the future of South Africa, the court also twice ruled on the question of
whether the final form of the nation's constitution met the principles established in the negotiations leading to the formation of the new government.
The court first refused to certify the constitution on several grounds, and
sent the document back to the drafting body, the Constitutional Assembly,
for more work.[4] Based on the court's ruling, the constitution was redone,
resubmitted to the court, and ultimately approved by it.[5]

Through its work, the Constitutional Court has firmly established
South Africa as a nation where there is a rule of law, not only in the sense
that established rules will be followed, but that fundamental and universally
held principles of justice will be upheld. Ismail Mahomed speaks of this role
of the court at the end of chapter 13.

But, perhaps more significant for this book, the court and its personnel
have also sent other messages to the nation.

Pius Langa

Pius Langa, who told of his practice in Durban and his work with the
murdered attorneys Griffiths and Victoria Mxenge in chapter 9, tells of his
view of the composition of the court:

∾ One aspect of the court is that we are all trying to facilitate transformation of the law in South Africa. The former judiciary was very unrepre-

sentative. It was glaringly white. People could not avoid noticing that the judges were drawn from one section of the population only, which merely emphasized how abnormal a society we were and we are. I say we are, because those aspects are still present. The composition of the Constitutional Court is at least a start. It has given impetus to the widening of the range of the pool from which judges are being drawn.

This is now replicating itself in other courts. More people who are not white are being appointed. We are, in a sense, playing a leading role in showing the way that South Africa should be and what the structures of justice, in particular, should be. It is very important that normality be brought about in those structures, which are cornerstones of our democracy.

Yvonne Mokgoro

In chapter 7, Yvonne Mokgoro told of her decision to become a lawyer after being arrested on the township streets. After qualifying as an attorney, she taught law at various universities. Her appointment to the court was a prestigious career step to a much-coveted position. Yet, it is a position she holds at some significant personal sacrifice. Her husband is director general (the chief administrator) of the North-West Province, in Mafikeng, some three hours drive from Johannesburg, where the Constitutional Court sits. The commuter marriage is a difficult challenge for people in visible, high-pressure jobs.

By the time I was told that I had been selected by the president, I don't think I looked at it as a matter of choice. I saw it as a duty that I had to carry out as a citizen of this country. I mean, we are talking about the need for change. We've always been involved in the struggle, and we've always advocated for change in all these various areas of South African life. When my husband and I talk about these things, we say, who do we expect should do these things if not us? We are the generation who will have to answer tomorrow if things have not been done. When I was faced with this reality at the last stage of the appointment, it was almost, in a positive sense, like a national call-up.

I didn't see it as a career move. The fact that it is a career move is just incidental. My idea was that this is a national duty that I have to undertake. I am going to set aside seven years of my life, I thought, to serve my country at this level. After seven years, I will know that I have done my duty. Then somebody else can move in and do the same.

Service, such as that of Yvonne Mokgoro, is important as an example to others who, for the first time, have opportunities in business and government far beyond anything available to them in the past. The actions of Justice Mokgoro and some other black lawyers have served to illustrate that a sense of duty ought to accompany new opportunity.

The Land Claims Court

Another innovation of the new South Africa was the creation of a Land Claims Court. Beginning especially in 1913 with an act limiting black land ownership, South African history is rife with instances where government edicts have deprived blacks of their rights in land. Not surprisingly, a high priority of the new government is the restoration of those rights. The Commission on Restitution of Land Rights, to which claimants must submit their claims, has been established. The Land Claims Court was created to approve settlements made by the commission and to adjudicate controversies that result from its decisions.

The decisions of the commission and the court are not easy ones. More than eighty years have passed since some of the land was originally taken. In many instances, the ownership of the land has changed hands many times. Where original rights cannot be restored, a right to alternative land can be offered. Where no land is available, financial compensation can be given.

Three out of the five judges of the Land Court are black: its president, Fikile Bam; Justice Moloto; and the more recently appointed Shehnaz Meer.

Bam, who described his ten-year imprisonment on Robben Island in chapter 7, had practiced as an attorney and advocate in several places in the country. Before his appointment to the court in 1995, he had been a member of a prestigious and virtually all-white law firm, Deneys Reitz.

Justice Moloto

Another black judge of the Land Court, Justice Moloto described his work with Steve Biko's organizations in chapter 7. After his banishment to

Bophuthatswana, Moloto practiced as an attorney in Durban before becoming director of the Black Lawyers Association–Legal Education Centre in 1987. He left the center in 1993 to become a contracts manager at Eskom, South Africa's electric utility.

He tells about the issues before the court with some trepidation. The court will have to sort out problems arising from the creation of the black homelands and the shift of communities from place to place in that process. It will also have to deal with urban areas where blacks were moved from communities such as Sophiatown in Johannesburg and District Six in Cape Town to make way for white areas. There were also instances of individuals removed from homes or farms if, as Moloto says, "in the wisdom of the government, you were in a place where you were not supposed to be." Whites were sometimes moved in this same process, but almost invariably with full compensation.

One of the issues the court must consider is obvious—is it feasible to restore the land or is compensation the only possible remedy under the circumstances? But there are other issues, including the reasonable use of the land. Farm or residential land may have since been developed as industrial property.

Moloto ponders the role that his political philosophy, heavily steeped in the black-consciousness teachings of Steve Biko, will play in his new judicial role:

> I do not want to tie in my political philosophy with my role on the court. I am not quite sure whether a political end can be served through the judiciary. I don't come to the bench with that in mind. I come to the bench resolved to administer justice the best way I can within my capabilities.
>
> However, in the majority of cases it is known that people were removed in pursuit of discriminatory legislation. It may be that a great majority of cases will have to be adjudged on the basis that the rights must be restored to the people.
>
> I want to believe that when that does take place, it will begin to empower a greater number of black people to engage in economic activity. It will enable them to be able to take their rightful place in the community as contributors to the economy of the country. They will be people who no longer lead a subsistence life, but who are in commercial and

industrial activities and are seen as major players in the life of the South African community. I think that a case can be made for such restoration.

There are whole tracts of land that have been taken away that people were using as agricultural land. People can again contribute in that area. There are lands which were taken where people had freehold title and could or would have developed those lands, either commercially or industrially, and were not able to do so because they were taken. The very fact of security of tenure is an important psychological boost for anyone wanting to go into business. Because people are now going to get title to their land and they know that that title is secure, they will be prepared to invest in the land. Such investment has not been possible since the removals.

The apartheid government shifted people into matchbox homes in townships and put people on government land. Because you knew you were not the owner, you just didn't do anything to improve the land. But with secure tenure, I think there is going to be a whole psychological change in the minds of black people, who will now want to invest in their land. In that way they are going to be major players in the community.

Some Other Judges

In the later days of apartheid, there were attempts by the government to persuade blacks to become judges of what was then the Supreme Court of South Africa,[6] the trial and appellate court with jurisdiction over more significant cases. Those blacks approached refused the appointment, expressing unwillingness to enforce the nation's existing racist laws. Ismail Mahomed declined the opportunity until 1991, after Nelson Mandela had been released and the ANC unbanned, when he felt the country was moving sufficiently in the right direction that he was willing to be in a position to enforce its laws.

The issue has now changed from one of persuading blacks to go on the bench to one of finding enough qualified blacks to fill available judgeships. The number of blacks qualified for judicial positions and high government posts is small. The impact of all the apartheid laws, particularly Bantu education, is still felt and will be felt for at least another generation.

Prior to the end of apartheid, no one could be appointed as a judge of the Supreme Court who was not a senior counsel. There are only a few black senior counsel. The rule has had to be changed so that more blacks would be eligible for a judicial appointment. Paralleling the experience in the United States, such appointments sometimes do not sit well with lawyers with more experience and seniority. In South Africa, as in the United States, black lawyers becoming judges often face the allegations, subtle or overt, that they lack real qualifications.

Furthermore, everything about the new positions occupied by these black lawyers is new to them—from the appointment process to the every-day conduct of their affairs. Educational deprivations and an absence of role models make difficult, demanding jobs even more difficult and demanding. Moreover, although racism is officially gone, lingering attitudes continue.

The experiences of two of the new black judges illustrate the point.

Mahomed Navsa

In chapter 2, Mahomed Navsa described the reclassification of his family from Indian to Coloured. He became a well-respected advocate on the staff of the Legal Resources Centre, heading the LRC's new constitutional law unit before his appointment to the bench in 1995. Navsa was one black lawyer who would have qualified even under the old rules, having been named senior counsel before his appointment to the bench. However, at age thirty-seven, he was far younger than the typical South African judicial appointee.

His initial appointment to the bench was as an acting judge. He describes his reaction:

> ∞ I was petrified. My commercial exposure was absolutely none. I'd be forced to deal with concepts I last read at law school, if then. I was exposed to a lot of pressure from black practitioners, senior practitioners, young people who urged me to do it.
>
> I came to the Supreme Court in Johannesburg, which is the busiest court in the country. It deals with a great amount of commercial litigation. I came in and I literally learned on the job. My second week here I was faced with a patents case. I was faced with an interpretation of the section of the act relating to third-party claims. We had never done any of that at the LRC. At least some of my black colleagues had had exposure to

family law and to criminal law. I had done a limited amount of criminal law related to the kinds of cases that the LRC did. But my field of expertise was human rights. So in the second week, when I was faced with patents and third-party law, I literally had to learn on the job and learn very fast.

There were a few judges here who were very helpful. One judge was very particularly helpful, not so much in terms of suggesting how I do things, but just in helping me when I was unsure about the practice in particular courts. Even though I might have had the book knowledge and I had read up enough about it, he would tell me how it really worked in court. I am indebted to him because it made that transition that much easier. I was incredibly frantic for the first six months. I would work until two every morning just to make sure. I also knew that there would be scrutiny. One must accept that there would be.

I knew that I was a standard bearer and that this was a pioneering job. There was incredible pressure. I was aware of the scrutiny. We mustn't kid ourselves. We were all in a new era in which the transformation of the judiciary and structures in society were in the forefront of public debate. The appointment of black judges, affirmative action, competency, dropping of standards, you name it, all went into the debates that were going on. I was acutely aware of that.

My appointment became permanent on 1 July 1995. I am less frantic now.

Lucy Mailula

Lucy Mailula told of her education in the state schools under Bantu education in chapter 4. She practiced as an advocate in Johannesburg before being named the first black woman judge of the Supreme Court in 1995. She was thirty-six years old and had not yet reached the status of senior counsel.

∞ It's very difficult to tell whether white lawyers and litigants react differently to me as a black woman. We have this etiquette in court, so I haven't really sensed any difference. However, I did receive a letter from a person who claimed to be a concerned citizen a few months ago. The man wrote that he was a black man and gave a post box. He said he had his own business but he didn't give a telephone number. He gave no physical address, nowhere where he could be contacted, except the post box. He wrote to say that he was a concerned citizen who was asked to come and testify in a criminal matter. He came to the Supreme Court and didn't know where to go. Security sent him off to the attorney general's office and he went to that floor, which is the same building as the Supreme Court. He got to the floor and was looking around trying to get someone to help him out. In one of the offices, he overheard this woman (the name on the door was Advocate So-and-so). She was on the phone and he overheard her talking to someone, saying words to the effect that "Ag, this does not matter. Sy is maar net 'n fucking kaffir meisie. (In English: "She's just a fucking kaffir maid.") So, if she can be a judge, I can be one too."

I got this letter and I looked at it and I said to myself, "Is it worth taking note of or does it belong to the rubbish bin?" I was concerned but after awhile I dismissed it as nonsensical. It was a typed letter. He gave a post box. A person who has his own business should have a telephone where you can contact him. But he did give the name of the advocate and I think I know the lady. I have never really had any dealings with her. She had never appeared in my court or anything.

Apparently this letter was also sent to the minister of justice, Dullah Omar's, office. So a few weeks ago, I got a call from the state attorney to say that the minister got this letter and he is concerned. He wants this to be investigated. I say, Well, then it means it is serious. I had dismissed it as somebody who was trying to see what my reaction was going to be and I just thought I shouldn't take it seriously. So the person from the minister's office says she was going to look into it. I told her to let me know what she found. She came back and said, That post box is nonexistent, maybe you were right to be less concerned with it.

The woman advocate told the state attorney that she is very upset. She says she has never uttered those words; she was never involved in that type of a conversation. She has since appeared in my court and has handled herself very professionally.

Certainly, there are still some people who believe that positions such as mine belong to white people. We are supposed to go and work on the farm or in the kitchen. But I would be disappointed if the author of this letter was someone who is an advocate, because then it means that they wanted to get this person in trouble and were using me. The investigation is at an end now. What concerns me, though, is the fact that the letter was probably written by an educated and sophisticated person. There are people who have failed to embrace the change in South Africa and the dream for a democratic, nonracial and nonsexist society.

Some Other Officials

Other black lawyers took positions in the government. Most prominently, Dullah Omar, whose history is set out in chapter 12, became minister of justice. Mathews Phosa, Phineas Mojapelo's law partner, became premier of the North-West Province. Others whose stories appear in this book who were appointed to government posts were Selby Baqwa and Pansy Tlakula.

Selby Baqwa

Baqwa practiced as an attorney and advocate in Durban for almost twenty years. In chapter 9, he described his defense of persons charged with treason. In 1995 he was named public protector of South Africa. The position, a new one under the constitution, is equivalent to that of a national ombudsman.

The appointment process was not an easy one for him. He needed the approval of 75 percent of Parliament. Previously affiliated with the ANC, which has 62 percent of the seats, Baqwa had opposition not only from the Nationalists, who control 20 percent, but initially also from the Inkatha Freedom Party. Inkatha was concerned about Baqwa's involvement in a task force investigating violence between the ANC and Inkatha in the province of KwaZulu-Natal. Ultimately, Inkatha changed its position and with the support of that party and the ANC, he squeaked by with 75.9 percent of the vote.

∞ I hope I can do important things as public protector. Here, the person in the street is usually thoroughly intimidated by the size of government bureaucracy, by the expertise that is available to government bureaucracy and the intricacies that present themselves. You have a situation when, for example, an illiterate person, who is indigent and from a rural area, is faced with a recalcitrant official who won't grant his pension. He will tell him that his forms are lost and so on and he wants a bottle of liquor as a bribe. This office is available for that kind of person. It is available to the people out there without any charge, without any bureaucracy or any procedures around it. The complainant may phone this office or call in person at the office.

Access to justice is far from adequate in this country. You have access to justice here on a short fuse for a person who has nothing. If you rely on Legal Aid [government-supported fees paid to lawyers for services rendered to persons who otherwise could not afford a lawyer], you have problems with a government which has no money, which means that getting such aid is not always certain. In this office, you can achieve results over the counter which could have cost the complainant thousands and thousands of rand and months and months of waiting in a court. When a person is not paid his pension comes here, and I call the official concerned, I inquire of him why he is not paying this person and I prove to him that his decision is incorrect where such is the case. Over the table I am able to get redress.

There was a case involving a small company owned by an Indian person in Cape Town which was being disadvantaged by a company which had had a contract for supplying coal to government over the years. This big company had pushed out the smaller company. If this small company went to court, it wouldn't pay less than a million rand. Instead they chose to lodge a complaint with my office. I called the chief director from the State Tender Board to my office. We discussed the problem. He agreed with my views, which were in favor of the complainant. The complainant was about to go out of business. The case was solved within a matter of weeks. You get those small pleasures where, over the counter, you just talk it over, logically substantiate your recommendation, and you achieve results.

But at another level, the government also established this office to promote government efficiency. We have had a problem with government efficiency in Africa, not only in South Africa. I am not so ambitious that I imagine that I am going to clean up government all over Africa. But in a sense, it is important to send a message to the present government officials

that, "Guys, previous governments in Africa and elsewhere have gone
down because of government inefficiency and not observing the proper
procedures and regulations. Let's not do it." They should know that my
office is one of the mechanisms to promote efficiency. It is my considered
opinion that efficiency is a sine qua non to an effective democratic dispensation. I think that if I can promote efficiency, we will not have that
recurrent dismal situation coming down to South Africa where people can
say, "Oh, yes. Another black government, what would you have
expected?" What did we fight for? Did we just want to take over the reins
of government and then go down the drain? No, you would like to see
sustainable development benefiting everybody in the country.

Pansy Tlakula

In chapter 5, Pansy Tlakula described her experience at the University
of the Witwatersrand. After obtaining her degree she became a law teacher
at the black University of Bophuthatswana. She also worked as director of
the Black Lawyers Association–Legal Education Centre in 1994. In 1995
she was appointed to the newly formed Human Rights Commission.

    ✑ The Human Rights Commission is so new it is difficult to talk about.
We don't even have proper premises. We operate from suitcases and the
boots of our cars. We are still talking about the structure. The general
charge of the commission is to look at all human rights violations. The act
[setting up the commission] talks about promotion and protection of
human rights in the country, creating a culture of human rights. We will
investigate human rights violations and try to settle them. If necessary, we
will take them to court. We also will advise government on what measures
to take in an attempt to promote human rights and monitor legislation at
all levels to see to that legislation does not contravene the constitution. So
the commission has wide powers. The commission is to have eleven members, but at the moment we are ten because one of us has also been
appointed to the Truth and Reconciliation Commission—Chris de Jager,
who represents the Afrikaner right wing. Apparently he is one of the few
reasonable right-wingers.

    There are three white people and the rest are black. Six are women, which is good. Four are lawyers. Helen Suzman, at age seventy-five, is the oldest member.

The appointments were strange in terms of political ideology because almost every political party is thought to be represented. In some instances they label people what they are not. Like me. They think that I represent black consciousness, even if I am ANC. There is Barney Pityana, who is the chairperson, who people think represents the ANC, when he is nonaligned. Before he went into exile he was black consciousness, because he became president of SASO after Steve Biko.

Ismael Semenya

In addition to service in governmental positions, some black lawyers have taken positions in nongovernmental organizations that have considerable clout with the new government. Ismael Semenya told of his activist student days at the University of the North in chapter 5. At the time of this interview, Semenya was director of the Black Lawyers Association–Legal Education Centre,[7] an organization whose views are now frequently sought by people in the government, especially the Department of Justice.

☞ It seems to me that part of the reason we are not seeing transition as fast we would want to see it is the need to inform these politicians on what legally has to be in place before certain things happen. For example, the Department of Justice has made various black appointments to the state attorney's offices. That decision has been taken to court and challenged as improper affirmative action. I have discussed the situation with the minister of justice. Obviously, he would want to make affirmative action appointments consistent with the law. It seems to me that the Legal Education Centre should be able to advise government on how to do these things to be consistent with the law.

We should be able to liberalize access to law, a difficult area for black practitioners. The BLA is now sitting with more than a hundred African law graduates who can't find placement in articles or in pupillage or even in industry. This is a vital human resource that needs to be harnessed to empower democracy.

The Justice Department is also seeking some guidance on how to create a human rights culture. Somebody needs to go and draw up programs that are going to help them do this. The Ministry of Safety and Security is battling with a program to legitimatize the police force. Members of the police are still not quite in tune with the human rights culture that this country wants to engender. From the BLA desk, I would hope to be able to design manuals that are going to change the standing orders, to design programs for the police on how they should behave in investigations—to change the culture of assaulting the culprit, letting him confess, and then taking him to court.

We have just reached a very critical area in the transformation of our country and if we don't try and bring the little contribution we can, history won't forgive us.

The situation of the growing number of black lawyers in private practice, to which Semenya refers, is the subject of the next chapter.

11

LAW PRACTICE IN THE
NEW SOUTH AFRICA

FOR THOSE lawyers who continue, at least for the time being, in private practice, the world of opportunity has theoretically opened to them. All the large white-dominated law firms now have at least a token black presence. Large corporations look for the opportunities to hire black lawyers—although the extent of their effort is the subject of debate, especially among black lawyers.

Yet most black lawyers still find themselves in the same kind of practices they had before there was a new constitution and Nelson Mandela became president of the Republic of South Africa. Most are still doing routine criminal and motor vehicle cases, with some domestic work thrown into the mix. Some are attempting to branch out into other fields, including corporate work. But progress is slow. In this chapter, some black attorneys and advocates talk about their current practices.

George Maluleke

George Maluleke described beginning his practice with a white practitioner in chapter 8. Success both in business and in his law practice has now made Maluleke one of the more successful black attorneys in the Johannesburg area.

∽ At the time my first firm broke up, around 1981, we didn't have much personal injury work. We did a lot more criminal work, a lot more general work, divorces, all sorts of things. Personal injury work by its very nature is very difficult work to build up if you are a young, up-and-coming attorney because it is very capital intensive. You've got to put in a lot of money. In South Africa, because of strict compliance with British ethical principles, we don't have a contingent fee system. But the only way you can do personal injury claims is by going on some contingency method because less than one or two percent of the people who are involved in car accidents can really afford to pay the full fee to take the matter up to Supreme Court level. So invariably, when you do that work, you have to finance it yourself.

To prove your claim, you've got to do the investigations and pay investigators to prove the merits—to prove the fault. Then you've got to pay medical doctors to establish the amount of damages. You would find that an average matter would cost you twenty to thirty thousand rand by the time it came to court or by the time you settle the matter. And this is money which you have paid by the time by the time you get your fees. It is not hard to imagine that if you have two hundred cases of that nature, you would have, at any one time, up to R700,000 or R800,000 paid into your cases. You've got to get it from somewhere. An overdraft from the bank would be directly related to the collateral you can put up. So it is very costly and things do go wrong. You could completely misjudge a matter and something comes up and you still realize that you shouldn't have gone that way. It happens very often.

But after 1984 or 1985, I think, personal injury work began to pick up. Since the mid-eighties, I have had a great amount of motor vehicle kinds of work. As of now, my firm has four lawyers, three partners. We have essentially a commercial practice. Two of us do personal injury work. We are in the process of trying to recruit one or two other lawyers. We are negotiating with them now. All of the lawyers are black. Ninety-nine percent of our clients are black.

In my work as an attorney I will have the need to employ counsel. We don't have enough black advocates. There are risks involved in contingency matters. You've put a lot of money in a case and you are disinclined to want to gamble with an advocate. What you do quite often is to team a black advocate with some senior white advocate in a complex matter. The only way that advocates learn well is when they are able to do work with a senior. I think that is very, very important. I do employ some black advocates regularly, including Ish Semenya and Vincent Maleka.

Phineas Mojapelo

Phineas Mojapelo, the former herd boy who described his clerkship with a white law firm in chapter 8, has continued to practice law in the small northern city of Nelspruit. He and his firm did a great deal of political work until near of the end of the apartheid era.

   ✑ In 1988 or 1989, when the funding for political cases began to dry up, we had started to emphasize other areas of work. I now do a mixed set of personal injury work and commercial work. Personal injury work does not know any race and in fact it is more black than anything. It accounts for the greater portion of my work. I do mainly plaintiffs' work. Of late, a few defendant's instructions trickle in, but that's not even 10 percent of my work. In commercial work, throughout the eighties and the beginning of the nineties, I represented black clients. But after the adoption of the new constitution, some big commercial corporations developed a practice of now and then sending instructions to black attorneys.

Now there is also some exciting development work. I was telling my friend George Maluleke the other day that I was given instructions to look into the development of an airport in the Hazyview area [near Nelspruit].

We are at a stage where we are now dealing with the whole land issue. That's exciting work and bit by bit there are other types of commercial work that are coming up. There is a movement of big corporate clients trying to look for black people to do business with. Those kinds of agreements are getting to be quite a common practice.

Timothy Bruinders

Timothy Bruinders is a successful young advocate in Johannesburg. In chapters 3 and 4, he told of his background and education as a Coloured person, and he described his early brushes with violence in the apartheid era in chapter 9.

∽ With Mandela's release and with the beginning transformation and the constitutional negotiations, there was less and less human rights work. I did a lot more labor work. The unions were paying fees, which in early years they obtained from foreign sources. Increasingly, unions are having to look for funding to themselves and their own membership. In the transition period, the unions were still able to tap foreign funding and so I was paid money that came to the unions from overseas. That kind of work you couldn't do at commercial rates; it was always at a much lower rate. You worked at a much lower rate than your opponents who were acting for management.

I act for both black and white clients. I think if I take the last year, I probably act for more black clients than I do for whites. But I do act for some white clients, including companies, mining companies. There has been a move by some of the bigger white firms to brief black counsel as part of, I suppose, affirmative action.

I don't find any discrimination against me by black African lawyers because I am not black African but rather "Coloured," under the former classification. Personally, in fact, I am quite insensitive on that level. It is not something that I think about too much. There are not many Coloured attorneys in Johannesburg, only a few. There are far more African attorneys. I don't get briefed by Coloured attorneys. There are just so few that they are insignificant. I get briefed by very few African attorneys. In fact there are African attorneys who, when they meet me, are quite surprised because my surname is not African and doesn't suggest that I am black. They often think it is an Afrikaans surname. So when they see me, they say, We always thought you were white. We didn't know you were actually black. But they do think of me as black. I know one or two black attorneys prefer briefing African advocates and feel more comfortable doing so. That happens and I am not part of any campaign to prevent that. There are some of my colleagues who happen to be Coloured and who are a lot more sensitive than I am. They certainly seem to feel it a lot more and complain about it.

Some Women Lawyers

The new South African Constitution guarantees equal treatment for women as well as people of all races. Affirmative action programs that benefit both blacks and women are underway. Such developments are beginning to make a difference for women lawyers, but the battle for gender equality is far from over. Attitudes among both blacks and whites must change. They will do so slowly. Problems such as the predominant role that women play both in childbearing and childrearing will present the same difficulties in South Africa as they do throughout the Western world.

Following are some thoughts from four women lawyers. Two are advocates, Kgomotso Moroka and Nona Goso. The other two are attorneys, Christine Qunta and Dolly Mokgatle. Some of the problems that they have experienced are those that any young lawyer, especially a young black lawyer, was likely to have faced. Other problems most certainly resulted from their gender.

Kgomotso Moroka

Kgomotso Moroka, after doing her articles at a white law firm, Bowman Gilfillan (chap. 8), became a magistrate in Bophuthatswana. She then moved to Johannesburg to become an advocate.

∞ I did my pupillage in 1989 and then opened my own chambers. And I starved for a few years! It was very difficult, those first years were very difficult. I remember just saying to my father, "Maybe I should just give it up because I think the bar is a very conservative place." I think lawyers are very conservative.

I think being female was very difficult. Some of my male colleagues were very supportive but others were not. We live in a very sexist society. We give a woman work and she owes you a favor, and some of the favors include payment in kind, if you get what I mean. It was very difficult to say, "Treat me like you treat the other advocates that you brief. Why should I be different? Why should I go to bed with you? You don't ask them to go to bed with you."

Those were difficult times, and there were times when I just sat in my room and I cried. But then I eventually said, "They are not going to get me down. I am going to make it." And I stuck it out. The lawyers who were looking for favors from me were black. Of course they were black. I never get work from white lawyers. Occasionally somebody will ask me to draft a plea or whatever, but I have never gotten a trial brief from a white firm. I meet my old colleagues from Bowman and they say, "We must brief you." That's about it.

Being black and female has made me realize my strengths and my limitations. It gave me an ability to concentrate on all that is positive about me, and all that is positive about human beings, and to accept that we are all fallible. I can't be too critical about other human beings because they are products of their own societal upbringing. When you talk about sexism, you must really be sure that society accepts blame for it. You must accept that society doesn't put up a fight on behalf of women to say, this is unacceptable. You complain, and nobody takes you seriously. This just taught me to fight my own battles my own way and say, I will succeed.

If the white man couldn't break us, the black male is going to do it. For all the other women lawyers coming behind, they need role models. They need to have women lawyers there. A lot of women going to the bar back then left and went to do other things. I think it is important that we have women at the bar so that other women can get the courage so that one day we will have women judges and that kind of thing. There is only one woman judge in the Supreme Court [Lucy Mailula; see chap. 10]. Yvonne Mokgoro is in the Constitutional Court; she never practiced law. How many black women are at the bar? The number is minimal. At the Jo'burg bar there are only the two of us. Others have come and gone. There is only one at the Pretoria bar.

Since she made these remarks, Moroka's practice has improved. She has served on important government commissions, including the Judicial Service Commission, which is responsible for the selection of judges. She was also one of two advocates representing President Nelson Mandela in his divorce case.

Nona Goso

Nona Goso taught at the University of the Transkei and practiced as an advocate in Umtata, the capital of that former homeland. She moved to Cape Town in 1994, where she opened chambers as an advocate.

  I don't have proper access to instruction from attorneys in my practice. There are very few black attorneys. I do get some work from them, but even then their practice is not very strong. Legal work is in white hands. So access to work when you are a black advocate in Cape Town is very difficult. People still believe in taking work to the white firms. But I have tried to turn that round. I work with the community a lot now. I am in the Woman's Coalition. I am in the civic organizations, residence associations. People are gaining confidence in me and they come directly to me for work. And I say to them, Go to so-and-so as your attorney, and I choose an attorney who will give me work. White attorneys are now beginning to give me work, but they are very cautious about it.

I had to fight to defend the Constitutional Assembly in the Industrial Court. [The Constitutional Assembly was in essence the Parliament of South Africa. Under the interim constitution, from 1994 to 1996, it was charged with the duty of drafting a new constitution.] The case related to whether the employees of the Constitutional Assembly are in the same position as the employees of Parliament in matters being taken to the Industrial Court. Someone from the Constitutional Assembly called me and said they were sending instructions to the state attorney to give me this brief. The case was to be argued on a Wednesday.

On the Friday before, I decided to call the state attorney to make sure that I got my brief over the weekend. I had other matters on Monday and Tuesday and I would have to prepare for Wednesday. At the state attorney's office, they said, firstly, the client is not supposed to speak to you directly. [Under South Africa's divided bar system, clients are supposed to contact attorneys, who in turn may employ advocates for courtroom work.]

I said, "I don't accept that. These are some of the rules that impede access and we need access to work. If the client prefers you, the client can always choose counsel. He can call you and find out if you are available on the particular date."

Secondly, they argued, You are not sufficiently senior. We have to look at more senior members of the Cape Bar to handle this sort of matter.

I said, "Well, if you are talking about my efficiency to handle the work, you can never know my efficiency if you don't give me work. I do hope that by saying what you are saying that you are not again trying to impede my access to work. Work should now be distributed equally amongst all lawyers from different persuasions."

The senior man at the state attorney's said to me, "I am meeting the minister of justice [Dullah Omar] this afternoon and I am going to raise this matter with him."

I said, "Please invite me to come along as well and present my own case."

And this man said, "I will come back to you."

He came back to me and said, "We will give this to Mr. Swart [a white advocate]. You will be junior to Mr. Swart; you both have ten years' experience."

So I said, "Fine, but please send me my brief."

I worked on the brief. Advocate Swart then called me to say, would we meet on Monday for a pre-trial conference. When I got there, they didn't have the slightest idea of the applicable laws. I had done my work and I said to them, go and read them. We can only discuss this matter when you have read those laws. I suggested that they take a point *in limine* [in this context, a legal motion to determine whether a court has jurisdiction to hear a particular matter]. The others said the point wouldn't work, but the reason was that they hadn't looked at the applicable laws. The meeting was rescheduled for the next day.

When we finally met the next day, they agreed with my argument. The point in limine was taken successfully.

I suppose my work on that matter has resulted in me now being instructed by the Constitutional Assembly to argue the validity of the new constitution.

Goso was part of a team of lawyers arguing on behalf of the government before the Constitutional Court that the final constitution met the constitutional principles set forth as guidelines. Among Goso's other cases was the representation of the young men charged and eventually convicted of the murder of an American student who had been in South Africa to help register blacks for the 1994 elections. She was junior to Justice Poswa in that case.

Christine Qunta

Christine Qunta described her exile in chapter 8. On her return to South Africa in 1993, she first worked in the legal department of a large insurance company, Sanlam. Her frustrations in getting that firm to give her the kind of work she felt she was able to undertake resulted both in her leaving to set up her own firm and in her writing of a book, *Who's Afraid of Affirmative Action.* She specializes in corporate work.

∽ I had no illusions when I opened my practice. South Africa is a place where economic power is still in the hands of whites. If you go into the areas of criminal law, where most black attorneys would go by default, I don't think you would have much problem. You would get lots and lots of work because the vast majority of people brought before the criminal courts are black. Of course, there is not as much money. If you are coming into the corporate law area, you are really asking for trouble.

For instance, I am the first African person to open in the center of Cape Town, in the central business district. People were previously not allowed to open in town because of the Group Areas Act. Even after the act came to an end, I suppose people just got used to being in the black areas. I decided if I am going to do corporate work, my clients are here, the big and small business, black and white. I don't really care what color my clients are. But it is difficult.

Most of my friends and colleagues say that I am brave, but I think maybe I am a bit foolish. One guy, a white guy, from the biggest white commercial firm in Cape Town, said to me, "Do you have foundation clients?"

I said, "Foundation clients?"

"Yes, clients to go with you."

I said, "No."

He said, "You want to open a practice and you don't have foundation clients?"

And he looked at me really incredulously, and I said, "No, I will just get them as I go along."

He just shook his head and he said to me, "I must tell you, you have a lot of guts."

I responded, "I have to have guts, because where will I get clients?"

I am a conveyancer. Here, unlike the States and Australia, you have to have a special exam to do conveyancing work. Not many attorneys are conveyancers. Conveyancing is quick money, that's for sure. But until a few months ago I was not even on the panel of attorneys listed for conveyances at the bank where I have my business account and my trust account. They turned me down when I sent them a letter of introduction in Cape Town. I was finally put on the panel by the Johannesburg office in January, but it is now the 22nd of May and they have not written to the Cape Town regional office to say, put her on the panel. They just keep on saying they are going to do it. I don't believe it is negligence. In South Africa, the standards are appalling, but I don't think here it is negligence. I believe it is deliberate stalling. I have now written to the chairman of the bank and told him what is happening. I rang yesterday to ask whether the chairman had gotten my note. They said it was on his desk, he has just come back from overseas. So I will see what to do, but I have just decided to take them on, and I will take them head on. I don't think they should be allowed to get away with the racism. If they get business from me, they must assist me.

Although I act now mostly for black businesses, I have got a few white clients. Sanlam is a client of mine. I have very good relations with them, ironically. I didn't sort of have a big bust and leave. I have good relations with at least two people there.

I act for a group of 103 fishing companies, West Coast Rock Lobster. They were referred to me by a big white firm here in Cape Town, Sonnenberg, Hoffman, and Galombik. They are the biggest commercial firm in Cape Town. I have had a good relationship with them because I initiated a program, as the Black Lawyers Association's Western Cape chairperson, where they give commercial classes to black attorneys in Cape Town.

Because of my dealings with that firm, when they have had conflicts of interest, they have referred people to me. It is quite interesting, because the people they referred were very conservative Afrikaner people, and they wanted the Sonnenberg firm to act for them because they are a big firm. They said, we cannot act for you because there is a conflict. They said, okay, we will go to Jo'burg and we will get a big firm in Jo'burg. So this one guy said to them, "Look, I don't whether you'll like this, but I am going to refer you to a lady who has got a small firm. She is a one-person practice, but try her."

And the lawyer rang me up to say, "Look, Christine, I have referred them to you. I don't know if they will come, but let's keep our fingers crossed."

It took three weeks; the lawyer twice rang to ask if they had contacted me. There must have been a lot of agonizing but finally they did come to me and, you know, they stayed with me. The man said to me when he first rang me up, he said: "Look, so-and-so referred us to you, can we come in and look you over?" That's what he said; those were his exact words!

So I said, fine, come and see my office. It's not a little hovel in Kayelitsha [a black township near Cape Town] or somewhere.

The next day when he came in, I said, "Now, are you satisfied?"

He said, "More than satisfied."

I now act for them. They are quite happy with me, and I get along with them. I think in the end, even though there is initial resistance because of race and being female, once they give you the work and they get to know you and you deliver, that is the important thing. If you do the work they will come back to you and those things sort of fall away. And I am hoping that that eventually will be the case. So I have a few white clients but, predominantly now, I have black businessmen.

I have a business plan for the next three years that would really get into doing big work. We would like to get into work involving restructuring of state assets. The government is going to privatize, or restructure state assets worth, I think, about eight billion rand. It is a major thing. I have linked up with other firms, one in Pretoria, one in Umtata. I am the tenderer of the proposal. We have also linked up with an American institute in Washington, D.C., to get expertise for restructuring, to involve people who have done restructuring elsewhere. I try and do quite a few training workshops just to upgrade my skills. I did a course in restructuring in Rome in 1994, and that was very useful.

So we are going for the big things. We are not going to say, okay, I am small, therefore I shouldn't tender for this. We will link up with other black firms. I don't believe in saying, I can't do that. If I don't have all the skills, I will go out and get the skills to supplement mine. I think that as black attorneys we should have that sort of positive ambition.

Since giving this interview, Ms. Qunta reports that her practice has prospered. Most of her corporate clients are businesses owned and managed by blacks. In addition to her Cape Town office, she plans to open an office in Johannesburg in 1999.

CHAPTER 11

Dolly Mokgatle

Dolly Mokgatle described her period of articles at a large white law firm in chapter 8. She joined the corporate department of Eskom, South Africa's giant electric utility, after working as an attorney in law firms, at the Centre for Applied Legal Studies at the University of the Witwatersrand, and on the staff of the Black Lawyers Association–Legal Education Centre. Mokgatle is a physically small person. With a smile, she describes herself as subject to three prejudices: she's black, she's a woman, and she's short!

∞ I went to Eskom in 1991. I was recruited for the job. Quite frankly, I hardly knew about Eskom. Eskom retains employment agencies. They instructed the employment agency to approach organizations such as the BLA to see if there were people who might want to apply for posts in Eskom.

I started as a junior legal advisor. I became the senior legal advisor within a period of ten months and I was promoted to chief legal advisor after two years. In November 1994, I was promoted to corporate legal consultant, and in July 1995, I was promoted to senior general manager in the Growth and Development Group, a position which I hold today. The legal department reports to me. Because of some internal circumstances, I am also acting legal manager and acting public affairs manager. I am also the chairperson of the Medical Aid Management Committee. I have a very tight schedule.

Beginning in 1992, Mokgatle began to receive numerous awards within the company based on the excellence of her work. In May 1995 she received the Chairman's Award, the company's highest accolade.

∞ All these awards came after a beginning that was very difficult for me. Before I came, Eskom had never had a black legal advisor, let alone a female legal advisor. I was employed by the head office but I traveled around quite a lot because Eskom is spread all over the country. I would have encounters with very conservative Afrikaners in remote parts of the country. So I had lots of problems trying to assimilate myself.

They would phone the Legal Manager and ask, "How can you send us a black woman?" He would say to them, "This is a legal advisor, whatever his or her color. She is going to advise you."

I found that the moment the people start knowing you, they change completely. They crucify you before they meet you, but they can be won over. My success is reflected in the awards that I won. When I walked in, I was first of all a professional. I didn't want to know about their political beliefs, and they dare not ask me about my political beliefs. I was there to do a job, and if they gave me a chance I would do it just as well as any legal advisor, white or male or whatever. I found that through my approach they actually warmed up and started respecting me. It wasn't that difficult in the urban areas because the people there were a little bit more attuned to change. But in the rural areas, it was extremely difficult.

I can illustrate that with one anecdote involving my representation of the transmission section of the company. Eskom generates, transmits, and distributes 97 percent of the electricity needs of the country. It has three major business areas: generation, transmission, and the distribution. The middle one is transmission. We were negotiating servitude with a farmer [in American parlance, negotiating an easement across land]. The farmer gave us problems. We got the servitude, but when we started building the line, problems arose. We stayed with those problems for a very long time, trying to negotiate a solution. This farmer was very abusive. He used to phone and hammer people.

He phoned one of my clients in transmission and yelled at him. The fellow said, "I think you should speak to Dolly Mokgatle, because she is our legal advisor in this whole thing."

Apparently the farmer said, Who? and they told him who I was.

He said, "How dare you! Are you white guys so weak that you can't solve your problems with me? Instead you send a black woman to solve your problems for you!"

He was so angry. But I won him over. One of the things that I did was to go to his house, to his farm right in the heart of the Free State, in Harrismith, to negotiate with him. I sat with him at his dining room table. He ended up calling me at home when he had problems with the line. He would call me like you would call a friend.

Those were very interesting times. Besides everything else, you encounter different-thinking people. Once they start to know you,

Afrikaners tend to respect you quite a lot. They are not as uppity as the white English-speaking South Africans. They are the first ones to praise you if you are doing good work for them. That's how I built up my relationships. Messages were going to my manager about my performance behind my back, and he was getting more and more pleased with me. It was important for him to get that feedback from the clients of the department.

Anyone familiar with the American legal scene will see clear parallels between the problems of African-American lawyers since the civil rights revolution of the 1960s and the problems of black lawyers in South Africa after the end of apartheid. The rise of women in the profession presents similar likenesses. Affirmative action programs have helped black lawyers get positions in government and large corporations. At the same time, those programs have take some of the most talented and most experienced African-American, as well as South African black lawyers, away from the private practice of law.

One would hope that the situation of both blacks and women will improve in South Africa, especially once their numbers reach such a critical mass that race or gender will no longer be as significant a factor in hiring and promotion decision. The rise of people like Dolly Mokgatle to a level of corporate management that gives them the responsibility both for the hiring of in-house lawyers and the employment of outside counsel is likely to change attitudes dramatically.

12

⚖

DULLAH OMAR

Lawyer for Robben Island Prisoners, Detainee,
Minister of Justice

To some extent, Dullah Omar's description of his early life tracks the stories of other lawyers interviewed for this book. His struggles as a young Indian through the South African educational system and in the early days of his law practice are similar to the descriptions given by other lawyers—African, Coloured, or Asian.

Yet, Omar's life is especially notable for a number of reasons. First, his work with Robben Island prisoners and with the leading antiapartheid organizations of his day was virtually unique. Second, his history is important because of the significance of the case that bears his name to the story of the fight against South Africa's draconian security laws. But recounting Omar's career is most useful because it provides the context in which this man operates, a man who is in a position to set policies that will define the legal profession in the country for decades to come.

I first met Dullah Omar in 1987, shortly after he was released from detention. We had dinner at an Indian restaurant in a Cape Town suburb and then went back to his house, where we watched the videotape of the speech that had probably contributed to his detention. Although it is ironic that this recently released prisoner would, in seven years, become the chief law enforcement officer of the nation, such a development is hardly surprising. It was clear, even when Omar had no more power than any other ex-detainee, that he was destined to become a leader in the new South Africa.

Omar was obviously respected by the leadership of the principal anti-apartheid movements—ANC, PAC, Black Consciousness, or other groups. Even though those leaders were seemingly politically impotent at the time—most were in prison or under banning orders—the day of their empowerment was not far in the future. Even more significant, the quality of Omar's mind, the depth of his commitment both to the antiapartheid cause and to justice and his ability to deal with people of all races, set him apart even from the other remarkable people with whom he was associated. His struggles and his ultimate success represent the best of the South African legal community.

Early Years

∾ I was born in Cape Town in 1934. Both my parents came from India. They eventually settled in Cape Town and lived in District Six. District Six, which has been very much in the news as part of the terrible story of apartheid in our country, has been very much part of my life.[1] I grew up there.

I attended a Muslim school in Salt River and I attended the high school in District Six, Trafalgar High School. At that time, even though there was segregation in our country, it was less stringent than it became later. So schools in the Cape were open to Coloured, Christian, Muslim, Indians. But there were separate white schools and separate schools for Africans and then schools for all the rest. So in a sense, our school was mixed. Trafalgar High had students of all population groups in the broader black community, Coloureds, and Indians.

Trafalgar was the place that opened my eyes to the reality of South Africa. In a way, my political career, or at least my involvement in the struggle, began when I was at Trafalgar. I was doing my final matric year in 1952. Nineteen fifty-two represented three hundred years of the coming of the first colonial invader. Jan van Riebeeck had come to the Cape in 1652. The apartheid government organized celebrations throughout the country—it was the first major festival in the country—and black organizations organized a boycott of the festival.

We students participated in that boycott. We had problems with some white teachers who were party to the celebrations. Today it looks very small and unimportant. But, for example, in one class our Afrikaans teacher requested us to write an essay on the van Riebeeck festival, and he identified a number of points which he thought we could cover in our essay. We were very upset. We met as a class, and we decided that we were not going to write that essay. We did not write it, and for us that was a very revolutionary step. We had always complied with what teachers and principals asked. The white school teacher stormed out of the class and went to the principal, who was a Coloured, and the Coloured principal supported us. We were very excited about it. What it meant was from then on we began to pay much more attention to what was happening in the country and to the need to resist oppression.

University Days

✑ I then went to the University of Cape Town [UCT]. I started at UCT in 1953 and completed my two degrees, Bachelor of Arts and Bachelor of Laws, by the end of 1957. That period, between 1953 and 1957, was also a very crucial period, because it was in that period that the National Party apartheid government, among other things, introduced legislation on the education front. Until then, blacks and whites wrote the same examinations, followed the same syllabus at schools. [Hendrik] Verwoerd [the principal architect of apartheid] had made it clear that there should be a conscious strategy in South Africa to develop separate cultures. This was not because he respected cultures, but because he wanted to create division. He wanted to break up the unity between the oppressed people which had been built up. I would say that his educational policy did succeed in some respects and created that division.

So my period at university was full of protest, full of struggle, full of resistance. We held marches, we protested, we had meetings, we agitated, we organized students, and it was therefore a very, very crowded and busy period for me. The wonderful thing about the liberation movement at the time, and I suppose even now, is that people who are dedicated to liberation and work hard in the struggle also turn out to be the best students. Even though they have very little time, they work hard and make effective use of their time, and they pass all their examinations. They read more than others because they want to understand the world, and understand what is happening. When they read about law, they want to understand the history of law.

So we were swept up by that kind of atmosphere and it was very exciting, even though things were tough in our country and people suffered a great deal. It was a period in which Pass Laws applied very harshly; Africans had to carry a pass and thousands of them were arrested every year under Pass Laws. And every day, we witnessed men and women being arrested for Pass Laws.

Articles and Starting a Practice

∽ I completed my university education and did articles, so as to become an attorney, in 1958 and 1959. I did my articles with a Jewish firm, an individual by the name of Kluk. He was a very kind gentleman who took me on. I had not been able to get articles. I had walked the street for a few months, but eventually found him and he agreed to take me. I earned R10 a month for a long time when I started, but for me the important thing was to just get through the articles.

I completed the articles and, because it was not possible to get a job with any other firm, I opened up my practice as an attorney. The strange thing about it is that my first act as an attorney was to break the law!

Africans were not allowed to practice as lawyers in the city. An African gentleman, Cadoc Kobus, had practiced in Cape Town, but had been ordered to leave the city. He closed down his practice, and he opened up a practice in Langa, an African township in Cape Town. When I completed my articles, because we were often together in the political struggle, we discussed the possibility of working together. We then agreed to enter into a partnership, which was illegal. I then went to work for him in Langa township for many months, and we then agreed to open up a partnership to enable us to open a practice back in Cape Town. I filled in my application forms. I lied about our relationship, and I said he was working for me. I lied under oath about a number of things. I, too, had to apply for a Group Areas permit because I could not practice in the city without a permit. So we had to tell a few lies on my permit as well. I managed to get a permit for one year, which I had to renew annually and which was renewed for a few years but then canceled. Kobus was my partner for a couple of years. Ultimately, because of harassment by Group Areas authorities and officialdom generally, we decided to end the partnership. He went to the Transkei.

For myself, when I opened my practice during the State of Emergency [1960, the time of the Sharpsville massacre], I consider that to be a turning point in my life. Until then I had not decided which way I wanted my legal career to go. I had no idea as to what I should concentrate on, what I should specialize in, so I was still finding my way. A role was simply thrust upon me by events.

We had the Langa march and I witnessed the march, I saw it, I joined in. The march, led by Philip Khosana, was quite a spectacular event. Thirty, forty thousand angry people marched to Cape Town from Langa, passed through many residential areas, many built-up areas, many shop windows, came into the city and not a single window was broken. Not a single stone was thrown.

They congregated outside Caledon Square police station for many hours. Then Philip Khosana was called in by the head of the police, who negotiated in connection with Pass Laws, because the demand was for an end to Pass Laws. Khosana and the other leaders agreed to lead the people back to Langa because the police just did not know what to do. He had been promised an interview the next day to discuss the grievances of the African people, and on the basis of that promise he reported back to the mass and led the people back to Langa.

I was there all the time. Walking back into my office was a very difficult thing. You couldn't just go on as if nothing had happened. It was very exciting because immediately after that the South African government announced the temporary suspension of the Pass Laws. It was highly significant, though it was a strategy just to defuse the situation.

In any event, after I opened my practice I was hardly in my office when the regional leadership of the Pan Africanist Congress [PAC] came to see me. They told me that the organization had been banned and that many of their people had been arrested. They asked me to act on their behalf. I agreed to act for them, and we were then to discuss details later. We discussed no financial arrangement, nothing. They left, and the next day I heard that they had all been arrested. By then, there was quite a

crackdown and many PAC members in many parts of the country were
arrested and detained. For the next couple of years, I found myself
defending PAC members under very difficult conditions. The State of
Emergency was a huge turning point in my life.

Representation of Robben Island Prisoners

ᔌ I found myself going to Robben Island because many people were sentenced and taken to Robben Island to serve their sentences. So from the
start, I started going to the Island, and I went to the Island for about
twenty-five years very regularly. In the process I acted for all the political
groups [ANC, PAC, Black Consciousness, and other groups].

It is almost an unknown chapter in my life because people who were
sentenced to the Island became forgotten people; nobody spoke about
them. The prison regulations forbade publication of matters relating to
them. I would go to the Island every week in order to defend one or other
prisoner. I would represent them on all sorts of charges—charges of contravening of a prison regulation, failing to obey a lawful command by a
warden, insulting a warden, being abusive to a warden, being threatening
towards a warden, refusing to work. I even had people who were charged
under the prison regulations with refusing to eat.

It was quite an experience because I used to go to the Island, go
through that process the whole day, and then get onto the boat again feeling terribly depressed and helpless. Yet I would come back and life
appeared to go on as normal, as if nothing was happening. Here I would
come back with all those things going on in my mind, things that I had
experienced, and nobody in the whole city of Cape Town knew a thing
about it. I was not allowed to publish it. This went on for years.

In the 1960s and 1970s apartheid was rampant and arrogant. Blacks
were made to feel in no uncertain terms that, if you are black, you have
no place in this society except as a servant. And so black lawyers suffered
that. Godfrey Pitje was one of the few lawyers who got up in court and
said, I refuse to stand at a bench or sit at a desk which is for blacks only.
He defied the apartheid rule [see chap. 1]. But all of us appeared in courts
where you had to sit at a specific bench. Often I would go to court in the
countryside and be subjected to all kinds of humiliations, which I would

tolerate because my central objective was to defend my client. I could make a big noise and walk out of court but then my client would have suffered, the people who needed me in that court would have suffered. So for the sake of our clients and to insure that we are there at least to protect them against the worst excesses of apartheid, we tolerated lots of humiliation.

The same thing happened when I used to go to Robben Island. To get to Robben Island, you have to get onto a boat which belonged to the government. As a black person, I was not allowed to sit in the areas where whites sat, protected from the harsh weathers of the Western Cape. The Cape is also known as the Cape of Storms and our sea between Cape Town and Robben Island is very choppy, with water gushing over onto the boat. Invariably, I used to stand outside and get soaking wet because I was not allowed to sit inside, where whites were. So it was fairly humiliating all the time, but because we were determined to do what we had to do, our humiliation took second place. The interests of our clients took first place.

On the Island itself, I was invariably subjected to a bodily search. My bag would be rampaged. In general, they were noncontact visits, which meant that there was a glass between you and your client. We fought that practice. In fact the prisoners themselves fought and refused to accept noncontact visits. After many battles, we were allowed contact visits. The visits were supposed to be within sight but out of hearing, which meant that there was a glass wall and a couple of warders watching you all the time. We assumed, correctly as we discovered afterwards, that our discussions were listened to.

So it was very difficult; there were no confidential discussions. We overcame that because we used to talk and we used to make notes. I would write one word and my client would know that he must look at that word, and we were able to converse in code. It was an art that we developed after many years of going to the Island.

As time went on, the prisoners on the Island themselves were very well organized on party political lines. There was a code of conduct which the parties had among themselves. There was great political tolerance in a sense. Of course, the groups fought each other as well—ANC, PAC, Black Consciousness Movement. I often came there in the midst of some of those battles. But looking back, in general, it was quite remarkable that they were actually able to have rules: for example, how they recruited members; how the parties conducted themselves; how the parties consulted with each other; how they communicated with each other.

The big challenge for people like President Mandela, Ahmed Kathrada, Govan Mbeki, and others [all leaders of the struggle against apartheid before, during, and after their imprisonment] was how to make contact with other prisoners. These leaders were cut off from other prisoners. It took them many years to develop lines of communication but they did. So a prisoner would come to me and sometimes take over an hour to battle to get a message across to me. It may have been something on which they had worked for a couple of months, to get across the prison, to get input from the leaders, and then to get out to me. I would then convey that message wherever it had to be conveyed. Sometimes we would battle to decipher it ourselves. On my next trip to Robben Island, I would say to some other prisoner, This is the message I got from ———. And I would write down the name and he would know immediately that it was one of his fellow prisoners.

So we were able to beat the system in many ways. That was very exciting. It was real meaningful work, and so we used those occasions in order to establish contact between the prison and the outside world. I used all my visits on the Island to promote linkage among the prisoners and between the prisoners and the outside world. It was for me one of the most satisfying parts of my work, although I often came back very depressed because there were so many brilliant people locked up and unable to make a contribution.

On occasion, there were charges that involved more than violations of prison regulations, criminal charges such as assaulting a warder, fighting with a warder. Then I would go to the Island to defend people in a normal criminal trial. The trial provided me with much more latitude and scope than where there were mere violations of prison regulations, because in a criminal trial you are presumed innocent until you are found guilty. You have the right to cross-examine properly. You have the right to call witnesses and all sorts of things.

So if a chap was charged with assault, they would bring a magistrate to hear the case. The magistrate would not apply the prison regulations.

He would apply the normal rules of criminal procedure. I would decide that, in mitigation, I wanted to call the accused's wife to give evidence. The accused had not seen his wife for a year. Or I might call his father or mother to give evidence. That threw the prison authorities into a big tantrum. The court, of course, had no way of saying that they were not going to allow it, because the criminal procedure provided that you were entitled to call witnesses.

Some magistrates were furious at the tactics we adopted and launched into attacks upon us. But we stood our ground and said we were acting in the interest of our client. On occasion, it meant that the prisoners saw their wives, even though the prison authorities always made sure that they were not able to touch each other. So it was also tragic because the accused would be in one part of the court and the witness would be brought in somewhere else. They would see each other and look at each other, perhaps shake their heads towards each other in greeting. The woman would give evidence and she would be whisked away. So it was very sad but at least they saw each other. I, of course, as counsel, was able to talk to them both. So I would see him, and tell him what she said, and tell her what he said. On occasion, you had the one warder who, at our request, would have allowed them to speak to each other for a short while.

But insofar as the mere contravention of prison regulations [as opposed to criminal charges] was concerned, those hearings were absolutely farcical. These were kangaroo courts. The warders were the judges, they were the prosecutors, and they were the witnesses. We used to fight, go through the motions of putting up a hell of a fight, knowing that we were going to lose.

The plus side of those representations was that I was able to spend a great deal of time with a client and discuss all kinds of matters—education, family, what was happening outside. It was a terrible thing not to get news. When I was in prison in 1985 for a very short period, two months, I was cut off from radio, cut off from newspapers. After one week of imprisonment, I was completely lost. You were bewildered. You didn't know what was happening in the world. You didn't know what was happening around you, and it affected you mentally. Psychologically you felt unsure of yourself because the world was passing you by.

The prisoners on Robben Island suffered from that for years—no newspapers, no radio. They resorted at times to stealing the newspapers of warders. Invariably the warders read the Afrikaans newspapers. They would steal a newspaper which was maybe three months old. They would then pass the newspaper to somebody who would then extract relevant articles, write them out in English and in other languages which people spoke on the Island. That little Island newspaper would then be passed around containing news that was three months old. But it was very exciting because as time went on they developed great expertise in stealing newspapers, getting the news translated, spreading it over the Island so that people at least knew a little bit of what was going on. Eventually they overcame this communications gap. So, knowing that these things were happening was quite exciting.

So at the end of a day, after a case would be finished, I would be whisked back to the boat. I would again stand on the deck of the boat, clutching a pole with my satchel lying next to me, both of us getting wet, satchel and me. I stood while whites were sitting comfortably inside drinking coffee. Nobody would bat an eyelid or thought that anything was wrong with it. The most menial white sat inside. They accepted it as normal, natural, God-given. I swallowed my own humiliation like many black lawyers did because of the greater cause we were serving. I would come back to the mainland and feel quite terrible, not for myself but for great people who were locked up. It looks like we did small things. I don't think we did very much to help our clients, but that was life for many years.

Political Trials

∞ The advantage of my Robben Island days was that I was able to meet a lot of people. I first met President Mandela on the Island. I also met Robert Sobukwe [head of the PAC]. When he was released, he was a sick man. He had cancer, and when he was taken to hospital he contacted me and asked me to act for him. So for a short period, I acted for Sobukwe as well.

To cut a long story short, in the 1960s many years were taken up by defending people who were charged with being members of the ANC, or members of the PAC, participating in the activities of banned organizations, breaking banning orders.

I defended the first sabotage trial in South Africa, which was the Poqo trial. There was an uprising in Paarl [a small city in the wine district, not far from Cape Town], which was also led by the PAC in '61 or '62 or thereabouts, when large numbers of migrant workers marched into Paarl. A few whites died in the process, shops were damaged and burnt, and so on. It was a protest, an uprising against inhuman conditions: pass laws, terrible wages, terrible conditions under which men had to live, single-sex quarters. The government then passed a law called the Sabotage Act with retrospective effect. It then charged about 120 men with sabotage. So they were charged with an offense which was only created after they had been arrested. South Africans regarded that as nothing. That was the very first sabotage trial I defended.

We received no funding for that representation. We could not get financial assistance because blacks had killed whites. The funders at the time said that I could only defend those who were not involved in the violence—not those who had participated in violence. I rejected those conditions. I said I was not a policeman, and I was not going to conduct a witch-hunt among a large number of people who had asked me to defend them. So we undertook the defense without the funds. We ran ourselves into the ground. There were five trials. I was only able to do the first one.

Those were very tough years; the sixties were particularly bad years. The apartheid regime ran rampant. It passed many laws, including the Suppression of Communism Act. The laws with regard to passes were tightened up. Laws were enacted on the labor front to prevent Africans from becoming part of trade unions, prohibiting strikes and all sorts of things. Africans were not allowed to take part in collective bargaining. Any attempt by Africans to organize themselves and to ask for meetings with employers in order to negotiate wages was regarded as treason. They would be instantly locked up and charged. A great deal of my work also revolved around defending African men and women charged under Pass Laws. The 1960s were very dark years.

In the 1970s things began to change because industrialization had proceeded apace and a large working class was developing in a number of towns. The 1970s witnessed the first significant worker uprisings in our country. By then, our universities had been closed to blacks. Bantu education was in full force. Hundreds of African teachers had been dismissed; a large number of Coloured teachers had been dismissed. Separate educational institutions were in place. The full fury of the Bantu education hit the African people. So, coupled with worker revolt, we saw the rise of the student movements.

From a political point of view, the 1970s heralded the inevitability of the downfall of apartheid—even though it took place twenty-five years later. The reason I say that is that the whole strategy of the apartheid government on education was designed to produce an African who would accept his place in society. Thousands of Africans throughout the country were forced out of school in order to enter the labor market completely unskilled. Many others were not able to reach standards which would enable them to go to university. The job reservation act, the apprenticeship act, and other laws prohibited Africans from becoming artisans, from becoming apprentices. There were no African electricians, no carpenters, no painters. They could not take any skilled employment. So Bantu education and the other laws did tremendous damage but they failed in their primary objective and that was to develop a slave mentality among Africans.

The 1976 Soweto revolt of students signaled the failure of the Bantu education policy. The 1976 events affected students in Cape Town and other places. Hundreds of students got arrested and I got involved defending students all over the country. That went on for a couple of years. In 1980 there was another student uprising, another student revolt. In the meanwhile, I had started helping workers form organizations. I acted for some trade unions which existed under very difficult conditions.

The way I managed to keep myself going financially was, firstly, I had a wife who was working. Farida was a tremendous source of support and strength. She and her family had a fruit and vegetable stall at the Salt River market. She kept the home fires going. She, by the way, was a sister of a woman who was also involved in the trade union movement. She was secretary of the Food and Canning Workers Union and she participated in the march of women to Pretoria in 1955. Two of her brothers-in-law were treason trialists in the 1956 treason trial. So there was some basic political consciousness in her family and herself. My wife was great support.

But the other thing was that I qualified in conveyancing and I did a lot of conveyancing work and estate work. I did administration of estates, which enabled me to pay my office expenses and keep myself going. Conveyancing is a type of work that you can do after hours, and if you have a good secretary you can do quite a lot of property transactions. So I did a great deal of that kind of work.

The 1980s saw the rise of the Black Consciousness Movement and I was asked to act for them. The first major organization was SASO [South African Students Organization] and a political wing, the Black People's Convention [BPC]. The BPC also formed an economic wing which was called the Black Community Programme [BCP]. It was a bold attempt to develop self-sufficiency among blacks. Looking back, maybe it was very naive, but blacks set up little businesses, little industries, little collectives of all kinds in an attempt to develop self-sufficiency. The idea was good, the vision was good, but clearly we were very naive about thinking how you could develop this. I acted for people in the BPC and for members of the Black Consciousness Movement. Then, when many of them were arrested and sent to Robben Island, I pursued my work at Robben Island. I identified strongly with the people I was representing, people like Peter Jones, who was a colleague of Steve Biko, and many others. Then, of course, there were many more terrorism trials taking place in the country so that took plenty of my time.

Arrest, Detention, and Liberation

∞ I moved to the bar in 1982. I was devoting almost all my time to political trials. I did a little bit of civil work here and there, but basically I was defending people charged with terrorism and all sorts of other political crimes. I continued my work on Robben Island and as things heated up I became more and more involved politically. Eventually I was arrested in 1985 and held under Section 29 of the Internal Security Act, not for a long period, merely two months, in solitary confinement. But it was bad enough.

I was held at Pollsmoor Prison. Even my family did not know where I was held. After I was released, I was around for a couple of weeks and then I was rearrested under the State of Emergency. Then, with thousands of others I was held at Victor Verster Prison. I was eventually released in December of the same year, 1985.

The legality of Omar's detention was upheld in a landmark decision of the Appellate Division of the South African Supreme Court, *Omar v. Minister of Law and Order*, 1987(3) SA 859(A). His original fourteen-day detention had been indefinitely extended under regulations authorizing such an extension without a hearing. The regulations also effectively prohibited access by detainees to any persons, including legal advisors and representatives. The court upheld the action and the denial of access to legal advisors despite strong administrative-law grounds calling for a different result. At the time, a legal scholar referred to the decision as a "political and legal disaster for South Africa, for South African lawyers and, above all, for the victims of apartheid."[2] Another speculated as to whether the decision portended a new judicial "dark age." [3]

The decision itself did not immediately affect Omar's freedom. He had in fact been released at the time that the appellate division reached its decision. Nevertheless, the precedent gave fuel to the government's policy of administrative detention of apartheid opponents and the reaction to it gave encouragement to those struggling against the system.

    ∾ I came out and the situation in the country demanded that we throw all our weight into the struggle, which I did in the Cape and elsewhere. I was elected to the position of chair of the United Democratic Front in the Western Cape soon thereafter. My own detention led to Cape lawyers organizing themselves for the first time. When I was released, the Democratic Lawyers' Organization was formed. It was allied with the BLA [Black Lawyers Association], but part of NADEL [National Democratic Lawyers Association]. I became the first president here and the national vice-president of NADEL. [NADEL and the BLA, both of which represent the interests of black lawyers in the country, eventually split and have frequently been rivals vying for membership.]

      Up to 1985, until my arrest, I saw my main role as being the role of a lawyer and, therefore, even though I was active politically, politics played a secondary role to that of lawyer. That phase went from 1960, the first state of emergency that I describe as the turning point, right up to 1985. Nineteen eighty-five heralded for me the beginning of a new chapter that was the primacy of the struggle for liberation—the primacy of direct resistance and a battle to overthrow the apartheid regime. That became the main objective in my life. Therefore, even though I continued to practice law and did my bit, politics began to play the dominant role.

Then, in the late 1980s, as things developed we began to prepare for negotiations. I was approached by the ANC to serve on its constitutional committee to prepare for those negotiations. We were anticipating what was going to happen and did a great deal of planning. I agreed, and I went to Lusaka and participated in the ANC constitutional committee.

As a result, I withdrew from practice as much as possible, left the bar, and went to the University of the Western Cape where I could work full-time on constitutional issues.

In late 1989 it became clear that the government would not be able to continue the way it was. We saw the release of Govan Mbeki, Walter Sisulu, and others. It was just a question of time before Mandela himself would be released. We were part of a massive defiance campaign which went on through the 1989 period. There were huge marches in Cape Town in defiance of apartheid laws. It was a very successful campaign.

President Mandela called me again to the prison and asked me to play a role in getting people to come and visit him from different parts of the country in preparation for his release. He was released and then with the ANC being unbanned, I joined the ANC officially and was immediately elected to the Cape executive. At a national congress, I was elected to the national executive, then elected to Parliament. I am still a member of the national executive committee and a member of its national working committee, which is a policy-making body of the ANC. I was named minister of justice in May of 1994 and that is the position that I now hold.

The Minister of Justice and the Legal Profession

∞ If one examines the present state of the legal profession, it reflects the legacy which apartheid has left us. The elections of 1994 brought change at a political level. The elections removed power from a white minority regime and made it possible for all the people of our country to participate in the electoral process. But the legacy of apartheid at the social and economic and institutional levels in the professions, in the occupations, and at every other level remains. The same applies to the civil service, the army, the police, the Justice Department.

All of us found ourselves in a situation where apartheid was very much alive. The same applies to the legal profession. Blacks are in a very tiny minority in the profession despite the fact that they constitute 65 to 70 percent of the population. We have a total of approximately 1,000 black lawyers, men and women—very few women, if I may say so—and so we are in a minority.

Black lawyers have over the years refused to cooperate with the controlling bodies of the profession, the bar council on the one hand and the law societies on the other. Our profession is divided between advocates or barristers on the one hand and attorneys or solicitors on the other. But both NADEL and the BLA have a membership which consists of advocates and attorneys. They are the only organizations organized along those lines.

The fact that blacks are in the tiny minority as lawyers is a reflection of what apartheid did to our country. It therefore means that we need to do a great deal of work to ensure that our legal profession, by and large, reflects the demographics of our situation. I'm not one who believes in quotas or proportions but I think that in a genuinely nonracial society in which there is real equality the picture would be very different. The personnel in our courts, in our professions, in various institutions, in business all over, would reflect the reality that the blacks are in a majority. At present, that is not so.

Where blacks do dominate, and where it is very clear, is in poverty, in homelessness, in children who have no shoes and clothes to wear. Poverty is to be seen and is equated with blacks in the same way that in the ownership of property and in every other area whites dominate overwhelmingly. When it comes to suffering, oppression, poverty, it is very clear who it was who suffered during the apartheid years. Now the legal profession reflects the same thing.

Secondly, we have had very little exposure to areas of law and practice of law involving company law, commercial law, or maritime law. Even in the field of property law, blacks have only recently been meaningfully involved, except in a few areas. The reason for that was very simple. Since the passing of the 1913 Land Act, Africans, black Africans, the indigenous people, were not allowed to own land in any of the urban areas of South Africa. Their occupation of land was restricted to what became known as the reserves, later known as the homelands or Bantustans. But in the rest of South Africa, 87 percent of our best land, property in urban areas, not a single black was entitled to own land. [Blacks were not permitted to own land in South Africa except in the homelands, which constituted 13 percent of the country.] Since blacks were not able to buy property, property transactions, registration of mortgage bonds, all work relating to property was outside the reach of black practitioners. Coloured and Indian lawyers were in a somewhat better position because Coloureds and Indians were allowed to own land. They were able to own their own houses in certain restricted areas, even though they too suffered under the apartheid regime. Our legal practices reflected the reality of the suffering of our people.

Most of us started off doing criminal work. In my case, besides doing the political work to which I have referred, I defended hundreds and hundreds of people over the years on charges of contravening Pass Laws or workers who were charged with having gone on strike, people charged with all kinds of crimes—theft, assault, rape, murder, and so on. Most black lawyers in our country would have relied on a criminal practice in order to survive. As time went on a little bit of conveyancing work involving property, administration of deceased estates, would have come to some of our lawyers. I did some work in that area myself, but most black lawyers would not have got much work in the field of administration of estates, for the simple reason that blacks had been completely dispossessed and most blacks had nothing to leave to their families when they died. Then there is a great deal of work for most lawyers involving intellectual property—copyright and so on. Very little of that came to black lawyers. So we had very restricted experience in legal practice and we have to address that question as well.

Black lawyers were in the forefront of human rights work over the years before the ending of apartheid because of their own experiences and the fact that they themselves suffered from violations of human rights. Black lawyers were prepared to take on cases involving violation of human rights. Some white lawyers did the same, but the profession as a whole remained a bastion of apartheid and defended apartheid. Today they claim otherwise, but both the bar and the side-bar in our country have a history of collusion with the apartheid system, although there were some white lawyers who excelled themselves in fighting for human rights.

I make that point because today, with apartheid gone, with a new constitution and a bill of rights, the old established legal profession has suddenly discovered that there is such a thing as a bill of rights and are becoming its biggest champions. But this is not because they want to bring rights to the poor but because they want to invoke a bill of rights to defend the privileges of the rich. The legal profession I think is faced with a big challenge in that regard: to identify who they serve, the interests of the rich or the interests of those who have been oppressed and exploited over the years. The attitude people have as to the kind of bill of rights we should have in our country reflects that kind of division.

We have a lot of work ahead of us to do. We need radical change in our country. There needs to be social and economic transformation which would end the poverty of our people and make it possible for more people to go to school in the first place. When you have 14 or 15 million people living in squatter camps, referred to as informal settlements—camps in which people have no sewerage and water and electricity in their homes but have to share communal facilities—it is very difficult for children to go to school and to study properly. If they do go to school, they drop out at an early age. So blacks start off with a huge disadvantage. Within the first ten years of the lives of [black] children, half of them fall out because of the social conditions under which they live.

I think one needs to make the point that political change in our country will not be meaningful to the overwhelming majority of our people unless there is meaningful social and economic change. It, of course, is not a single event. It is a process but that process has to go on and has to go on meaningfully. The fact that we are part of a world economic system which makes it very difficult for our own country to determine economic policies freely in a way which would benefit people is a huge problem.

Nonetheless, even within the framework of that limitation, social change has to take place. That is the first thing.

Secondly, our school system needs to be overhauled. Our Ministry of Education is busy doing that, but again it is going to take time to create real equality and access to education. We still have a situation where whites, who are a small minority, enjoy the best facilities in the country. Millions of blacks share very poor facilities and at times no facilities at all. In rural areas and on farms, the position is particularly acute.

Our whole educational system and the allocation of resources need change. I say that our government is attending to that, but again it is going to take time. But that has to take place to make it possible for a broader pool of people to develop the minimum educational qualifications to enable them to go to law school.

Thirdly, we need to reexamine the training and the university qualifications with regard to law. We need to look at the content of our law degree and the time period of the law degree. We have been doing that. It is perhaps the easiest of the three problems that I have mentioned now. At university level, there are now many more black students, black men and women, and I know that we are now in a much better position. We will be producing more black lawyers.

Our situation produces strange contradictions. The maintenance of an inequitable social system produces a contradiction. Over the last couple of years, we have produced a large number of black law graduates. However, they are walking the streets. They cannot get articles, they cannot get pupillage. If they want to open a practice, they do not have the capital. They cannot get jobs. As minister, I have intervened in the situation and approached funders to make some cash available for us to provide support for these graduates. At the same time, we have approached lawyers so that we could place black graduates with lawyers to do their articles or pupillage. We are seeking funds to keep them going for a year or two while they go through their courses and then help them set up practices. There is a scheme which we have initiated in order to do that.

We have also called a couple of legal forums. When I became minister, I initiated a number of broad consultations with all the players. We brought together the judiciary, people from the magistrates profession,

prosecutors, other areas of the justice department, all lawyers' organizations, paralegals, representatives of advice offices, some representatives
from civil society, to look at the various issues relating to transformation
of the justice system in our country.

I initiated a meeting between all the law faculties in South Africa. We
called them together, no matter how progressive, reactionary, or whatever
they may be. We found a great deal of goodwill and a general preparedness to look at the issue. What we have done is to look at legal qualifications and what people need to go into legal practice. We did not restrict
that discussion to the elite, the academic community alone. We involved
the same people who had been involved in the legal forum. Based on that
discussion, the law faculties and law deans got together again and looked
at legal qualifications.

I initiated a number of other steps which did not require lengthy
debate. The first was to remove Latin as a requirement for the law degree.
I immediately initiated legislation and last year Parliament passed a law to
abolish Latin as a requirement. Secondly, during the years of National
Party rule, they had brought in a law that prescribed that you need English and Afrikaans—at least one course each at university level—to qualify
for practice as a lawyer, either an attorney or an advocate. Now, while language is important, we have eleven official languages and I did not understand this bias in favor of the English and Afrikaans languages. So I
brought in legislation that abolished that requirement as well.

The law deans made a recommendation that we should replace the
present system with one in which there is a straight four-year LL.B.
course, Bachelor of Laws degree, to be followed by one year of practical
training which could take a number of forms. The idea is that that one
year of practical training would replace articles or pupillage and at the end
of the five-year period, according to this plan, the persons who obtained
the degree would have been trained academically in the theory and
knowledge of law and they would have developed practical experience.
They would then be able to enter the profession. That is the present state
of continuing discussions on the issues of legal education, articles, or
pupillage. There is no agreement on the nature of the practical training in
the law schools.[4]

Particularly from the ranks of the BLA and NADEL, there was a request that we should reexamine the system of articles and pupillage. Now personally, I must say that I benefited from articles. I also practiced at the bar, and I benefited from pupillage. You learn a great deal by learning from people who have been in practice for many years. You learn practical things. But while it is useful, many of our people cannot afford it. They cannot afford the time; they battle through university in the first place. It is almost the last little hurdle, which makes a very big difference. So we have reexamined the whole question.

Both NADEL and the BLA have also held a view for some time that the professions, the bar and the side-bar, need to be fused. As part of NADEL, I subscribed to that view and I do think there is room for movement in that direction. I think, however, it is a complicated question. It is not going to be easy. In other jurisdictions which have the same history as ourselves, the fusion of the professions did not actually lead to practitioners abandoning the dual nature of the profession. An informal bar developed and so you have the broad profession and the informal bar. The bar is very strong in our country and advocates, black and white, would, I think, in general like to retain the present system where you have a divided profession. Therefore, for me simply to move towards issuing a diktat or passing a law making provision for one fused profession will not produce positive results. I think we need a great deal more discussion.

I personally think that some of the discussion has lacked depth on the side people who practice at the bar. There is only concern about the retention of the bar and its maintenance. We have a very elitist system. For example, in the past, before our new democratic order, the only people who qualified to sit as judges in the Supreme Court were people who practiced as advocates. They would have had to have practiced there for many years, and would have to be senior counsel, to have taken silk. So judges were drawn from a very small, select group of people. So it was a very elitist system. Now in terms of the new dispensation, we have widened the pool; you need not be a senior counsel in the first place. Secondly, attorneys can now be appointed to the bench and academics may be appointed to the bench as well. So we have widened the pool considerably and during the past year we have appointed academics and attorneys to the bench. Incidentally, in the last year we appointed sixteen permanent judges to the Supreme Court and eight of them are black. So it is a big change. We appointed more judges who are black in one year than the whole of apartheid South Africa did throughout its history. It is not enough. We need to continue the process, but we need to increase the pool.

I did have Parliament pass a law last year to give attorneys or solicitors audience rights in the Supreme Court, which is also a dramatic break from the past in our country. There was resistance from the bar and also from our Supreme Court to such a move, but the side-bar welcomed it. After the law was passed and attorneys started going to the Supreme Court, things have just got back to normal and the world hasn't come tumbling down.

The debate over a fused profession should be shifted so that the central emphasis should be on access to justice. The reality is that the overwhelming majority of people in our country have had no access to justice and indeed no access to the profession. It therefore meant that people had to find their own ways of resolving problems in their communities. When that happens they develop ways which enable them to take the law into their own hands, and ultimately that leads to the use of violence as the ultimate method. So one of the contributory causes to violence in our country and the cultural violence is the fact that the majority of people have never had access to justice in an organized sense of the term. Therefore, our priority is to create mechanisms and procedures in all commu-nities wherever they are which would enable people to resolve their problems and disputes and regulate their lives, where they need to be regulated, in a way which would be seen to be fair. I think that is the simple object of our justice system at the moment. Because that now does not exist we are looking at ways and means of bringing it about.

I believe that the legal profession has a big contribution to make, but if they are to fulfill that role then the way they look at themselves has to change. Instead of asking what is in the best interest of the profession, you need to ask, How can we ensure that we deliver access to justice to the people of our country, and then to adjust ourselves accordingly.

There were other dangers lurking for Omar, even apart from the constant risk of detention he faced. In 1990 a judicial inquiry called the Harms Commission probed seventy-one cases of politically motivated violence against antiapartheid activists by an underground government organization. Among the plots disclosed was the charge that the government tried to kill Omar while he was in prison by substituting poison pills for his heart medication. No charges were ever brought based on these allegations.[5] Omar notes: "During my years of practice, all kinds of other things happened to me. Shots were fired into my house. Plans were hatched to kidnap my daughter, but I was tipped off in time and was able to take precautions. Motorcar wheels used to come off. Clearly they were tampered with." He also reports that, after he had been made minister of justice, a person known as Peaches Gordon asked to see him. Gordon said he had once been paid to kill Omar and that he now came to apologize.

> ✑ I offered him a cup of tea (unpoisoned), which he accepted. Over tea he explained to me that he was paid to shoot me. He took steps to do so. One reason that he was unable to carry out his assignment was that at the time I was constantly being followed by the security police of the apartheid regime. Their constant presence (though that was another form of harassment and intimidation) prevented him from carrying out his assignment. What a contradiction! What an irony! Thereafter he was asked to poison me by substituting my heart tablets. As you know, he did not succeed.

Nor have Omar's troubles ended in the new South Africa. Crime is rampant in the country. As the nation's chief law enforcement officer, much of the burden of doing something about street crime falls on him. Some people and organizations want to take matters into their own hands. The most prominent of those is an organization called PAGAD, a Muslim organization devoted to self-help in the fight against crime. Many have called them vigilantes. They have placed particular pressure on Minister Omar, himself a Muslim.

Whatever the pressures on him, Omar is the primary focus of transformation of the legal system. Access to justice by individuals and access to the legal profession by aspiring students are both subjects with which he must deal, while attempting to react to the mounting wave of criminal violence.

13

⚖

PAST, PRESENT, AND FUTURE

Overcoming the Challenge

I N THE preface to this book, I posed the following questions: How could South Africa's black lawyers become professionals under an educational system diabolically structured to keep them as hewers of wood and drawers of water? What enabled their spirit to persevere under circumstances that would have caused most of us to resign ourselves to our governmentally designed destiny?

There is no single answer to either of these questions. The answers are undoubtedly different for each of the individuals whose story is told here. Yet, certain commonalities exist. There is one overriding explanation: the persons I interviewed possess, without exception, extraordinary intelligence and ability. All have remarkable drive and dedication to succeed, usually not simply for the benefit of themselves and their families but also for their people—the blacks of South Africa.

In addition, most black lawyers came from families who, although rarely as well-off as the average white family, valued education. The pattern of the lawyer who is the offspring of one or two teachers is a common one. The black lawyers interviewed were also more likely to have come from a relatively stable family environment—a two-parent family—than many of their black countrymen.

Good fortune and timing, as in any success story, played a role. In the days before Bantu education, some of the older lawyers got their elementary and secondary education from church schools. And some lawyers received their university education before South African government effectively closed the doors to white universities. Occasionally, a young black person came to the attention of a white teacher or someone who could offer financial aid. Cataclysmic national events, most prominently the 1960 Sharpeville massacre and the 1976 Soweto uprising, may have shocked the individual into a socially conscious legal career. Amazingly, even imprisonment could provide such inspiration—as well as the time for useful study. Given the state of Bantu education, confinement with such role models as Nelson Mandela was a painful, yet ironically better, alternative.

Given the history of South Africa, such role models were few, but their influence was powerful. Mandela and Oliver Tambo stand out. Even though in prison or exile during the formative years of most of the lawyers interviewed, Mandela's and Tambo's success as lawyers and their dedication to the cause of ending apartheid showed that law could be both an acceptable profession and a means for helping one's brothers and sisters. Although not a lawyer, Steve Biko was also an enormously important influence. Biko preached black consciousness—the need for black persons both to be aware of their blackness and to seek to create their own destiny. In later years, the Black Lawyers Association and other groups, as well as the admiration and moral support of families and friends, gave black lawyers the sense of community they needed to exist in a hostile society.

However, neither personal characteristics, nor good fortune, nor role models, nor the support of community could totally negate the oppression of apartheid on black South Africans. The South African government attempted to insure that blacks would not become educated enough to create a problem. And official South African culture has told blacks, virtually their entire lives, that they are a people apart and distinctly inferior. They have grown up in a culture in which race was the primary defining factor for one's entire existence. These deprivations, in addition to severe economic disparity and the predictable emotional effect of hundreds of years of discrimination and persecution cannot have left these individuals unscarred. Still, although they have every right to be, the lawyers interviewed are not bitter. Indeed, most are irrepressibly open and warm. These remarkable people not only survived apartheid, they succeeded despite it.

CHAPTER 13

The New South Africa

On many levels, the change in South Africa since 1994 has been remarkable. Instead of a government exclusively composed of members of the white minority, a nonracial government dominated by the black majority is in power. Nelson Mandela, who was once such a pariah that his very name was made unmentionable, has served as the first president of the newly constituted Republic of South Africa. Although many whites have questioned his policies and the effectiveness of his political party, the African National Congress, in running the nation, Mandela himself is enormously popular with people of all races. Blacks dominate the national Parliament and the parliaments of most of the provinces.[1] The great majority of government ministers are black.

The old homelands have been reincorporated into South Africa itself. Their corrupt regimes have been replaced by democratically elected provincial governments. All these areas, except for KwaZulu-Natal, are controlled by the African National Congress.[2]

Under the terms of the negotiations—under which the Nationalist Party agreed to hold general elections with full suffrage—the old bureaucracy, as well as the judiciary and magistracy, have remained in place. This means that the nation is largely still run on a day-to-day basis by the old white establishment. However, steps to bring blacks into the administration of the country, particularly law enforcement, are progressing and the face of government operation is likely to be very different in just a few years.

From a legal standpoint, there have been enormous strides. The apartheid laws are off the books and have been replaced by antidiscrimination legislation and affirmative action programs. Most significantly, rather than parliamentary supremacy, there is a new constitution that guarantees fundamental rights to people of all races and a Constitutional Court to enforce its dictates. This court, composed of some of the most outstanding legal minds in the country, if not the world, has vigorously upheld the letter and spirit of the document.

Yet, many serious problems still exist. Indeed, the problems of South Africa are so severe that history cannot yet label the transformation a success. The legacy of the apartheid era will have a serious impact on the nation for decades, perhaps a century, to come.

Crime seems to exist unchecked by the police, especially in the larger cities, and most particularly in the Johannesburg area. Ordinary citizens, black and white, venture out of their houses in constant fear of criminal attack. Carjackings, sometimes resulting in death to the victim, are a scourge, particularly in Johannesburg. One is not even safe in the sanctity of his or her electronically gated house. In 1996, Arthur Chaskalson, the president of the Constitutional Court, who is mentioned frequently in many of the interviews in this book and is enormously respected by people of all races, was robbed in his Johannesburg home. The police, largely the same people who patrolled the nation under the apartheid regime, seem unequal to the task. Efforts are being made to reform and retrain law enforcement personnel, but the task is a difficult one that is progressing slowly. With the rising fear of crime has come a desire on the part of South Africans of all races to get tough on the criminals, with a resulting cry to diminish some of the rights included in the new constitution. For example, there is considerable sentiment for a return to the death penalty.

A significant factor in the horrendous presence of crime in the nation is, of course, the continuing wide disparity in economic conditions. There is a huge gap between rich and poor, and most of the poor are still black. Indeed, the economy of South Africa is still almost exclusively in the hands of the white minority. Only a tiny percentage of black Africans could possibly be classified as upper middle class.[3] Affirmative action programs in major corporations have brought some blacks into relatively high positions. But for every black who has entered the corporate board room, there are hundreds of thousands whose lives are at the subsistence level. There is no family, no racial history of involvement in industry, other than as menial laborers.

Segregation of public facilities, known in South Africa as petty apartheid, is now gone. Blacks can and do enter restaurants, movies, beaches, golf courses, and other places that at various times were barred to them, at least as guests as opposed to workers. Yet, as a trip to one of Johannesburg's or Cape Town's upscale shopping malls will demonstrate, most of the people attending the movies, eating at restaurants, and generally functioning as part of a first-world, urban society are white. Blacks, for the most part, do not have the resources to participate in these activities. Even if they could afford it, most still feel uncomfortable in what to them is an alien world, even though it is part of a country in which they are by far the largest racial group and which they now fully control politically.

The educational opportunities for blacks are certainly better than under the old regime. Schools are now totally desegregated and affirmative action programs are beginning to be successful at the formerly white universities. But, although these opportunities exist, long years of Bantu education have left vast educational gaps between the great majority of blacks and their white counterparts. Black children at the beginning of their school careers may have the same opportunities as white children, if they can overcome the heritage of parents who are likely to be illiterate. But those who began in the Bantu educational system before 1993 are still at an enormous disadvantage. Furthermore, almost twenty years of antiapartheid struggle—characterized by school boycotts—have left even the best and the brightest blacks without a solid educational foundation. Thus, as blacks move into government positions and into business, they have neither the education nor the experience of their white counterparts.

The Legal Profession in the New South Africa

The legal profession reflects this state of affairs. There are relatively few black lawyers. The number of black attorneys and advocates still hovers around the 10 percent level. There are even fewer black advocates. Most blacks are still struggling with marginal practices concentrating on criminal, motor vehicle, and domestic work.

The control of the economy by the white population is obviously still the primary factor affecting law practice. However, there are other impediments as well. Language is a problem for many black Africans. There are now eleven official languages in South Africa—English, Afrikaans, and nine African languages. Theoretically, any of the languages can be spoken in court and interpreters, although of varying degrees of competence, are available. However, the judges and magistrates speak English or Afrikaans as their primary language. Very few know any African language. To be effective, a lawyer must be able to articulately address the judge in one of the white languages. History has made most blacks more comfortable with English than with Afrikaans, but many still struggle with either language. It will be many years before the language skills of most blacks equal that of white lawyers.

As Dullah Omar indicates, the system of articles or pupillage also presents a problem for black lawyers in the new South Africa. A few larger law firms have had black clerks for many years, as the experience of Phineas Mojapelo, Kgomotso Moroka, and Dolly Mokgatle illustrates (see chap. 8). However, even those firms can accommodate very few individuals. Other white firms have now opened up to blacks, but the number of available positions is small compared to the number of lawyers seeking to qualify. There are so few black attorneys that the opportunities for articles with them is very limited.

Pupillage presents somewhat less of a problem because the time is shorter, four months as opposed to the two years of articled clerkship. However, a career as an advocate is usually not the preferred option for an aspiring black lawyer. The nature of the bifurcated profession has meant that most blacks opt to become attorneys rather than advocates. To be an advocate has meant that you are dependent on attorneys for case referrals. Attempts have been made to change that situation, including the granting of audience in the higher courts to attorneys. Nevertheless, old patterns are difficult to break. Most court work is still done by advocates.

The white establishment is still firmly in control of the governance of both branches of the legal profession. The law societies (which govern attorneys) and the bar councils (which govern advocates), if not exclusively white, are dominated by the same white leadership that had control under the old government. Election to the councils of these organizations has been difficult for black lawyers. Although they are numerically part of the majority race in the nation, they are very much a minority among lawyers. Whites seem to be willing to have blacks be part of these organizations; they seem most unwilling to give up their control of them.

The relationships between black lawyers and white liberal lawyers continues to be uneasy. The Legal Resources Centre continues its work representing the underprivileged of the nation. Its leadership is now more reflective of South Africa's racial makeup. Yet, the rivalry between white lawyers involved in human rights litigation, such as those at the center, and black lawyers still exists. Only a tiny fraction of black lawyers maintain close relationships with their white counterparts. Fear of white control over decision making is a legacy of apartheid, even though the political tables have been turned.

The control of the profession by whites has continued the already existing suspicion and has fueled accusations of racism in the administration of qualifying examinations. Justice Poswa, the senior counsel from Durban, comments:

> ∞ Even blacks with a better background generally fail the exams. There are those who fail because they never got adequate training but I don't know why most others fail. The perception, and I want to put it no more than that, is that these examinations are being used as a means of maintaining a white cartel of lawyers—that is, keeping out black lawyers in the profession. Some of the best students, who should have done well, just don't do well in these exams. It is almost a rule that they must fail. The odd one passes. There may be no truth in that suspicion. It may well be that they genuinely fail, but blacks have no control over this whole process. Our white colleagues tell us what has gone on. So it is very easy to be suspicious in these circumstances.

As Poswa suggests, the suspicion is unlikely to go away until there is either black control of the process or the same percentage of blacks pass the examinations as do whites.

The vast majority of judges and magistrates are still white. Although efforts to recruit black judges continue with some sense of urgency, there are few black lawyers qualified for the position. As noted in chapter 10 and as Minister Omar comments in chapter 12, junior counsel, attorneys, and academics are now eligible. A great number of black lawyers have the intelligence, inherent ability, and temperament to be judges. But there are few experienced blacks, even in this wider group. Very few have the experience to be able to handle the broad range of difficult problems that confront a judge at any level. Furthermore, each black who becomes a judge diminishes the number of experienced blacks in the general practice of law.

The economic gap between blacks and whites means more than simply that blacks have less money. Most black lawyers have little experience in even rudimentary business transactions. Neither they nor anyone in their family has ever run a business. Black Africans formerly were not permitted to own property, so most will have no experience with real estate transactions, the bread and butter for many lawyers in the United States and elsewhere. Even relatively senior black lawyers have most usually had practices limited to criminal and motor vehicle work. Business people may be convinced to turn to an experienced black lawyer for some of their work. It is most difficult to convince them to turn to a newly qualified lawyer, especially one without business sophistication.

Similarly, the fact that they were excluded from government work until the Mandela administration has caused blacks to be unfamiliar with legal matters involving governmental action. The new constitution may be just as new to white lawyers as to black, but at least the whites have had experience in working within a government of some kind.

The lack of either business or government involvement not only limits the black lawyer in doing that kind of work. It also means that he or she has had very little experience in running an organization of any kind, unless it involved protest. Concepts such as planning and budgeting are often entirely new to many of the blacks who find themselves either in a position that requires such activity or advising a client who needs to be thinking about such things.

Although black lawyers have had role models, they have had few mentors, at least with regard to the kinds of work they are now called upon to do. They are politically aware, they know how to organize a protest at a university, but they usually have had little contact with people who have been involved in the kinds of law practice that are now available to them. Even in those rare instances in which large white firms brought in young people like Phineas Mojapelo or Dolly Mokgatle, their experiences were limited and colored by the large gap between the races.

The absence of mentors and continuing sexism among both whites and blacks make the role of black women lawyers even more difficult, as illustrated by the comments of the women lawyers in chapter 11. Women who have succeeded in the practice of law and who continue to combat the double discrimination of race and sex are truly remarkable people.

Adding to these problems are the continuing, and in some senses heightened, racial tensions among black groups. In this book, I have treated all black lawyers the same—African, Indian, and Coloured. Under the new

South African law, no such categories are recognized. But differences exist, and these differences are exaggerated as black Africans, by sheer weight of numbers, become the dominant group in South African society.

Those people formerly classified as Coloured often believe they are between two groups. Many believe that they will be a forgotten people under the black African–led government. Timothy Bruinders refers to the concern expressed by other Coloured lawyers about their relationships with black Africans (chap. 11). Racial politics reflecting this unease at least in part explains why the Nationalist Party remains in power in the Western Cape, which contains the largest concentration of people formerly classified as Coloured.

Indians also find themselves caught in the middle. While many Indians were among the most active antiapartheid fighters, many others were small business owners servicing the black community. These individuals have both been viewed as exploiters of the black community and have been disproportionately the victims of crime. There are several government ministers of Indian descent in the Mandela government, including Dullah Omar, reflecting the prominent involvement of Indians in the struggle that led to the ascendancy of the ANC. However, criticism of their power is often heard among black Africans.

Some Indians, including Pingla Hemraj, the nation's first black woman prosecutor (chap. 8) have considered emigration:

> ∞ I don't know what the future holds for me. Once in about two or three months, I think I want to emigrate. I am very scared of bringing up children here. I see so much of this violence, more than what is in the newspaper. Every brief that lands on my desk has somebody killed in the most awful manner. I don't want to bring up my children here. I don't want my family to grow up here because I don't know how safe we are going to be. I don't know how safe we are right now. I've looked at emigrating to London and I've looked at America. I couldn't think of going anywhere else. I haven't looked at Canada yet. I certainly couldn't go east. In India, there are far too many lawyers and I would never make enough money. My problem with emigrating is that I don't want to leave this practice that I have built up. It took me the best part of fourteen or fifteen years to get where I am. I am afraid that I am not optimistic about what is going to happen in the country.

Not all Indian lawyers share Pingla's concern. Indeed, on many days, she feels much more optimistic herself. But the underlying situation gives cause for concern.

The Future

Things will progress slowly for black lawyers. Some of their problems are directly tied to the nature of the South African economy and its domination by the white minority. If efforts by the government to bring some of the nation's wealth to its black majority are successful, that success is certain to benefit black professionals of all kinds, especially lawyers. The process, however, is likely to be a long one. Patience will be required before there is substantial improvement.

Other difficulties for lawyers arise from language problems, previously unequal educational opportunities, the articles system, and control of legal institutions by whites. Law schools are beginning to put in a revised curriculum that will permit an individual to receive an LL.B. degree in five years. Such an accelerated program will permit more blacks to qualify more quickly. Improvements in primary and secondary education for blacks will eventually yield significantly higher numbers of people who have both the language and other skills to make good lawyers.

Alternatives to articled clerkships, such as service with organizations like the Legal Resources Centre, are already possible. Other plans are being seriously discussed both by lawyers' groups and through the auspices of the Ministry of Justice. There is a real possibility that some additional practical training will be provided through the law schools so as to at least reduce the period of articles.

If the number of black lawyers increases and their education improves, many of the most significant issues will be resolved. White businesses will be more willing to give them work. Black businesses will increase in number and economic clout and presumably those businesses will hire more black lawyers. Until that time, the government can help by making sure that more of its work is being channeled to black lawyers. If there are not black lawyers with experience in particular kinds of work, blacks can be paired with seasoned white lawyers until experience is gained.

A generation may pass before there are enough black lawyers qualified to be judges—even under the newer standards for judicial selection that permit persons other than senior counsel to be selected—so that the number of black judges begins to reflect the population of the nation as a whole. Efforts can be made to train exceptional young lawyers for the bench, but for the most part, judicial selection may have to wait until today's lawyers gain more experience. Again, if patience prevails, the situation will turn around by itself.

The eventual domination by blacks of all segments of South African society is preordained, given the numbers of people of each of the races in the country and the removal of the artificial racial barriers of apartheid. Thus, black Africans will eventually dominate both the bar and the judiciary, almost regardless of what steps the government now takes. The only question is when this will happen and whether the blacks who take over positions of leadership will have the time to prepare themselves for the positions they will certainly hold.

In talking about the political philosophy of black consciousness as it applies to the legal profession, George Maluleke, the successful Johannesburg attorney, puts the matter in perspective:

> ∞ In 1985, a priest friend said, "There is no real serious difference between black consciousness and what is ANC policy. While we are worried about Africanization and making everything as black as possible, there is no wrong in trying to cultivate a nonracial culture. Because, whatever way you look at it, even though the ANC may appear to be nonracial and even white-dominated in its approach, it can only have a black government because of the sheer weight of numbers." And I told him after the 1994 elections, "How right you were." The people you have in government may not be as black nationalistic in a narrow sense as maybe some of us would have liked. But they cannot change their blackness. Because of the sheer weight of numbers, there is no way to avoid change now. In fact, what you can do about it is to try to deal with it in a more balanced rational manner and without the hysteria of race definitions.

Assuming South Africa survives as a constitutional democracy and progress is made on a continuing basis, competent, well-educated blacks will control every aspect of South African society, including the legal profession and the judiciary.

The Rule of Law

Oddly, both the transformation of South Africa in these difficult years and the nature of the nation that will emerge are aided significantly by one aspect of the old South Africa and the traits of the people who ran it. There are numerous references in this book to unfair laws and draconian efforts by the government to protect its undemocratic hold on the people of South Africa. But there are also many instances in which, despite clear opportunities to do so, the government followed its own legal processes, even if it was not in its interest to do so. Dikgang Moseneke (chap. 6) talks at some length about using what he calls the Calvinist proclivity of the Afrikaner to follow rules to the advantage of his clients. Dullah Omar (chap. 12) describes defending prisoners on Robben Island. If they were charged with criminal offenses, they were entitled to a full trial, with witnesses to be called on their behalf, even if it was clear to the magistrate that these witnesses were only being called to permit the prisoner to have some contact with their families. Fikile Bam (chap. 7) notes that Nelson Mandela was given the right to study law under the old rules, and the prison authorities couldn't take that right away from him when new rules went into effect.

All South African lawyers, black and white, were used to a rule of law, in the sense that existing processes were to be followed. The value of such an approach, particularly when applied to a set of laws that are nonracial and democratically enacted, cannot be lost on these lawyers. The value of an independent judiciary, ready and able to enforce rules even against an executive branch that would rather not go through the bother of a court challenge, is apparent to all South African lawyers.

Adherence to a rule of law does not always mean harsh justice. Rather, it may simply mean the establishment of a regularized process that is conducted in accord with internationally recognized standards of decency. Illustrative of South Africa's devotion to a rule of law in this sense is its Truth and Reconciliation Commission. This commission was formed by the Mandela government, not to punish perpetrators of apartheid era crimes but rather to fully inform the nation of what had occurred in those years. The theory was that the commission could bring healing to the nation through exposure of the truth. Perpetrators of crimes could apply for amnesty in exchange for a full accounting of their activities. The commission, despite the able leadership of Archbishop Desmond Tutu, has not been without controversy. Many blacks believe that it has stood in the way of justice and that a Nuremberg-style trial would have been more appropriate. Others, especially whites, believe that nothing has been served by digging up the sins of the past. Many of both races say simply that the commission has been ineffective.

Whether the Truth and Reconciliation Commission has been a useful tool in the transition from apartheid to democracy remains to be seen. Yet, the attempt to rely on this process with the expectation that the decisions of the group would be widely respected by all the concerned parties reflects the respect for legal process that exists in both the white and black legal communities.[4] Also reflective of the new South Africa, both black and white lawyers participated in the proceedings, both as members of the commission and as lawyers for those appearing before it.

Black lawyers, such as those whose stories appear in this book, understand what it means to have a working legal system and to have that system adhere to a rule of law. Having such a tradition and having lawyers who will certainly be in a leadership position in the government of such a nation, can only give one a positive view of the future of the nation.

In 1994 Ismail Mahomed, who appears several times in this book, was named deputy president of the Constitutional Court. In 1997 he was named chief justice of South Africa, thus becoming the nation's highest-ranking judicial officer. In an interview conducted prior to his selection as chief justice, he told me:

∞ We are entering a phase in this country where, for the first time in our legal history, a parliament is no longer supreme, the constitution is. For us, that's a revolution. Brought up in the doctrine of parliamentary sovereignty, where Parliament could do whatever it wanted, it is a mighty challenge for a human rights culture. For the first time there is a parliament which is elected by universal adult franchise and which is accountable to all people. I see enormous challenges.

My eighteen months or so on the Constitutional Court have been a very satisfactory time. I think that black people, black lawyers, are able to embark on careers, find a fulfillment and satisfaction which is completely beyond the comprehension and dreams of all of us who practiced throughout this century. It's the most challenging and most exciting time for black people. They will bring to the law not only their own sensitivity, their own understanding of the law in operation, but their own emotional content, which is very rich. Of all the careers which may be open to black people in this country as a result of what has happened since 1990, law must be among the most exciting and most fulfilling and the most stimulating. For me, it's an enormous privilege to be able to live and work in this time. After all, I had thirty-five years of apartheid practice where we found we were getting nowhere. Suddenly the gates have opened, the heavens are smiling on us, and I'm feeling alive and creative and tall. It's a wonderful time.

NOTES

Chapter 1

1. Mogoba has now retired as bishop of the Methodist Church of South Africa. As of this writing, he was the head of the Pan Africanist Congress. He comes up again in Dikgang Moseneke's story of imprisonment on Robben Island (chap. 4).

2. Buthelezi ultimately became head of the Inkatha Freedom Party (IFP) and a political rival of Nelson Mandela. Discussions of the often bloody conflict between the ANC and the IFP appear in several other places in this book. As of this writing, Buthelezi serves as Minister of Home Affairs.

3. Dr. Motlana appears elsewhere in the book as the father of one of the lawyers interviewed, Kgmotso Moroka (chap. 4), and as the head of the black financial giant, New Africa Investments, Inc. (chap. 6).

4. Sobukwe was later a head of the Pan Africanist Congress.

5. Further discussion of the difference between attorneys and advocates is contained in chapter 8.

6. Mandela graphically describes his own time as a lawyer in Johannesburg in his autobiography, *Long Walk to Freedom* (New York: Little, Brown, 1994).

7. Sophiatown was a black section of Johannesburg. The government cleared the area of blacks in the 1950s. A new white suburb called Triomf (Afrikaans for "triumph") took its place. See Allister Sparks, *The Mind of South Africa* (London: Mandarin, 1990), pp. 188–89; Don Mattera, *Sophiatown: Coming of Age in South Africa* (Boston: Beacon Press, 1987).

8. The history of Gandhi's time as a lawyer in South Africa is recounted in several sources, including Ela Gandhi, *Mohandas Gandhi—The South Africa Years* (Cape Town: Maskew Miller Longman, 1994); Robert A. Huttenback, *Gandhi in South Africa: British Imperialism and the Indian Question, 1860–1914* (Ithaca: Cornell University Press, 1971); P. S. Joshi, *Mahatma Gandhi in South Africa* (Rajkot, India: Author, 1980); The film *Gandhi* (1986) contains a fictionalized account of his removal from the train.

9. See Vincent Maleka, 4 *African Law Rev.* 20 (1993).

Chapter 2

1. Nelson Mandela describes his years at Healdtown in his autobiography, *Long Walk to Freedom*, pp. 31–37.

Chapter 3

1. See, for example, Shamil Jeppie and Crain Soudien, *The Struggle for District Six: Past and Present* (Cape Town: Buchu Books, 1990); Richard Rive, *"Buckingham Palace," District Six* (Cape Town: David Philip, 1986); Dollar Brand, "Blues for District Six," in *Seven South African Poets: Poems of Exile,* ed. Cosmo Pieterse (London: Heinemann, 1971), p. 5.

Chapter 4

1. See William Beinart, *Twentieth-Century South Africa,* (Oxford: Oxford University Press, 1994), pp. 153–54.

2. Gail. M. Gerhart, *Black Power in South Africa: The Evolution of an Ideology* (Berkeley: University of California Press, 1978), p. 255, quoting from Muriel Horrell, *A Decade of Bantu Education* (Johannesburg: South African Institute of Race Relations, 1964), p. 6.

3. Gerhart, *Black Power.* See also Leonard Thompson and Andrew Prior, *South African Politics* (New Haven: Yale University Press, 1982), p. 116.

4. Thompson and Prior, *South African Politics,* p. 116.

5. Ibid., p. 117.

Chapter 5

1. For further discussions of the Extension of University Education Act and its effect on the black community, see Gerhart, *Black Power;* Thompson and Prior, *South African Politics.*

2. As a member of the Constitutional Court, Mahomed participated in the unanimous decision that declared capital punishment unconstitutional under the new South African constitution and wrote a vigorous concurring opinion: *S. v. Makwanyane* 1995(3) SA 391 (CC).

3. His mother is Ellen Kuzwayo, author of *Call Me Woman* (Ravan Press, 1996), a captivating story of what it is like to grow up black and female in South Africa. At this writing, she is the oldest member of the South African parliament.

4. See, for example, "The Truth about Steve Biko," *New York Times,* 4 February 1997. Samples of Biko's writing espousing his philosophy of black consciousness are contained in *I Write What I Like: Steve Biko, A Selection of his Writings,* ed. Aelred Stubbs, (New York: Harper and Row, 1978). See also N. Barney Pityana et al., ed., *Bounds of Possibility: The Legacy of Steve Biko and Black Consciousness* (London: Zed Books, 1992).

5. Semenya was counsel for Winnie Madikizela-Mandela in her divorce from the state president and in her appearance before the Truth and Reconciliation Commission.

Chapter 6

1. The 1979 opinion of the Supreme Court of South Africa, in which the court decided that Moseneke should be admitted as an attorney, corroborates his version of the charges against him. The court concluded that he "was not in any way . . . involved

in any actual acts of violence, sabotage, rioting, force or compulsion or threats of such conduct and no ammunition, arms, weapons, or any other dangerous objects were found in his possession, custody or control."

2. Mogoba had been one of Moseneke's teachers at Kilnerton. He ultimately became bishop of the Methodist Church in South Africa and later leader of the Pan Africanist Congress.

3. Ironically, Godfrey Pitje, who was a more deeply religious person than Dikgang Moseneke, had a banning order that prohibited him from attending any church services (see chap. 1).

Chapter 7

1. Steve Biko's philosophy and death are also discussed in chapter 5.

2. Dikgang Moseneke described his representation of Zwelakhe Sisulu in chapter 6.

3. The life and murder of Griffiths Mxenge are discussed by Justice Pius Langa in chapter 9.

Chapter 8

1. As of 1997, the Supreme Court is now the High Court.

2. There are two branches of the University of Natal, one in Durban and one in Pietermaritzburg. All the other lawyers whose stories appear in this book attended the Durban campus.

3. The case was the trial of Andrew Zondo, described by Lewis Skweyiya in chapter 9.

Chapter 9

1. Chaskalson is now president of the Constitutional Court.

2. See, for example, two excellent books describing many of the major antiapartheid legal controversies: Richard L. Abel, *Politics by Other Means: Law in the Struggle against Apartheid, 1980–1994* (New York: Routledge, 1995) and Stephen Ellman, *In a Time of Trouble: Law and Liberty in South Africa's State of Emergency* (Oxford: Clarendon Press, 1992). Although Ismail Mahomed's prominent role in one case is examined by Abel, not a single black African lawyer is mentioned as having a significant role as a lawyer in any of the matters discussed by either author.

3. For a full description of the trial, see Fatima Meer, *The Trial of Andrew Zondo* (Harare: Baobab Books, 1988).

4. The questions and answers are from Baqwa's memory. No transcript is available.

5. All the questions and answers are based on Mahomed's memory. No transcripts are available for the cases discussed in this excerpt.

6. She is also the author of *The Trial of Andrew Zondo* (see note 3, above).

Chapter 10

1. The term was lengthened in the final constitution from the seven years provided in the interim constitution.

2. Mahomed resigned from the court in 1997 to become Chief Justice of South Africa. Pius Langa became deputy president of the court. The vacancy left by Justice Mahomed's departure was filled in 1998 by Zakeria Yakoob, a black South African of Indian ancestry. Justice Yakoob had obtained prominence as an advocate in Durban despite the fact that he has been blind since the age of sixteen months.

3. *State v. Makwanyane* 1995(3) SA 391 (CC).

4. Certification of the Constitution of the Republic of South Africa 1996, CCT 23/96 (6 September 1996).

5. Certification of the Amended Text of the Constitution of the Republic of South Africa 1996, CCT 37/96 (4 December 1996).

6. The name of the court was changed in 1997 to the High Court.

7. Semenya has now returned full-time to his practice as an advocate.

Chapter 12

1. See Timothy Bruinders's description of District Six in chapter 3.

2. Lawrence Baxter, "A Judicial Declaration of Martial Law," 3 SAJHR 317, 318 (1987).

3. David McQuoid-Mason, "Omar, Fani, and Bill—Judicial Restraint Restrained: A New Dark Age?" 3 SAJHR (1987).

4. At this writing, the South African law schools have all adopted a new degree program that permits a student to receive an LL.B. degree in five years. Questions as to the nature of the one-year practical training after the law degree remain under discussion.

5. "S. African Squad Plotted Deaths, Witnesses Say," *Chicago Tribune,* 6 March 1990; Scott Kraft, "Bombs and Baboon Plots by Secret Army Unit Admitted by S. Africa," *Los Angeles Times,* 6 March 1990; John F. Burns, "Military's Power over South Africa: The Lid Is Off," *New York Times,* 11 March 1990.

Chapter 13

1. The Nationalist Party controls the Western Cape, the province in which the city of Cape Town is located.

2. KwaZulu-Natal is controlled by the Inkatha Freedom Party of Mangosuthu Buthelezi.

3. South Africa has roughly 31 million black Africans and about 5.2 million whites. In a 1996 government survey, a total of 65,000 whites reported that they had a monthly income of R12,500 or more a month (roughly $2,750). Just 4,000 black Africans reported incomes at that level or above.

4. Of the people called before the commission, the only prominent South African to ignore its summonses was former president P. W. Botha. Botha was prosecuted criminally for his failure to appear.

GLOSSARY

advocate	trial lawyer with full audience in the South African courts; equivalent to the British barrister
Afrikaner	Afrikaans-speaking white South African—often of Dutch or French Huguenot descent
apartheid	vast scheme for separating races in South Africa
articled clerks	individuals serving an apprenticeship before becoming attorneys
attorney	office lawyer; equivalent to the British solicitor; traditionally had audience only in the lower courts; now may qualify for audience in the High Court
baas	boss (Afrikaans); term used in apartheid days by blacks to address whites
banning order	punitive order limiting movement of an individual; most banning orders restricted an individual to contact with one other person at a time.
Bantu	name used by apartheid-era South African whites to describe blacks; considered offensive
Bantu education	policy establishing a separate educational track for blacks
Bantustans	*see* homelands
bar	collective term for all advocates
bar council	governing body for advocates
B.Iuris	a three-year law degree that usually would not entitle graduate to practice as either an attorney or an advocate but might permit the graduate to be involved in law-related work
B.Proc.	four-year law degree that would entitle graduate to qualify as an attorney, but not an advocate
board examination	qualifying examination for attorneys

263

brief	instructions from an attorney to an advocate
bursary	scholarship
bushveld, or veld	rural areas of South Africa
candidate attorneys	articled clerks
chambers	offices shared by a group of advocates
Coloured	apartheid-era racial classification, often designated people of mixed race
combi	minibus
Constitutional Assembly	group, consisting of the houses of Parliament, charged under the interim constitution with drafting a permanent constitution
Constitutional Court	court set up under the new constitution to review the constitutionality of legislation and administrative acts
counsel	*see* advocate
Eskom	large, government-run electrical utility
Group Areas Acts	legislation establishing the areas in which various racial groups could live
High Court	*see* Supreme Court
homelands	areas set aside for black citizenship; also called Bantustans
Indian	black South Africans of Indian or other South Asian descent
Industrial Court	court dealing with industrial matters
influx control	system of apartheid laws governing rights of blacks to locate in particular areas within South Africa
in limine	motion dealing with a preliminary matter in a court case
instructing attorney	attorney referring a case to an advocate
Internal Security Laws	series of laws enacted by the apartheid government to stifle opposition
job reservation	jobs reserved for members of particular racial groups
Judicial Services Commission	commission set up under the new constitution to select judges
kaffir	highly derogatory term for blacks
Land Claims Court	court set up under new constitution to deal with land claims

law society	governing body for attorneys
LL.B.	postgraduate law degree required to practice as an advocate
location	rural area set aside for blacks
magistrate	lower-court judge
matriculation	(matric)—final year of secondary school; a matric certificate permitted the individual to enter university
maths	mathematics
Nationalist Party	ruling party during apartheid era
native commissioner	official in charge of black affairs
Northern Sotho	*see* Sepedi
Pedi	African tribal group
Pass Laws	laws establishing the need for blacks to carry documents proving their right to be in a particular part of the country
principal	lawyer in charge of education of a pupil or articled clerk
pro deo	payment to court-appointed lawyers in criminal cases
professional assistant	nonpartner lawyer in a South African law firm; equivalent of an associate in an American firm
pupillage	apprenticeship served to become an advocate
public protector	ombudsman position set up under new South African constitution
Queen's counsel	*see* senior counsel
rand	South African currency; also sometimes used to refer to the area around Johannesburg
Rivonia trial	1963 trial in which Nelson Mandela and others were sentenced to long imprisonment
senior counsel	experienced advocate(s); usually senior counsel appear in court only as the leader of a team that includes a less experienced lawyer (junior counsel); also called Queen's counsel, or silk
Sepedi	African language spoken by Pedi or Northern Sotho tribal group
SeSotho	language spoken by Sotho tribal group
Sharpeville massacre	1960 uprising in Sharpeville township
side-bar	collective term for all attorneys

silk	senior counsel; to "take silk" is to become a senior counsel
Soweto uprising	1976 uprising in Soweto townships
Sotho	African tribal group
Special Branch	police charged with enforcement of Internal Security Laws
squatter camps	areas to which blacks have moved without legal right to the land
standard	school grade level; standards 1 through 10 are equivalent to U.S. grades 3 through 12
State Tender Board	government commission dealing with contracts between government and private persons
State of Emergency laws	various sets of laws enacted by apartheid-era Parliament to impose tight security measures
Supreme Court	highest court of South Africa; the Supreme Court has both a trial and appellate division; now called High Court
Telkom	government-owned telephone utility
third-party case	motor vehicle liability case
township	urban area set aside for a nonwhite group (separate townships would exist for blacks, Indians, and Coloureds)
Tswana	African language and tribal group; the language is properly called Setswana
veld	countryside
Wits	the University of the Witwatersrand
Xhosa	African language and tribal group; the language is properly called isiXhosa
Zulu	African language and tribal group; the language is properly called isiZulu

PEOPLE

The following list includes South African lawyers and activists mentioned more than once in the interviews. The race of each individual is listed because it is relevant to this book. The author apologizes to the individuals for this designation, recognizing that many of them would believe their race irrelevant to whatever contribution they made to the struggle against apartheid.

Biko, Steve (black)
> leader of the Black Consciousness Movement; murdered by police in 1977

Bizos, George (white)
> antiapartheid advocate; represented Nelson Mandela

Browde, Jules (white)
> antiapartheid advocate

Buthelezi, Mangosuthu Gatsha (black)
> leader of the Inkatha Freedom Party leader; rival of Nelson Mandela

Chaskalson, Arthur (white)
> antiapartheid advocate; director of the Legal Resources Centre; later president of the Constitutional Court

Dugard, Prof. John (white)
> professor of law at the University of the Witwatersrand; director of the Centre for Applied Legal Studies

Fischer, Bram (white)
> antiapartheid advocate; represented Nelson Mandela; died in prison

Gandhi, Mohandas Karamchand (Mahatma) (black)
> Indian leader who spent almost twenty-two years in South Africa

Kathrada, Ahmed (black)
> President Mandela's parliamentary counselor

Kentridge, Sydney (white)
> antiapartheid advocate; later acting justice of the Constitutional Court

Kuny, Denis (white)
> antiapartheid advocate

Maharaj, Mac (black)
> minister of transport in the Mandela administration

Mandela, Nelson (black)
> state president of South Africa; symbolic leader of the antiapartheid
> struggle through twenty-seven years in prison

Mandela, Winnie (black)
> former wife of Nelson Mandela; leader in the ANC

Mbeki, Govan (black)
> ANC leader and fellow Rivonia defendant with Nelson Mandela;
> father of current deputy president, Thabo Mbeki

McQuoid-Mason, David (white)
> professor and dean at the University of Natal (Durban), faculty of law

Mogoba, Stanley (black)
> antiapartheid activist; later bishop of the Methodist Church of
> South Africa; later head of the Pan Africanist Congress

Motlana, Dr. Nthato (black)
> antiapartheid activist and business leader

Mxenge, Griffiths (black)
> attorney; assassinated in 1981

Mxenge, Victoria (black)
> attorney; assassinated in 1985

Phosa, Mathews (black)
> activist lawyer; later premier of Mpumalanga Province

Sisulu, Walter (black)
> ANC activist in prison with Nelson Mandela

Slovo, Joseph (white)
> lawyer and head of the South African Communist Party; later
> government minister

Sobukwe, Robert (black)
> leader of the Pan Africanist Congress

Suzman, Helen (white)
> antiapartheid member of South African Parliament

Tambo, Oliver (black)
> head of the ANC in exile; law partner of Nelson Mandela

Unterhalter, Jack (white)
> antiapartheid advocate

PLACE NAMES

Alexandra	large black township adjoining Johannesburg on its northeast
Amanzimtoti	small town south of Durban
Athlone	Coloured township in the Cape Flats near Cape Town
Atteridgeville	black township near Pretoria
Baragwanath	part of Soweto; location of large hospital serving blacks
Benoni	small town east of Johannesburg
Bloemfontein	capital of the Free State Province and judicial capital of South Africa
Boksburg	suburb east of Johannesburg
Bophuthatswana	former independent homeland
Botshabelo	teacher training institution in what is now Mpumalanga
Braamfontein	part of Johannesburg, north of the central business district; location of the University of the Witwatersrand
Bridgetown	Coloured township near Cape Town
Bryanston	Johannesburg suburb
Cape Flats	area east of Cape Town containing many Coloured townships
Cape Town	second-largest city and legislative capital of South Africa
Ciskei	former independent homeland
Danielskuil	small mining town near Kimberley
Diepkloof	part of Soweto
District Six	part of Cape Town; blacks were removed from this district in the 1960s
Dube	part of Soweto
Durban	large port on the Indian Ocean
Eastern Cape	South African province

Eastern Transvaal	former province, now Mpumalanga
Edenvale	small town near Johannesburg
Flagstaff	small town in the Transkei
Galeshewe	black township near Kimberley
Gauteng	South African province in which Johannesburg and Pretoria are located
Germiston	small city just southeast of Johannesburg
Grahamstown	city in the Eastern Cape
Grassy Park	Coloured township near Cape Town
Harrismith	city in Orange Free State
Holy Cross	small town in the Transkei
Jan Smuts	airport serving Johannesburg and Pretoria; now Johannesburg International Airport
Johannesburg	largest city in South Africa
Kayelitsha	black township near Cape Town
Kempton Park	small town near Johannesburg; site of constitutional negotiations
Kimberley	city and diamond-mining center in the Northern Cape
Kruger National Park	enormous game park in northeast South Africa
KwaZulu	nonindependent homeland
KwaZulu-Natal	South African province
Langa	black township near Cape Town
Lebowa	nonindependent homeland
Leeukop	prison near Johannesburg
Lesotho	independent country in the middle of South Africa
Mafikeng	city in Bophuthatswana
Mamelodi	black township near Pretoria
Mariannhill	small town in KwaZulu-Natal; home of St. Francis College
Mmabatho	city in Bophuthatswana near Mafikeng
Mpumalanga	province of South Africa; formerly Eastern Transvaal
Natal	former province; now KwaZulu-Natal
Nelspruit	small city in northeast South Africa, near Kruger National Park
Nebo	small town in Northern Province
Northern Cape	South African province
Northern Province	South African province; formerly Northern Transvaal
Orange Free State	South African province

PLACE NAMES   271

Orlando East	part of Soweto
Paarl	small city in the wine district near Cape Town
Pietermaritzburg	large city in KwaZulu-Natal
Pietersburg	capital of the Northern Province
Pineville	black township in Springs
Pokwani	small town in Northern Province
Pondoland	part of the Transkei
Port Elizabeth	city in the Eastern Cape
Port Shepstone	small city south of Durban
Potchefstroom	small city southwest of Johannesburg
Potgietersrus	small city near Pietersburg, in the Northern Province
Pretoria	administrative capital of South Africa
Queenstown	small city in the Eastern Cape
Qumbu	small town in the Transkei
Reiger Park	Coloured township near Johannesburg
Rivonia	Johannesburg suburb
Robben Island	notorious prison offshore from Cape Town
Roodepoort	small city just west of Johannesburg
Rustenburg	small city west of Pretoria
Salt River	Cape Town suburb
Sandton	Johannesburg suburb
Scottburgh	small town south of Durban
Sekhukhuniland	part of the Northern Province
Sharpeville	black township near Vereeniging
Sophiatown	former section of Johannesburg from which blacks were removed in the 1950s
Soweto	large group of black townships southwest of Johannesburg
Springs	city east of Johannesburg
Stellenbosch	city and Afrikaans-speaking university near Capetown
Swaziland	independent country northeast of South Africa
Tembisa	small town between Johannesburg and Pretoria
Transkei	former independent homeland
Transvaal	former South African province in which cities of Johannesburg and Pretoria were located; now divided into several provinces, among them Gauteng Province, present location of Johannesburg and Pretoria
Tsolo	small town in the Transkei

Turfloop	town in Northern Province; site of University of the North
Umtata	capital of the Transkei
Umzimkulu	small town near the Transkei
Vaal	river near Johannesburg; also refers to an area near Vereeniging; the name of the former Transvaal province is derived from its location north of the Vaal River
Venda	former independent homeland
Vereeniging	industrial city just south of Johannesburg
Verulam	Indian area near Durban
Walmansthal	district of Pretoria
Western Transvaal	area west of Johannesburg
Witwatersrand	area around Johannesburg; also the University of the Witwatersrand

SOUTH AFRICAN UNIVERSITIES

Each institution is followed by its racial status under the apartheid laws. Except for the Afrikaans institutions, the principal language of instruction for all universities was English. The Afrikaans universities are specifically noted.

Medical University of South Africa (MEDUNSA)
    black, medical school near Pretoria
Pretoria University
    white, Afrikaans, Pretoria
Rhodes University
    white, Grahamstown
University of Bophuthatswana
    black, Mmabatho
University of Cape Town (UCT)
    white, Cape Town
University of Durban-Westville
    Indian, Durban
University of Fort Hare
    black, Ciskei
University of Natal
    white, branches in Pietermaritzburg and Durban
University of the North
    black, Turfloop
University of Potchefstroom
    white, Afrikaans, Potchefstroom (near Johannesburg)
University of South Africa (UNISA)
    no racial classification, largely correspondence university, Pretoria
University of Stellenbosch
    white, Afrikaans, Stellenbosch (suburb of Cape Town)
University of the Transkei
    black, Umtata

University of the Western Cape (UWC)
     Coloured, Bellville (suburb of Cape Town)
University of the Witwatersrand (Wits)
     white, Johannesburg
University of Zululand
     black, KwaDlangezwe

LAWYERS INTERVIEWED

*Numbers indicate chapters in which excerpts
from the interview appear.*

Norman Abraham, 8
Fikile Bam, 2, 5, 7
Selby Baqwa, 3, 5, 9, 10
Timothy Bruinders, 3, 4, 5, 9, 11
Nona Goso, 11
Pingla Hemraj, 5, 8, 13
Pius Langa, 9, 10
Tholie Madala, 8
Ismail Mahomed, 2, 5, 8, 9, 13
Lucy Mailula, 4, 10
Vincent Maleka, 5
George Maluleke, 5, 8, 11, 13
Matilda Masipa, 7

Phineas Mojapelo, 2, 5, 8, 11
Dolly Mokgatle, 3, 4, 5, 8, 11
Yvonne Mokgoro, 4, 7, 10
Justice Moloto, 5, 7, 8, 10
Kgomotso Moroka, 4, 5, 8, 11
Dikgang Moseneke, 6
Mahomed Navsa, 3, 10
Dullah Omar, 12
Godfrey Pitje, 1
Justice Poswa, 5, 8, 9, 13
Christine Qunta, 7, 11
Ismael Semenya, 5, 10
Lewis Skweyiya, 2, 7, 8, 9
Pansy Tlakula, 5, 10

INDEX